Dancing for Busy People

by

Calvin Campbell

Ken Kernen

Bob Howell

Cover Illustration

Helle Urban

1st Edition 1995

2nd Edition 2003

Library of Congress Number: 2003102151

ISBN 0-9615404-2-7

Printed in the United States

Dedicated to

Mrs. Dorothy Stott Shaw

Whose love of the dance inspired

all three of us

To Willard & Nancy
Thanks for supporting
the Kids

WALTZ WITH ME, DARLING

Waltz with me, darling, before we go home,
Light in my arms as a handful of foam,
Light in my arms as the moonlight that spills
Over the magical hills.

Grandmother danced in a happier day.
Under her hoopskirts her slipper toes play
Under an arbor of smilax and rose,
With a step and a step and a close.

Bring back dear Grandmother's gladness a while;
Her light little feet and her bright little smile;
Waltz with me, darling, beneath a big moon,
To a sweet little three-quarter tune.

Lilacs in blossom have scented the air,
Stars in your eyes and a rose in your hair;
Waltz with me, darling, with wings on your feet!
Nothing was ever so sweet - so sweet.

Dorothy Stott Shaw

Table of Contents

Contra Dances

Recommended Teaching Order

1. Circle Left/Right
2. Forward & Back
3. Swing
4. Promenade Single File
5. Arm Turns
6. Couple Promenade
7. DoSaDo
8. Allemande Left
9. Right & Left Grand
10. Star Right/Left
11. Pass Thru
12. U-turn Back
13. Courtesy Turn
14. Ladies Chain Two/Four
15. Right & Left Thru
16. Separate
17. Split the Couple/Ring
18. Roll Away 1/2 Sashay
19. Lead Right/Left
20. Circle to a Line
21. Bend the Line
22. Star Promenade
23. Wheel Around
24. Grand Square
25. Star Thru

95 % of the dances in this book use only the terminology (basics) listed above. Definitions, styling, timing and teaching tips for each are provided in Appendix A. Information included with individual dances provide additional needed details.

Note : See Appendix B for a teaching plan.

Dancing for Busy People

This book is based on several premises. First, many people want to dance, but they have a limited amount of time to learn how to dance. Second, many people will try dancing if the dance program is quick to learn and fun to dance. Third, dancing to good music is more important than mastering complex footwork. Fourth, it is fun to dance with friends and to be part of a group.

The dance program presented in this book is designed to provide a wide variety of dancing experience through the use of a combination of square dances, mixers, contra dances, couple dances, quadrilles, line dances (solo), etc. that use a common set of terminology or dance movements throughout all of the dances. The goal is to provide the maximum amount of dancing with the minimum amount of instruction.

This book is a reference tool for both new and experienced dance leaders. If you are a new leader, just starting out, you will find a complete program laid out in the following pages. You will not have to be a dance expert with a great deal of experience before you start. You will be able to learn and then teach dances using very few technical terms. Each dance movement can then be used in many different dances. The amount of dance knowledge needed to provide a long term program of entertaining dances is minimal.

If you are an experienced dance leader, this program will provide resources to present a diverse dance program that will meet the needs of a large audience. The average person entering a dance program usually has a very limited amount of time to devote to mastering complex body and foot movements. Most of them just want to have fun to good music. Building a dance program with a limited number of basic dance movements and a large variety of dance formations and music makes the most productive use of the knowledge dancers gain. More people become willing to learn to dance and they dance longer. There are enough dances presented here to provide variety and challenge for a program lasting for years.

History

In 1986, a worldwide group of dance leaders met to discuss the changing recreation desires of the American public. It was obvious that the size of dance instruction classes was decreasing and the attendance at dance functions was becoming smaller. Many reasons were cited for this decline. Dancing was no longer a part of the curriculum in elementary and secondary schools so more and more adults had little experience in dancing. Job and social pressures gave people much less time to devote to any one hobby. Entertainment options had expanded to the point where dancing was not able to successfully compete for people's time because of the extended amount of time it took to learn to dance.

A committee, organized under the International Association of Squre Dance Callers, felt that a program needed to be developed which could be easily taught and easily learned in a few short sessions. Following this learning period, functions would be provided where people could attend as frequently or infrequently as desired and still be able to dance comfortably most of the dances presented during any one program.

An initial program was devolped to provide six to eight lessons, but over time we discovered that a large population of people within the United States prefered to not be obligated to attend more than three or four lessons of two hours in length. This book is based around the recommendations of the original committee and modified to meet the desires of the public for three to four lessons or less.

Advantages of Limited Terminology

Dancing using a limited number of dance movements is certainly not new. Numerous events are held every night around the world where people arrive knowing little or nothing about dancing and dance a whole evening with a minimal amount of instruction.

This program is just a little more ambitious. It assumes that many people are willing to learn a few basic movements well enough so that they do not have to be taught over during every dance. Then the leaders have the opportunity to walk-thru dance routines in a shorter period of time and to introduce the people to more dances. More dancing means more fun.

The advantages for the dancer include: Not starting from the beginning every night. Not having to go through an extended lesson period before being able to enjoy their new hobby. The ability to learn at any pace dictated by jobs, children, and/or other responsibilities. The enjoyment of being able to dance as often or infrequently as desired and not feel "left-behind". The challenge to use their dancing skills in a diverse set of dances to different music and with a different feel.

Dancing for a Lifetime

Generally, people do not dance regularily throughout their life. They may learn as youth, have to stop for a time to make time for jobs or children, etc. and then return to dancing later in life. People also tend to move from place to place and may dance with many different groups of dancers.

The terminology used in this book is universal throughout most of the dancing world where Americans dance. The skills learned will enable people to participate in dancing for a lifetime. They form the foundation for learning more complex dances when desired. They provide the base of knowledge to enjoy dance, as a recreation, at any level of participation.

Learning How to Dance

It is important to give people a variety of options on how to gain enough dance experience to enjoy being part of an organized dance group. The goal is to have everyone learn a small common group of dance terminology that can be used in a large variety of dances. There are many ways people can acquire the necessary dance skills.

Learn one night at a time – Many dance leaders operate programs where people can start any time they wish to join.The learning sessions are planned so the dances taught during any one session can be learned by people attending for the first time. On the other hand, people attending consecutive sessions will find they will learn new dances and movements each session. Over several sessions everyone will acquire the same overall set of dance skills. Under this system, people can attend on an infrequent basis and only need to remember which sessions they need to attend to catch up. **See Appendex B for a complete example program.**

Progressive lessons – People are expected to enroll at the start of the series and attend all the sessions in the series. This enables the group to progress as a unit and the leader does not have to review each movement each night.

Once a week – Evening lessons held once a week for three to four weeks will work for many people. You may want to consider holding lessons in the morning, early afternoon, or during weekends. Many people are primarily daytime learners.

Three or four consecutive days – Many people who will not or cannot sign up for several weeks of lessons will often set aside a week to learn how to dance. There is an additional advantage in this schedule. Retention of dances learned the previous day is much higher than dances learned the previous week or further in the past.

Learn while on vacation – Teaching dancing in a vacation atmosphere has the advantage of giving people the chance to enjoy each other's company while doing other recreational activities.

Community education programs – Universities, community colleges and recreation departments are usually receptive to new class offerings. Short courses of 3-4 weeks or less fit very nicely into the typical school or recreation department schedule.

Learning How to Teach

This text book contains many pages describing teaching techniques. There are both general and detailed instructions for teaching specific dances. It is very important to recognize that new dance leaders do not have to master everything described before embarking on becoming a dance leader. Many organized dance groups have multiple dance leaders. Some specialize in one dance type, some in another.

Many CDs, records and tapes have tracks where the dance instructions are performed by professionals. In this case, the dances are taught by the dance leader and then the dance will be called, prompted or cued from the recording. This not only helps the dancers, but also helps dance leaders to learn by example.

The definitions described in Appendix A include teaching hints and techniques. It is very important to be able to describe any movement using several different choices of words. Strive to be concise in your description and remember that a demonstration is essential for some people. Almost all of the dances used in this program should be able to be learned with no more than 3-5 minutes of instruction.

Watch and listen to people who are effective teachers. What do they say and what do they do? Many video tapes are available which show an instructor teaching the dances. Study and emulate the examples where students appear to learn effectively.

Finally, tape record yourself and try to critically follow your own instructions from the viewpoint of someone who does not know how to dance. Did you give enough direction? Too much direction?

Reaching the Customer

One of the most successful ways to start a dance group is to find existing organizations (churches, service groups, lodges, recreation departments, etc.) who are willing to sponsor a recreational dance group.

Many companies are becoming concerned about the welfare of their employees and their families and will provide space and even financial support for social dance groups. Many of these same companies will permit people outside of their work force to join a company sponsored dance group.

Educational institutions often permit social groups to use their facilities. If these functions can be tied to student body events, the cost of renting the facilities can be reduced. Dancing used to be a part of the curriculum of most schools. Budget cuts have reduced this activity considerably. Fortunately, volunteers are still welcome. Dances that require partners become valuable about the age when boys begin to find girls are interesting (about the 4th grade). Before that, you are better off to use dances that do not require opposite genders to dance with each other as partners.

Community style dancing can be very popular at the middle school, high school and college levels. It provides an easy way for boys and girls to interact, socially, without the pressure to date or commit to a relationship. You will notice that many of the dances, in this book, do not require male-female partners.

Senior citizen communities or groups are excellent sources for dancers. These people often have more flexibility in their schedules and may prefer to learn during daytime hours with parties in the early evenings.

The Heart of Community Dancing

The success of any dance program, *designed for busy people*, lies in the ability to keep people interested and still stay within a skill plane that encompasses a large number of people. Limiting the amount of special terminology people need to learn is one way to keep the skill plane avil-able to more people. The use of a broad range of music and dance formations provides additional ways to keep people interested without exceeding the skill level of the average dancer.

Dancing and Formations

This topic sounds very dull and formal, but it is the key to the success of a social dance program. Most people are accustomed to operating as part of teams in other environments. One of the most satisfying aspects of human interaction occurs when people recognize that contributing to the success of a team can be very emotionally rewarding. Dancing as part of a dance group can provide the same rewards.

Line Dancing (solo dancing) is one of the most popular forms of social dance. The dances are usually done in groups, with all the people facing the same direction. Most people tend to form lines. Even though you may see some variations in styling and even some added steps, the measurement of success, in this environment, is whether you can dance the steps, as written, and essentially keep up with your line. When dancers succeed, there is an emotional high that follows.

Dancing in a square involves coordination with seven other people, but does not require much footwork. Instead, the emotional reward comes in being in the right place at the right time while moving in a geometric pattern. This involves the cooperation of all eight dancers in the square. Sometimes, all eight people are moving at the same time. There is also much satisfaction realized from the ability to be able to understand what the caller is requesting and to do it with precision and grace.

Contra dances and most other prompted dance forms, such as trios, quadrilles, etc., add still another dimension of enjoyment. In these dance forms, people are expected to dance in time to the music. When it is done properly, everyone moves through the dance pattern at the same pace and the whole floor of dancers move together.

The key to all of these dance forms is the positive reward of dancing in formation and being part of a team, and in working in cooperation with other dancers to produce something that is more beautiful and satisfying than dancing alone. When the dance is finished, you feel closer to your companions and you experience a large emotional lift.

Since much of the enjoyment of the dance is moving through the floor pattern formed by the choreography of the dance, very few instructions are needed by a leader to describe any one dance. Every time people are placed in a different formation or arrangement of ladies and men, the dance pattern is new and unfolds in a different way.

Using Music as a Tool for Enjoyment

Music creates and/or changes moods. It is a critical factor in providing plenty of variety without exceeding the skill level of the average dancer at a function. Many people experience problems in attempting to move gracefully to music. Any time footwork is involved, the success rate, of a dance, falls off dramatically. For that reason alone, the dances recommended for this program require little more than the ability to walk in time to the music. Even people who can't walk in time to the music may get much enjoyment moving in a pattern to music.

Once the dance pattern is learned, the dancer can enjoy dancing to the music and stop worrying about how they appear. They feel more secure, as part of a group, and perhaps less vulnerable. This means the music must be good. Different styles of music appeal to different groups of people. The goal in a program which employes many different dance forms is to also provide variety in music styles, rhythms and arrangements. Not everyone will like everything, but everyone will have their favorites.

Most of the dances, in this manual, list a recommended recording. Many have several recommendations. Which recording is used will depend on the makeup of the group and the environment. For example, a leader may choose to use very different music, for the same dance, in different environments. Elements such as room temperature, floor covering, age, mobility, altitude, and where the dance occurs in the program, become part of the considerations.

As a leader, you should recognize that dancers quickly associate some dances with a specific recording. When the music is played, the dancers expect a specific dance to follow. Sometimes you can successfully substitute another recording or another dance routine and sometimes the dance and the music are so closely associated that you should not try to change anything.

Friendships are Critical

Most people have limitations on how much they can or wish to learn about dancing. When they have either satisfied their interest in learning or have reached their limitations in dancing ability, then other factors take over and some people will quit dancing. Many of these people can be retained, as dancers, by the careful cultivation of other reasons to stay with the group.

A very strong factor in retaining dancers, over an extended period of time, depends on the friendships that are made within the group of dancers and the support these friends give each other. People will continue to attend dances if they feel they have the support of friends. They will often come to dances even when they cannot dance, for some reason, if they have the opportunity to see and visit with friends.

The promotion of friendships among dancers should be an active part of every set of lessons and every dance a leader conducts. This can be enhanced by the dance material chosen, but it must be continued through every aspect of an evening or long term planning of a recreation program.

The dance material chosen for the evening is the obvious point to start. The leader(s) must know the capabilities of each of the dancers. Then they must plan a careful blend of dances that includes fun, learning, surprise, nostalgia, excitement, tenderness, sadness, challenge, and relaxation. The dance leader is like a conductor of an orchestra. To get the best out of the orchestra, he or she must know the capabilities of each instrument. They must draw on the strengths of all the instruments and get everyone to work together as a team.

The dancers play a strong role in the success of any dance function. They must be willing to try new dances. They must take an active role in seeing that everyone feels successful. Most of all, they must be friends with each other and support one another. Much can be achieved by smiling and enjoying whatever happens. Part of the success formula must be strong support of the dance leadership and the people who handle other details of running the dance.

If dancers are to become friends, then they must be given the opportunity to cultivate these friendships. Teaching dance styling where people are encouraged to smile at each other, make eye contact at various points during each dance, and be aware they are dancing as part of a coordinated team effort will help. Dancers will feel a lot less need to do-their-own-thing when they feel they are part of a team and dancing, as part of that team, is part of the fun.

Events should be provided outside of the dance program to cement friendships. This can often take the form of going out after the dance to someplace for refreshments. Pick a place where people can sit around large tables. Plan the ending time of the dance to allow this type of activity to take place without keeping people out too late.

Another way to promote friendships is to take off an evening from the usual dance schedule and do something different as a group. Dance leaders should play a prominent role in this activity. It will give them the opportunity to get to know people on a one-to-one basis and for people to feel they are also friends. Finally, don't get too serious about the dancing. That's not what it is really all about.

We live in a world of competition most of the time. Dancing needs to be one of the places where we can escape and relax with friends.

Parties, Themes and Dancing

Parties and themes form an important part of providing reasons for people to attend the dance rather than sit at home and watch the television. Community style dancing, with the very large variety of music and dance formations available, is an excellent medium for building themes for parties. For example, many of the dance routines can be adapted to Christmas music. Numerous Israeli dances can be used during the celebration of Hanukkah. Almost any holiday can provide a theme for a party.

People often enjoy dressing up for a special occasion whether it is a Hobo night wearing the "grungees" or an elegant "cotillion" where the ladies all wear long dresses and the men wear coats for, at least, the first dance. It is part of our need to occasionally be actors or actresses and to play a role that is not part of our everyday and often humdrum life.

If you hold a formal dance, you might even consider printing a formal program for the evening and provide each lady with a pencil and small version of the program neatly folded into a small booklet that can be carried on her wrist. Early in the evening, the men are expected to arrange and sign up for dances with different ladies. Of course, the men need to make certain their partners and the single ladies get to dance as much as they desire.

Refreshments and decorations can do much to enhance the setting of a dance. On special nights, the refreshments need to fit the theme. There are usually several people in every group who love to bring special snacks. Find them and work with them. On the special theme nights the light refreshments should probably be available during the dance. This means the dance program will need to have additional time built in where people have the time to enjoy the goodies.

Lighting is particularly important. If you can control the lighting in your hall, dim the lights during certain dances. Try placing candles on small tables. This encourages people to sit down in small groups and talk. Put table cloths and a center piece on each table.

On some evenings, consider having a special ceremony or a presentation. Something short, no more than five minutes in length. A simple circle and lighting of candles can do wonders to make people feel good and closer to each other.

Many people enjoy ballroom dancing. Keep some old favorites and some country-western music available. Play it during rest times. You may be surprised how many people will get up and dance.

By now, I hope you are realizing that a community dance is not only the dancing, but also the setting, the costumes, the refreshments, and, most importantly, the friends. It is a time to forget the outside world and just spend time enjoying life.

Once you have a successful theme or activity you will probably want to continue it as a tradition. Refine the theme every year, but be sure you keep what is best from year to year. People look forward to these and will tell their friends about them. It will keep them coming back.

Fundamentals of Calling/Prompting/Cueing

Dance leaders must be able to communicate directions to dancers on the floor. There are many ways of doing this. One of the most obvious methods is to demonstrate the steps and then play the music and expect the dancers to remember the steps. This is very effective for short simple routines, but as the dances become more complex, more effective methods are needed.

The next method is to demonstrate a dance and then to assist the dancer's memory by adding some spoken directions during the dance. While this method is very useful, once again, there are limitations. The dancers must remember most of the dance and when various steps or moves occur in relation to the music.

The third method is to describe each dance with a series of short easily learned commands or basics and then tell the dancers what to do just before they need to do it. This technique is known as prompting, cueing or calling a dance. Even though there are differences in the mechanics of calling, prompting and cueing the various dance forms, several elements are common to all. The techniques unique to leading each dance form are described later. The following fundamentals apply to all the dances.

Rhythm

The dance leader must understand the relationship of the dance movements and the music. The dancers will be moving to the rhythm of the music and the leader must be able to hear the same rhythm and be able to identify basic elements related to the structure of the music. The first element is the musical beat, the underlying rhythm of a tune. Play a square dance hoe-down record or singing call and see if you can walk in time to the music. You should be able to pick out a background beat that tells you when to take each step. If necessary, ask a companion if you are walking to the beat of the music.

Next, listen to the music and see if you can identify an 8-beat phrase. In most square dance or contra dance music there are usually two stronger beats within each 8-beat phrase, one on the 1st beat of the phrase and one on the 5th beat of the phrase.

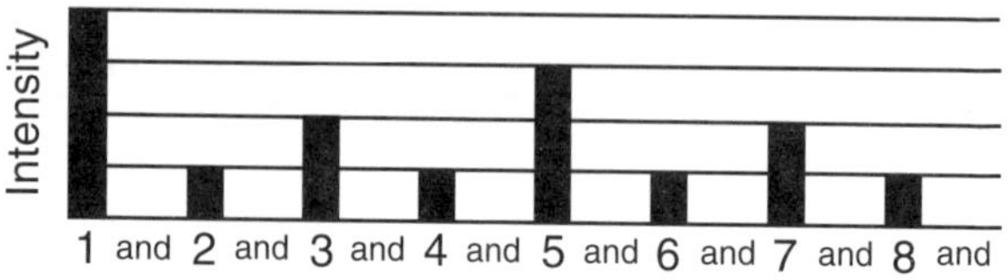

Try counting 1 and 2 and 3 and 4 and etc. in time to the beat of the music. You should be able to hear the start of each 4-beat segment (half phrase). Try reciting the following nursery rhyme to the music:

Little boy blue come blow your horn; the
1 and 2 and 3 and 4 and

sheep's in the meadow, the cow's in the corn
5 and 6 and 7 and 8 and

You should be able to anticipate the start of each phrase (1st beat) and the 5th beat (half phrase) and begin speaking the words of the rhyme exactly on the 1st or 5th beat of the phrase. After practicing the rhyme for awhile, try a simple dance prompt such as the following square dance routine:

Allemande Left with your left hand
1 and 2 and 3 and 4 and

right to your partner and Right and Left Grand
5 and 6 and 7 and 8 and

If you find the exercises above are relatively easy, then you can probably expect to be able to learn how to call/prompt/cue dances quite easily. If you can only hear the beat and cannot identify the musical phrase, you may still be able to call square dances, but you will find it to be quite a challenge.

The ability to identify the musical phrase is critical to prompting contras, trios, quadrilles and to cueing round dance mixers. The leader must be able to correctly identify the beginning of each phrase and to deliver the dance commands prior to the start of each musical phrase.

Line dance routines may not conform to an 8-beat structure and the music may deviate from it as well. The leader picks when to start and even though it is highly desirable to start on the beginning of a musical phrase, it is not critical in many of these dances. As long as you can feel the beat of the music, you can probably line dance.

Vocal Clarity

A dance leader must both be heard and understood or the dancers cannot dance. Part of vocal clarity depends on the acoustics of the hall and the quality of the amplification equipment. Another part of vocal clarity depends on the voice qualities of the leader. Here are some of the key elements to achieving clarity

1) Keep your mouth open and mobile. Your voice must have a large opening to pass through. Use plenty of air when you speak. This moves a larger volume of air across your vocal chords and produces more volume. This will also keep your vocal cords from becoming sore.
2) Each word must be spoken distinctly and separated from the other words. Form each word with a beginning and an end. Do not slur words together. Speech habits formed in many regions of the country tend to run-the-words-together. Break this habit.
3) Project your voice. Don't shout but imagine you are speaking to someone in the back of the room. Push the words toward them, but let the microphone do the work for you.
4) Let your enthusiasm show through with tonal changes. Words spoken in a monotone tend to run together. Tonal changes help to separate the words and make the call more interesting to hear.

Command

Command could be defined as "Don't ask . . . tell!" Every dance description has certain command words which must be emphasized. Command must be tempered with persuasiveness. You should tell the dancers what to do in a manner that makes them want to follow the command. Inspire, don't demand. The leader must indicate clearly who is to do an action and what action is to be done. For example:

Head Two Couples . . . (Who)
Right & Left Thru . . . (What)

Emphasizing command words may be enhanced by several means:

1) Increase the volume of your voice on the key command words. In the example, emphasizing the word "Head" alerts the head couples that the following action will be danced by them. The "what" por-

tions of the call must all be emphasized.

2) Use changes in vocal pitch or volume.
3) Repeat part of the command. In "Allemande Left with your left hand", adding the second "left" reinforces the fact the left hand will be used.
4) Vary the method of delivery. Change from chanting the call to speaking special commands you want to emphasize.

The Relationship of Your Voice to the Music

Most instructions for dancing are delivered in the normal vocal range of the leader. This is fortunate because many people can hear the rhythm and recognize the tune associated with a piece of music, but they cannot sing along with the music.

When calls, prompts or cues are spoken, much can still be added to enhance the delivery of the instructions to the dancers. Good rhythm and clarity are still essential. Changes in volume and projection are used to emphasize commands and some enthusiasm must come through. The technique is generally referred to a voice inflection calling or prompting.

Square dance callers often use an added technique. They pitch their voice to harmonize with the musical chords of the music being used. The vocal notes used are the same as those used in the chord structure of the music. This may sound difficult, but for most people it is natural.

Pick out a square dance hoe-down record you like. Hum a note that sounds "on-pitch" with the music. This will normally be the dominant note of the musical chord. Pick out a note above the dominant note and another note below the dominant note that do not seem to clash with the music and hum a little tune composed of just these three notes. Chances are you will have picked two other notes in the chord. Now, try adding words to the "hum" and you will produce a chant. If your companions confirm that this chant does not clash with the music, you are calling "on-pitch."

Each piece of music has a chord progression. The leader must be able to hear when the chord changes and change the musical chant. This means developing several little chant tunes to fit various pieces of music. With practice, you will also gradually learn to use more notes in the chord pattern.

Timing

Timing refers to the number of beats of music allowed between the delivery of a call or a prompt and the delivery of the following call or prompt. The ideal goal is to provide dance commands timed so that the dancers never have to hurry or wait at any point in the dance. Each dance basic takes a minimum number of beats of music to complete comfortably. These are listed in Appendix A. In set pattern dances, such as contras and trios, the choreographer should carefully match the dance movements and the music. In square dancing, the timing can change depending on the formation, size of the set, reaction time of the dancers, etc., but it is always relatively predictable.

Problems arise when dancers are either not given enough time or given too much time to complete an action comfortably. When a call is delivered too far ahead of the expected action, the dancers try and hurry the previous action to catch up. If the call is delivered too late, the dancers will finish the current action and then have to stand and wait for the next instruction. The result is stop-and-go dancing. The trick is to achieve a careful balance between the two.

Word placement of the dance commands is very important. The commands should be delivered 2 to 4 beats ahead of when the dancers are expected to begin any given action. The caller must know how many beats of music are needed to comfortably complete any basic movement from any position or formation. From there, it is a matter of study, practice and experimentation. The objective is to keep the majority of the dancers moving smoothly. Be sure you are monitoring the whole floor and not just a few "good" sets.

Calling Square Dances

Calling square dances differs considerably from the technique used in the other dance forms presented in this manual. The other dance forms have fixed dance routines and are often done to the same music every time. The leader must prompt or cue ahead of the points in the music where the dancers are expected to execute the movements of the dance routine.

In square dancing, the dancers start to move as soon as they recognize the call. The job of the caller is to keep the movement flowing smoothly and not necessarily to have the dancers dancing on the phrase of the music. The process is usually referred to as patter calling.

The option of the dancer ignoring the phrasing in the music presents an interesting situation for both the caller and the dancers. Many dancers will enjoy square dancing long before they appreciate the other dance forms. They don't have to worry about when to start and stop. They just move to the rhythm of the music and leave the timing up to the caller. This style of dancing even appeals to people who are convinced they have two left feet. In square dancing, all dancers have to be able to do is to walk.

The caller has several more options open in square dance calling than are available in prompting or cueing. Every movement has a recommended minimum number of steps for completion. These are listed in Appendix A. It is very important for the square dance caller to know how many steps it takes to complete each move comfortably for each of the configurations listed. However, the caller can adjust the number of steps allowed for each command, above this minimum, to fit the conditions of the environment. If the floor is slick or the room is hot or the people have some sort of physical limitations, the caller can give the dancers more time to complete each movement.

The caller can also use choreography that is not timed to fit a set block of music. Dance routines can be any length necessary to finish an interesting dance pattern. The pattern can even be altered as it is being danced with more movements added in or taken out.

Prompting Dances

The descriptions for all the quadrilles, contras, mescolanzas, Sicilian Circles, trios and mixers in this manual are organized into lines which describe the action danced in 4 to 8 beats of music. Most of the dance routines are 64 beats of music in length because the majority of the music used for contra dancing is organized into 64-beat tunes. Exceptions are noted in the descriptions of the dance.

The instructions or prompts (cues) for prompted dances are normally spoken during the last 2 to 4 beats before the start of the following phrase. The prompts should be spoken in cadence with music and should be finished on or just before the last beat of the phrase and just prior to the start of the phrase where the dancers are expected to begin the described action.

Each of the prompted dances in this manual have a sample set of prompts. Dashes are used to mark the beats of music where no words are spoken. Most of the time the prompter will wait the first 4 beats of the phrase and then speak the prompt on the last 4 beats of the phrase. For example, in the following line, count to 4 and then say the words on beats 5-8. The dancers will start the action on beat 1 of the following musical phrase.

1-8 - - - -, Turn your partner Right Hand around

Compare the wording for the same 8-beat phrase in the '*Prompts*" section and the '*Description*' section for each dance. Notice that the prompts always come ahead of the action. The description tells you the details about what the dancers should be doing during each 8-beat phrase.

Most music, used for prompted dances, will have an 8-beat introduction before the melody begins. To start the dance correctly, the prompter should wait for the first 4 beats of music and then speak the *Intro* prompt during the last 4 beats. If the music does not have an 8-beat introduction then the prompter should first tell the dancers what to do and then start the music.

Once the dancers are in motion, you will usually wait 4 more beats of music and then give the prompt for the next action on beats 5-8 of the phrase while the dancers are completing the previous movement. It will help to silently count out the number of dashes on every prompt line.

Cueing Dances

Cueing dances is very similar to prompting. About the only difference may be in the amount of information delivered. Dances that are cued are usually taught by a demonstration on the floor. When the music is started, the dancers are normally familiar with the dance routine. The leader only needs to provide a minimum of spoken directions during the dance.

Final Thoughts

All the above are tools-of-the-trade. Remember, to be a well-rounded instructor/entertainer, you should eventually know how to call square dances, prompt contras and/or quadrilles and cue simple rounds, mixers, line and no-partner dances. All play definite roles in providing an evening of dancing entertainment.

Programming a Beginner Dance

A beginner dance may consist of anything from the first night of a class to presenting an evening of entertainment for a father-daughter banquet. The majority of people who attend will know little or nothing about dancing. They are there to be entertained. It's your job to see they have the maximum amount of fun.

Most of the people who schedule dances of this kind want square dancing featured as a major part of the entertainment. As such, you need to introduce square dance terminology and square dance style music early in the program.

Even though the dance may have been advertised as a square dance or a "Hoedown" you should still use a variety of dance forms. The same basics used in a circle, a square and a contra line feel different. Add still more variety by changing music styles and you can entertain a group for several hours with very few basic movements.

Getting Started

If the hall is large enough, have everyone choose a partner and form one large circle with the lady on the man's right. If people are bashful about picking a partner, have them line up with the girls/ladies on one side of the hall and the men/boys on the other. Join them into couples by walking the two lines down the center of the hall so that the lady is walking on the man's right hand side. At the end of the hall *Promenade* everyone to the left into one large circle. Play the music at a low level so the people can move to the music but, still hear the instructions. If there are extra women, you can usually convince them to pair up. If there are extra men, you will most likely have problems getting men to dance with men. Don't fight it. Keep the dances short and get the extra men dancing in the next dance.

If the hall is large enough, the first dance should be done in a large circle. It is much easier to control the dancers in one large circle and to spot any problems. Any people who arrive late can step in and join a big circle with very little interruption of the dancing.

The choice of dance material should be simple basics such as *Circle Left, Circle Right, Forward & Back*, etc. The goal is to get the people moving comfortably to the music. Simple gimmicks such as *"Run to the middle with a great big shout"* will help get the people into the spirit of the dance.

If the crowd is too large to accommodate in one large circle, you can either use several smaller circles or squares. Several smaller circles with a varying number of couples usually works best. The number of couples in each circle is unimportant and they take less time to organize that squares of four couples.

From this point on, the best approach will depend on the mixture of males and females. If the mixture is fairly even, you can teach *DoSaDo, Swing, Arm Turns* and *Promenade* from a circle. It will be necessary to demonstrate some basics, but keep the instruction time to a minimum.

If the mixture is heavily one gender or the other, then some people will have to be willing to dance the role of the opposite gender. Your job will be to make this as easy as possible by choosing terminology and dances that minimize potential problems. For example, women are usually willing to *Swing* with other women, but men are usually unwilling to *Swing* with other men. Either eliminate *Swings* or substitute something such as a *Elbow Swing* or a *DoSaDo.*

The dances on the following pages are all designed to be used under beginner party conditions. The routines are provided for practice and to show the variety of dances that can be done using a very few basic terms. You will need to judge what material to use depending on the age mixture of the group, the dancing area, the size of the group and probably many other factors.

Dancing in a Big Circle

The dance routines are only examples and can be rearranged several different ways. The square dance patter has been broken down into 8-beat phrases with suggested wording and dash marks indicating a suggested wait time between commands. The amount of wait time suggested is the maximum ever needed. As you gain experience as a caller and the dancers gain experience in dancing, you will need to adjust the timing to keep the movement smooth and natural. There are several ways to fit the words into the 4-beat half phrases. You may want to underline the first letter of the word that starts each beat to help you practice.

You need to put some careful thought into the teaching sequence. Some dance movements such as *Circle Left/Right* and *Forward & Back* require little explanation and can be taught without stopping the music. On the other hand, *Swings* and *Arm Turns* need a quick demonstration.

The first dance routine is designed to acquaint people with the partner position. You will need to teach *Swing* and tell the man to put his partner on the right hand side before the *Circle Left*. Show *Arm Turns* with a quick demo.

1-8 All join hands & Circle Left, - - - -
9-16 - - Circle Right, - - - -
17-24 Promenade Single File, - - - -
25-32 All the ladies turn around, - - - -
33-40 Turn your partner Right Hand Around. - - - -
41-48 Turn your partner Left Hand Around, - - - -
49-56 Swing your partner 'round & 'round, - - - -
57-64 Join hands & Circle Left, - - - -

The second dance routine adds dancing with the corner or left hand lady. If some people are having problems, change the routine. *Swing* and *Promenade* the corner lady after turning the previous partner *Right Hand Around.* This provides everyone with a new partner.

1-8 All join hands & Circle Left, - - - -
9-16 Circle Right - - - -
17-24 Promenade Single File, - - - -
25-32 All the men turn around, - - - -
33-40 Turn this lady Left Hand Around, - - - -
41-48 Turn your partner Right Hand Around, - - - -
49-56 Turn left hand lady Left Hand Around, - - - -
57-64 Swing your partner - -, - - - -
65-72 Join hands & Circle Left, - - - -

In the following dance routine, you may want to stop the action just after the *Promenade Single File*, tell the men to move up beside their partner on the inside of the circle, and show them the proper hand hold for a *Couple Promenade*.

1-8 Join hands & Circle Right, - - - -
9-16 Promenade Single File, - - - -
17-24 Men move up beside your partner, - - - -
25-32 Promenade your partner, - - - -

Dancing in a Square

Squares can be formed from a big circle by several methods. If you have everyone dancing in a big circle you can have the couples peel off in groups of four couples. Start with the couples directly in front of you and proceed around the circle in both directions.

Another option is to have everyone *Scatter Promenade* all over the floor and then find one other couple and *Circle Four.* Then have each foursome find one other foursome and *Circle Eight.*

It is very important that all people who want to dance are given the opportunity to dance. If some people are left over after forming squares, you may need to encourage other couples standing on the sidelines to join the people who are dancing. If this is not successful, it is possible to call for a square with only three couples or even a square with five couples. Just use dance routines that do not require numbered couples or the identification of head or side couples.

Once they are in squares, the first task is to get everyone acquainted with the square formation. You will have to point out home position for the men. It is often a good idea to use the same dance routines you just used in the big circle, but adapt them so the couples *Promenade* to a home position before they *Circle Left* again.

1-8 Circle Left around the ring, - - - -
9-16 Face your corner & DoSaDo, - - - -
17-24 Face your partner & Swing your own, - - - -
25-40 Promenade this lady home, - - - -,
- - - -, - - - -

In the next two routines, dancers change partners. The ladies move from man to man and *Promenade* to different home positions. You may want to demonstrate the *Swing* and the *Promenade* again. End the set with everyone back with their original partner.

1-8 Swing your corner 'round & 'round, - - - -
9-16 Promenade around the town, - - - -
17-24 - - - -, Right back home & settle down
25-32 - - - -, - - - -

1-8 Face your partner DoSaDo, - - - -
9-16 Go back to the corner & Swing, - - - -
17-24 Promenade around the ring, - - - -
25-32 - - - -, Right back home & square your set
33-40 - - - -, - - - -

The First Singing Call

Singing calls can be sung or prompted. Even if you choose to prompt the dance, it is still important to use a singing call record. Pick a singing call record with a strong melody. If you choose to prompt a routine, you might consider **"First Night Quadrille"** (Pg. 120).

Here is a good singing call routine. The first routine (Intro/Break/End) is used to start the dance, used again in the middle after the figure has been called twice, and used at the ending after the figure has been called twice more.

<u>Singing Call Intro/Brk/End</u>

1-8	**Join hands & Circle Left , - - - -**
9-16	**- - - -, - - - -**
17-24	**Circle Right - -, - - - -**
25-32	**Turn your corner with a Left Hand Around**
33-40	**Now your partner DoSaDo, - - - -**
41-48	**Same lady Swing -, - - - -**
49-56	**Promenade around the ring , - - - -**
57-64	**- - - -, - - - -**

The figure below is repeated 4 times. Each time the man gets a new partner. The timing provides extra time for the *Promenade.* If the dancers are arriving at home position too quickly, a *Swing* can be added at the end. The exact wording will vary with the music used.

<u>Singing Call Figure</u>

1-8	**Four ladies Promenade inside the ring, - - - -**
9-16	**Come back home & Swing, - - - -**
17-24	**Four men Promenade inside the ring, - - - -**
25-32	**Come back home & Swing, - - - -**
33-40	**Turn your corner by the Left, - - - -**
41-48	**DoSaDo your partner, - - - -**
49-56	**Promenade the corner, - - - -**
57-64	**- - - -, - - - -**

Rest Breaks

By now, the group has probably been dancing for about 12-15 minutes. Some groups will need a rest break, at this point, and some won't. It's a judgement call. If the dancers are having fun and do not appear to be tiring, let them dance. If the group includes several older people or certain sets are having problems, give them a rest break.

Mixers

Mixers give people a change of pace and a choice of resting or dancing. They are usually done from a large circle with all the couples facing around the hall in a counterclockwise direction. **"Hyll's Phrase Craze"** (Pg. 255) uses a *Swing* and a *DoSaDo.* The dance changes partners and can be taught in 2 minutes or less.

Changing the Formation with Contras

A contra dance will give the dancers a complete change of pace and introduce them to a totally different style formation and music. The two contras, suggested below, use the same starting formation and could be danced one after the other or one contra could be used at this point in the program and the other contra later in the program.

"NoName Contra" (Pg. 147) uses lines composed of four to six couples with the men on the prompter's right and the ladies on the prompter's left. It can be danced with more of one gender than the other. All people really need to remember is which line they return to after each prompt.

Many of the people may recall doing some sort of a **"Virginia Reel"** in the past. The **"Virginia NoReel"** (Pg. 146) eliminates the reel portion, for now, because some people have a very difficult time learning the reel movement.

The arch in a **"Virginia NoReel"** is a two hand arch. The only other problem may occur on the *Arm Turns*. Each *Arm Turn* finishes with the person standing back in their home line.

The published timing of the figure works well for six couples. If there are more that six couples in any contra line, additional time will need to be allowed for the extra couples to duck thru the arch. An interesting variation for this dance is to have the top two, three or four couples slide to the foot at the same time. The same number of couples make the arch.

No-Partner Dances

If you choose to dance two contra dances in a row, the group has probably been dancing for about 30-35 minutes. Some people can hardly wait to dance some more and some people need to rest. It's a good time to put in a no-partner dance (solo or line dance).

The first no-partner dance should be very simple. Remember, all of the dancing up to this point has only required the ability to walk. Now, you are expecting them to be able to do something complex with their feet. You will need to build their confidence in their ability.

Don't expect everyone to participate. Some people are very reluctant to do dances they perceive as difficult. Let them watch and they may be willing to try later. Be prepared to repeat the same dance later in the program. Once people learn a dance routine, they will want to do it again.

No-partner dances are usually taught with the instructor on the floor facing the same direction as the dancers and all facing the front of the room. A short demonstration will usually get the people moving. If the crowd is large, demonstrate the routine from several places in the room, so people can see what you are doing with your feet.

The first recommended routine is**"Amos Moses #1"** (Pg. 272). Use the first routine until most of the people can do it. Introduce the second variation **"Amos Moses #2"** (Pg. 274) as something that can be added if you wish to be adventurous.

Don't hurry. If several people are having problems with the first routine, stick with it for the entire record and introduce the second variation when your repeat the dance later in the program.

Back to Squares ?

If the dance is advertised as a hoedown or a square dance, it is time to square dance once more. You have the choice of teaching some new figures, repeating some of the previously used figures, or a combination of the two. It is usually wise to at least start out with a repeat of some of the earlier material. Some new people may have joined the group and some people may have forgotten what they learned. Once you are confident the dancers are back into the 'groove', feel free to show them something new.

Numbering the Couples

Identify each of the couples by position number. The couples are numbered counterclockwise starting with the couple with their back facing the caller. Have them hold up their hands, as they are numbered, so you know they know who they are. Then put on the music and let them dance.

1-8 Couple #1 Swing your partner, - - - -
9-16 Couple #2 Swing your partner, - - - -
17-24 Couple #3 Swing your partner, - - - -
25-32 Couple #4 Swing your partner, - - - -
33-40 Join hands & Circle Left, - - - -
41-48 Promenade back to home, - - - -
49-56 - - - -, - - - -

In the following dance, the next couple should start their *Swing* just after the previous couple passes them. The time from counts 33-48 allows a comfortable amount of time for the last couple to reach home position.

1-8 Couple #1 Promenade outside the ring, - - back to home
9-16 Couple #2 Promenade outside the ring, - - back to home
17-24 Couple #3 Promenade outside the ring, - - back to home
25-32 Couple #4 Promenade outside the ring, - - back to home
33-40 - - - -, - - - -
41-48 - - - -, - - - -

The next dance was adapted from an old figure named the **"Arkansas Traveler."** It can be called for each of the men in turn. It also works well to have both the head men or side men move at the same time. If you have all four men move at the same time, it gets a little hectic. You can change the order the man visits each lady. You don't even have to come back to the partner each time. Have fun with the idea.

1-8 First gent turn the right hand lady with a Right Hand Around - -
9-16 Back to your partner with a Left Hand Around, - - - -
17-24 To the opposite lady with a Right Hand Around, - - - -
25-32 Back to your partner with a Left Hand Around, - - - -

33-40 To the corner lady with a Right Hand Around, - - - -
41-48 Back to your partner & DoSaDo, - - - -
49-56 Promenade, - - - -
57-64 Back to home & square your set, - - - -

Most of the square dance material, thus far, has been arranged in 32-count modules so they can also be used in a quadrille or singing call. The two routines below work together very well in a quadrille. Alternate 1st & 3rd and 2nd & 4th for the best effect. Remember, in quadrilles, you will need to prompt ahead of the music.

1-8 1 & 3 couples Forward & Back, - - - -
9-16 Same four Circle Left (or Right) **, - - - -**
17-24 All the way back home & Swing, - - - -
25-32 - - - -, - - - -

(Repeat for 2nd & 4th couples)

1-8 1st & 3rd couples bow & Swing, - - - -
9-16 Promenade outside the ring, - - - -
17-24 All around the set you roam, - - - -
25-32 Come on back & Swing at home, - - - -

(Repeat for 2nd & 4th couples)

If you wish to change partners, use the following routine.

1-8 Face your corner & DoSaDo, - - - -
9-16 Swing this corner & Promeno (Promenade), - - - -
17-24 - - - -, - - - -
25-32 - - - -, Come back home & square your set

Take Stock of Your Progress

How is the program going so far? Do most of the people seem to be understanding the terms? Is there something that needs to be repeated? Is there a dance that the people seemed to enjoy more. If so, you might want to consider repeating this dance.

What is the environment like? Is it getting hot in the hall? Is the floor sticky or slick? How is the energy level of the dancers? Are people starting to sit out more? Are there children present? If so, do you need to provide a dance for them?

So far, only seven dance basics have been used. These are *Circle Left/Right, Forward & Back, DoSaDo, Swing, Promenade Single File, Couple Promenade* and *Arm Turns*. Only one special step (Sashay which is a sliding step) other than walking has been used. The dancers have danced in a large circle, and in a square formation a couple of times. They have danced one or more contras, a no-partner dance and a mixer. With rest breaks, you should be between 1 and 1.25 hours into the program.

What should you choose to dance next? You could put in another contra dance. You could dance in a big circle again. You may feel it is time to interject another no-partner dance or perhaps a mixer. The choice will vary with the group.

It is important to recognize that as carefully as you might prepare your game plan, circumstances may change that plan. Stay flexible and be prepared to entertain the dancers for the rest of the program without using any more basics.

Try Out a Trio

Trios are very valuable when the balance of men and ladies or boys and girls is lopsided. They can be done with any combination of males and females. "**Wild Turkey**" (Pg. 210) **"Theil's Trio**" (Pg. 211) and **"Do-Ci-Dizzy"** (Pg. 212) use the same seven basics we have been using thus far. "**Theil's Trio"** even borrows some moves and the music from **"Hyll's Phrase Craze Mixer"** which was used earlier.

Another Mixer

One of the keys to the success of any beginner party is the quality of the music. The **"Hyll's Phrase Craze Mixer",** done earlier, requires a special piece of music. "**Molly Mixer"** (Pg. 251) can be done to any of your favorite singing call records. You might want to use different music for different age groups. If the group is largely older, pick out a tune that might be associated with their youth. If the group is younger, use a tune that is more modern.

Jiffy Mixer (Pg. 260) is excellent for functions with young children. It is also very popular with teenagers.

Several Quick-teach Solo Dances

The country and western scene has produced many tunes that are ideal for solo (line) dancing. The **"Texas Freeze"** (Pg. 272) was probably one of the original solo/line dances.

The **"Hully Gully"** (Pg. 274) routine is a little different. The routines starts and ends at a different point in the tune each time. In spite of this, it dances very well to many tunes.

How About Some More Square Dancing?

The first consideration for additional square dances should be to repeat some of the dance material used earlier in the program. Remember, for most of the audience, this may be their first exposure to dancing of this type. They will not mind repeating the same dance material twice in the same program.

If you choose to repeat some dance material, your choice of music should be different. If you used a snappy hoedown tune earlier, try to use something with a smoother feel this time.

A clever way to interject variety is to have the couples *Scatter Promenade* all over the floor. Find another couple and circle four. Now do some *Arm Turns, DoSaDo, Swing* and *Scatter Promenade* again. Find another couple and do it again. Finally have the circle of four break and form a circle of eight. The dancers will have great fun dancing movements they already know.

Finally, here are several more bits and pieces for square dance routines that make use of the same seven basics in different ways.

1-8 **1 & 3 couples Promenade Half - - - -**
9-16 **Same four Circle Half, - - - -**
17-24 **When you get home Swing, - - - -**
(Repeat for 2nd & 4th couples)

1-8 **Ladies/**men **to the middle & Circle Left/**Right, **- - - -**
9-16 **Come back home & Swing, - - - -**
17-24 **Men/**ladies **to the center & Circle Left/**Right
25-32 **Come back home & Swing, - - - -**

1-8 **1 & 3 DoSaDo, - - - -**
9-16 **Same two form a two hand arch, - - - -**
17-24 **2 & 4 ladies tunnel thru the arch, - - - -**
25-32 **Swing the opposite man, - - -**
33-40 **Ladies tunnel back, - - - -**
41-48 **Swing at home, - - - -**

The same figure can be called with the men tunneling through the arch. If some people have trouble getting though the arch, have the couples forming the arch not touch hands at the top.

1-8 Couple #1 stand back to back, - - - -
9-16 Walk away from your partner halfway around the set - -
17-24 Partner DoSaDo - -, Couple #3 make a two hand arch
25-32 #1 duck thru the arch & Swing at home, - - - -

In the routine above, notice directional words are used instead of introducing a new basic called *Separate.* It takes a little longer to say, but it avoids making the dancer learn a new basic.

Other Dance Party Material

As you can see, it is quite easy to construct a two hour program of entertainment without having to spent much time teaching. Check the basics used in the dances at the front part of each section. The first seven basics on pages 34-47 contain over 40 square dances. Check out the simple little gimmicks printed on pages 46 and 47.

There are also other dance formations that can be used. "**First Night Sicilian Circle"** (Pg. 226) and "**Scottish Man 'O' War"** (Pg. 227) can be danced in either a large double circle or in a small group setting.

If needed, you can teach some more dance basics. *Allemande Left* is really only a traditional name for for a *Left Arm Turn*, but it is a term many people have heard. Adding it takes very little teaching and people will enjoy dancing exactly the same dance routine as was done using *Left Arm Turn.*

Probably the next basic of choice should be *Stars. Stars* are fun and easy to teach. They have so many variations in so many dance forms that you could spend probably and entire hour just exploring this one basic.

Planning a Long-Term Dance Program

Once any group dances more frequently than 4 times a year, a dance leader faces new responsibilities. Fortunately this book is written specifically to support this role.

Typical dancers who attend a long-term dance program want to dance some old favorites and to learn something new every night. The dance leader's challenge is to provide these ingredients for dancers who come to every dance as well as those people who only show up once-in-a-while.

It is essential that the leader keep track of what dances and/or basics are used for each event. It helps if you will also make notes on which dances were a special hit and which dances may have presented problems. Then, at the next function or even the next several functions, you can refer to these notes in planning the program.

Don't feel rushed to hurry on to new material or to teach new basics. Let dancers enjoy exercising their skills. The dances in each section of the book are arranged in approximately the same order as used in the recommended teaching order shown just after the table of contents and followed in the square dance section. Many times, it will be more beneficial to pick out a dance which uses a different formation or a different piece of music than to teach a new or different basic dance movement.

When you decide to introduce something new, keep in mind that small changes can make a big difference. Research the dances in all sections to pick out dances which compliment each other. As an example, if you are going to teach a heel and toe step for a mixer, you might want to consider using this same step in a contra dance either during the same program or in the following program.

Read and re-read and re-read the text material scattered throughout this manual. You will find tidbits of information that will become valuable time and time again.

This book contains several hundred dances using a wide variety of formations and music. With just a little imagination and skill, any dance leader should have adequate material to provide interesting and varied dance programs for years. Also, as you gain in skill you will find even more material or be able to invent your own.

Square Dances

Square dancing evolved from early English country dance forms that the French and others transformed into the quadrille, cotillion, and finally the square dance. The American contribution was to transform these rather rigid dances into the free form choreography and style used today. In the process, Americans invented the caller to replace the dance master, accepted a wide range of music for dancing, and spread square dancing all over the world.

The dances in this manual use only a very limited set of square dance movements (basics) out of a very large vocabulary. The goal is to provide an interesting cross section of square dance choreography without burdening the dancers with an extended learning period. The same basics are also used extensively in other dance forms in the manual. Together, they form the base for the Community Dance Program.

The majority of square dancing is done in squares composed of four couples starting in the formation shown to the right. The men are illustrated as squares and the ladies are illustrated as circles. The small black squares indicate the direction each person is facing. The positions in the square are numbered starting with the couple with their back to the caller and progressing counterclockwise around the square. The caller is shown at the bottom of the diagram.

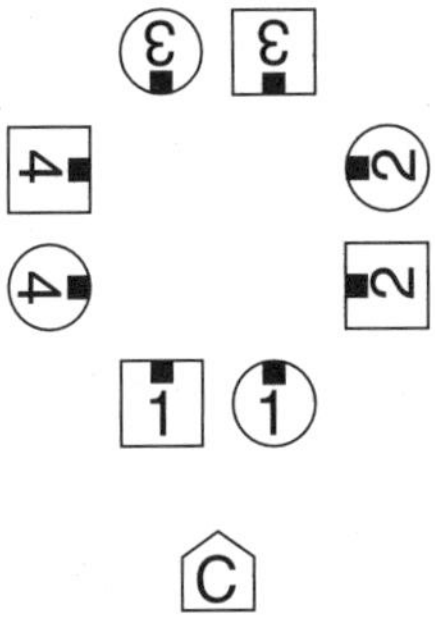

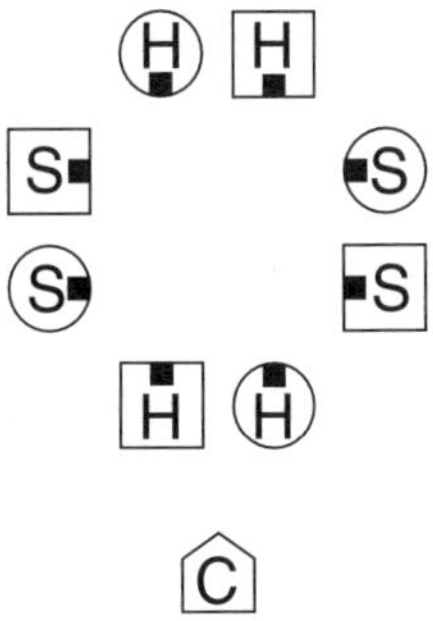

Directions can also be given to head couples or side couples. The Head couples either have their back to the caller or are facing the caller. The Side couples are on the sides of the square as shown to the left. Couples 1 & 3 are also Head couples and couples 2 & 4 are also Side couples.

The dance material in the Square Dance and the Contra Dance section of this manual are closely coordinated. Leaders will find it beneficial to use both in teaching new movements (basics) to dancers. The squares enable the dancers to gain skill in moving without having to concentrate on the timing. Contra dances give the dancers a chance to polish up their timing and styling.

Square Dance Music

Music used for square dancing is usually not strongly phrased. Some callers do use Jigs and occasionally a Hornpipe, but the majority of square dance tunes are Reels and other musical arrangements that have evolved specifically to compliment square dancing.

The main feature of all good square dance music is a solid beat for the dancers to move to and a 4-beat musical structure that enables the caller to deliver the calls in time with the music. This is often referred to as the *boom-chuck* sound.

Square dances are also danced to tunes where the words are sung instead of chanted or called. These are singing calls. The dance routines are designed to fit within one time through the melody which is almost always 64 beats in length. Most recordings used in square dancing are designed specifically for square dancing.

Even though many of the old 'standard' tunes are still very popular, country western and blue grass music have had a strong effect on square dance music in recent years. New sounds and instrument combinations are creeping in all the time. Whether this is good or bad depends on your viewpoint and the desires of you and your audience. As always, it is wise to provide a broad selection of sounds.

Because the timing of movements in square dancing does vary, the square dance routines in this manual are not written to strictly fit a 4-beat or 8-beat phrase. Instead, the complete wording of the calls is either left up to the caller or a suggested wording is given that generally fits a 4-beat half phrase. The caller then uses the techniques described in "The Fundamentals of Calling/Prompting/Cueing" starting on page 11.

The calls are separated by a (...) to show where the caller should pause for a few beats before giving the next command. In some cases, extra words or directions are provided. For example, in the line: **Head ladies/**men **turn the opposite lady/**man **Right/**left **Hand 1/2 Around,** several pieces of information are implied. First, the basic action is a *Arm Turn* halfway around. The caller can choose to have the men do it or the ladies do it. Second, the caller has the choice of the *Right Arm Turn* or a *Left Arm Turn*. This is a way of providing a number of variations for a dance routine in a compact format.

Organization of the Dances

The square dances, in this manual, are organized by the number and difficulty of the basics (movements) used. Definitions for these basics are provided in Appendix A.

The square dances provided under each named basic can include any terminology (basics) used up to that point in the square dances. For example, routines provided under *Arm Turns* include *Circle Left/Right, Forward & Back, Swing* and *Promenade Single File* because these basics have all been used in earlier dances. Routines provided under ***Arm Turns*** do not include *DoSaDo* because this basic has not been introduced in the sequence of dance routines printed in the manual to this point.

The dances under each featured basic are divided into several subgroups. The first two subgroups are **Patter-Big Circle/Square-Easy** and **Patter-Square-Easy**. The first subgroup has several routines that can be called from a large circle of couples. These are easy-to-dance patterns designed to give people confidence in dancing newly learned movements.

Next, several routines are presented from the square formation. They are still easy level routines, but the description identifies heads, sides, corners, home, etc. Keep in mind routines in **Patter Big Circle** can also be used in squares.

The next group is classified as **Patter-Square-Medium.** These routines should not be used until the dancers are dancing each basic comfortably. They are also excellent for use at dance functions where people attend on an infrequent schedule. They can all be taught in a short period of time and add variety to a program.

Patter-Square-Unusual and **Patter-Square-Difficult** dances should be reserved for groups that are very comfortable dancing the less challenging material. All of these figures should be walked-thru before each use.

Singing Call - Intro/Brk/End and **Singing Call - Figures** are dance routines timed to fit the 64-beat musical organization of most square dance singing call records. These same dance routines can be used in patter calls as well.

Circle Left/Right

Teaching Tips—On *Circle Left/Right,* be sure people are facing slightly toward the direction of travel. The men should be dancing holding their palms up and the ladies palms down. The people should take gliding steps and try to move smoothly with little or no bobbing up and down.

Patter - Big Circle/Square - Easy

Join hands Circle Left...
Circle Right...
Into the center with a Hey Hey Hey!*...
Back right out & Circle Left...etc.

* Substitute "Into the center with a Great Big Shout!" or "Into the center with a Ho Ho Ho!" Allow time for the people to walk to the center and back out comfortably. Make it fun.

Patter - Square - Easy

Men to the center & Circle 4 all the way back home...
Ladies center & Circle 4 all the way back home

Heads center & Circle 4 all the way back home...
Sides to the center & Circle 4 all the way back home

Head couples Circle 1/2...
Side couples Circle 1/2...
All 8 Circle Left to home

Almost anyone who has every played children's group games already knows how to *Circle Left* or *Circle Right.* The goal of the "Run to the center with a Great Big Shout" is to break-the-ice. People realize it's OK to dance and they can actually do something in time with the music. The "Hey Hey Hey" or "Ho Ho Ho" will almost automatically turn into a *Forward & Back.*

Notice that one of the figures listed above has (etc.) at the end of the routine. This is your indication that the figure does NOT end with all the dancers in the home position with their partner. You will need a *Promenade* home or do something else of your choice to return everyone to home position.

Forward & Back

Teaching Tips—Show the *Forward & Back* as 3 steps forward and swing the free foot forward on the 4th count and then back up 3 steps and touch. Have the dancers walk into the center 3 steps and say "Whoa" and then back up 3 steps and say "Hey." This will help to emphasize the correct timing of the movement. You can also have the men go forward and stomp their foot and then the ladies go forward and clap their hands.

Patter - Big Circle/Square - Easy

Everybody Forward & Back...
Circle Left...
Everybody Forward & Back...
Circle Right...
Now just the ladies Forward & Back...
Just the men Forward & Back

Patter - Square - Easy

#1 couple Forward & Back...
(Repeat for couples 2, 3 & 4)

Heads Forward & Back...
Sides Forward & Back

Good styling and courtesy points, associated with each basic, should be taught as soon as the dancers understand how to dance any movement. For example, on a *Forward & Back*, there are usually people on the opposite side of the set who are also moving *Forward & Back* as in the dance routine above. You should encourage the dancers to look at these people and to nod or curtsy to them. It's the little added touch that changes the movement from walking like a robot to dancing.

Forward & Back can be used any place a leader feels the dancers need to have time to stabilize and/or recognize where they are in a formation. *Forward & Back* can be added into many of the dance routines on the following pages. For example, pick out several places where two couples are facing across the set and put in *Forward & Back*.

Swing

Teaching Tips—A *Swing* should be taught by a demonstration. The walk-around version is probably best for beginner's. Be sure the arm and hand positions are demonstrated. Have the couples lean back into their partner's arm. When a *Swing* is completed, the man should place the lady on his right hand side and face the center of the set.

Patter - Big Circle/Square - Easy

Swing your partner...
Put her on your right & Circle Left...
Men Swing the lady on your left...
Go back & Swing your own...
Put her on your right & Circle Left...etc.

Circle Left...
Swing the lady on your left...
Put her on your right & Circle Left...etc.

Patter - Square - Easy

Couple #1 Swing your partner...
Couple #2 Swing your partner...
Couple #3 Swing your partner...
Couple #4 Swing your partner...
Join hands & Circle Left...etc.

Heads to the center & Circle 4 halfway around...
Swing...
Sides to the center & Circle 4 halfway around...
Swing...etc.

(Repeat entire figure to return everyone to home position)

Heads/sides **Circle 4 once around...**
Swing at home

Men Circle 4 once around...
Swing at home...
Ladies Circle 4 once around...
Swing at home

Promenade Single File

Teaching Tips—Precede teaching *Single File Promenade* with a *Circle Right.* The dancers will already be traveling the correct direction, counterclockwise, with the lady in the lead.

Patter - Big Circle/Square - Easy

Circle Left…
Circle Right…
Promenade Single File lady in the lead…
Ladies turn around (U-turn Back)**…**
Swing…
Put her on your right & Circle Left…etc.

Circle Left…
Circle Right…
Promenade Single File…
Men turn around (U-turn Back)**…**
Swing the lady behind you (Partner change)**…**
Put her on your right & Circle Left…etc.

Patter - Square - Easy

Head/side **couples Swing…**
Promenade Single File around the outside halfway…
Single File Promenade (Pass right shoulders)
down the middle to home…
Swing at home

Patter - Square - Medium

Put the ladies/men **in the center back to back*…**
Men/ladies **Promenade** (Single File)
around the outside track…
Back home & Swing

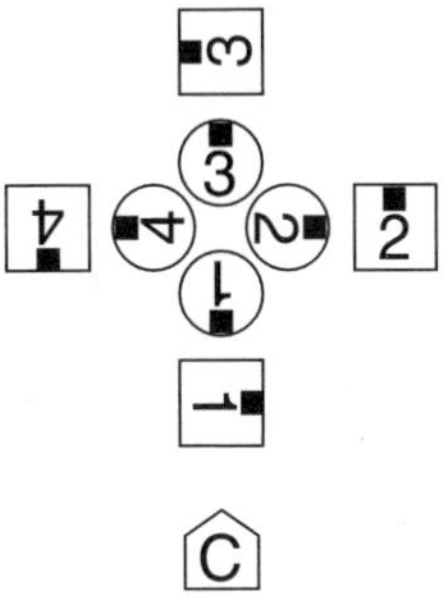

*The ladies/men step into the center of the set and face out so that all four people are back to back. The men/ladies *Promenade Single File,* around the outside of the group of four counterclockwise.

Arm Turns

Teaching Tips—Show the correct forearm grip for *Arm Turns* and the imaginary rotation point between the pair. Be sure the dancers understand to grip the opposite person's arm firmly, but not tightly.

Patter - Big Circle/Square - Easy

All join hands & Circle Left...
Circle Right...
Promenade Single File...
All the ladies turn around (U-turn Back)**...**
Turn your partner Right Hand Around (Arm Turn)**...**
Turn your partner Left Hand Around (Arm Turn)**...**
Swing your partner...
Join hands & Circle Left...etc.

All join hands & Circle Left...
Circle Right...
Turn your partner Right Hand Around (Arm Turn)**...**
Turn your partner Left Hand Around (Arm Turn)**...**
Swing your partner 'round & 'round...
Join hands & Circle Left...etc.

All join hands & Circle Left...
Circle Right...
Promenade Single File...
All the men turn around (U-turn Back)**...**
Turn this lady Left Hand Around (Arm Turn)**...**
Turn your partner Right Hand Around (Arm Turn)**...**
Turn left hand lady Left Hand Around (Arm Turn)**...**
Swing your partner...etc.

Circle Left...
Turn your partner Right Hand Around (Arm Turn)**...**
Turn corner Left Hand Around (Arm Turn)**...**
Turn partner Right Hand Around (Arm Turn)**...**
Swing the corner (Partner change)**...**
Put her on your right & Circle Left...etc.
(In squares, repeat 3 more times to get partner back.)

Patter - Square - Easy

Heads/sides **go Forward & Back...**
Turn the opposite Right/left **hand 1/2 Around** (Arm Turn)**...**
(Repeat the routine 1 more time to return everyone to home position)

Head ladies/men **turn opposite lady/**man
Right Hand 1/2 Around (Arm Turn)**...**
Heads Forward & Back...
Side ladies/men **turn opposite lady/**man
Right Hand 1/2 Around (Arm Turn)**...**
Sides Forward & Back...
4 ladies/men **Circle 4 half around...**
Swing partner...
Promenade Single File to home...etc.

Patter - Square - Medium

Put the ladies/men **in the center back to back...**
Men/ladies **Promenade** (Single File) **the outside track...**
Turn partner Left Hand Around (Arm Turn)**...**
Turn partner Right Hand Around (Arm Turn)**...**
Turn corner Left Hand Around (Arm Turn)**...**
Swing partner...etc.

Turn corner Left (Arm Turn)**...**
Put the ladies in the center back to back...
Men Promenade Single File around the outside...
Turn same lady once & a half (Arm Turn)**...**
Put the men in the center back to back...
Ladies Promenade Single File
around the outside track...
Turn same man by the left (Arm Turn)**...**
Swing partner...etc.

A diagram for putting men or ladies in the center back to back is shown under *Promenade Single File* (Pg. 37). Remember to walk-thru the pattern before using the figure. The goal is to have the dancers be successful in dancing the figure.

Couple Promenade

Teaching Tips—In an alert group, teaching a *Couple Promenade* can be done with the couples continuing to *Promenade Single File.* Otherwise, have the people stop in *Single File Promenade* position. Then have the men step to the inside of the circle and move up to stand beside the lady ahead. Without turning, the men should reach over and shake right hands with this lady. Hold on to the right hand and reach under the lady's arm and shake left hands. Start walking. The men should have their palms facing up and the ladies palms should be facing down.

Patter - Big Circle/Square - Easy

Join hands & Circle Right...
Promenade Single File...
Men move up beside your partner...
Promenade your partner...etc.

Circle Left...
Face your corner & turn her
Left Hand Around (Arm Turn)**...**
Go back & Swing your own...
Promenade this lady...etc.

Patter - Square - Easy

Swing your corner round & round (Partner change)**...**
Promenade around the town...
Right back home & settle down
(Repeat until everyone is back with their partner.)

Face your partner DoSaDo...
Go back to the corner & Swing...
Promenade around the ring...
Right back home & square your set
(Repeat until everyone is back with their partner.)

Head/side **couples Promenade 1/2...**
Same four Circle 1/2...
When you get home Swing

Couple #1 Swing...
Promenade outside the ring back to home ...
Couple #2 Swing...
Promenade outside the ring back to home ...
Couple #3 Swing...
Promenade outside the ring back to home ...
Couple #4 Swing...
Promenade outside the ring back to home

Time the above call so the next couple is starting the *Swing* just after the last couple has passed them on the *Couple Promenade.* When done properly, the couples appear to peel off the square in one continuous motion. The routine can also start with any one of the couples.

#1 lady Promenade outside the ring...
Home you go & Swing...
#2 lady Promenade inside the ring...
Home you go & Swing...
#3 couple Promenade the outside...
Home you go & Swing ...
#4 couple Promenade the inside...
Home you go & Swing ...
Couples 1 & 3 Promenade outside...
Couples 2 & 4 Promenade inside...
Home you go & everybody Swing...
Side couples Promenade outside...
While the head couples Promenade inside...
Circle up eight & don't be late...
Partner Swing...
Promenade home

You can mix the order in the above calls anyway you please. To play fair with the dancers, there should be some pattern that will allow everyone to participate. Even if you make a mistake it still will usually be fun.

All join hands & Circle Left halfway around & you stop right there...
Go eight to the middle & come right back (Forward & Back)**...**
Circle to the Right go around the track...
Go eight to the middle & give a shout...
Wink at your partner then back right out
Swing your partner 'round & 'round...
Promenade go around the town...etc.

Head/side **couples Promenade 1/2...**
Go Forward up & Back...
Now Circle Left on the inside track halfway round & back right out...
Side 2 couples Promenade 1/2...
Go Forward to the middle & Back...
Now Circle Left on the inside track halfway around then back right out...
Swing your partner 'round about...
Promenade home

"Arkansas Traveler"

1st & 3rd Forward & Back...
Turn the opposite lady Right Hand Around...
Your partner left (Arm Turn) **when you come down...**
Corners all with a Right Hand Around...
Partners all with a Left Hand Around...
Promenade corner...etc.
(Repeat for sides and then repeat two mores times, once for heads and once for sides.)

The Arkansas Traveler is a traditional square dance with many variations. In all of them, the men *Arm Turn* the ladies in some sequential order. The men then *Arm Turn* their partner between visits to each of the other ladies. With these conventions as a base, any number of dance routines can be designed around the same idea. Just be careful the traffic pattern does not have opposing men interfering with each other. This is very important when all four men are moving at the same time.

Patter - Square - Unusual

 # 1 lady cross the set & Circle up three with the opposite pair ...
 # 2 lady cross the set & Circle up three with the opposite pair...
Stop those circles where you are ...
 # 1 gent cross the set...
Swing your lady 'round & 'round...
While couple #3 Promenade 1/2 ...
 # 2 gent cross the set...
Swing your lady 'round & 'round...
While couple #4 Promenade 1/2...
Circle up eight (Left) **& around you go...**
Swing your partner...
Promenade...etc.

Singing Calls

Singing call tunes are usually played through seven times. Each tune is 64 beats of music in length. The **Singing Call -Intro/Brk/End** routines are used to begin the dance and do not have a partner change.

Following this, a **Singing Call - Figure** is used twice. Usually the figure rotates the ladies one position to the right or the left. This gives the ladies the opportunity to dance a different position in the square.

The **Intro/Brk/End** routine is used again in the middle and the **Figure** is repeated two more times. On the seventh time the **Intro/Brk/End** routine is used once again.

It's important to use singing calls from the first learning session on. Select tunes that encourage the dancers to sing-a-long at certain points in the record. Use dance routines that allow the dancers to relax and just enjoy the music.

Singing Call - Intro/Brk/End

Circle Left all the way around...
Circle Right all the way around...
Everybody Forward & Back...
Swing...
Promenade

Join hands & Circle Left...
Turn your corner with a Left Hand Around (Arm Turn)**...**
Now your partner Right Hand Around (Arm Turn)**...**
Corner Left Hand Around (Arm Turn)**...**
Back to your partner & Swing...
Promenade around the ring...
Back home & Swing

Circle Left full around...
Circle Right full around...
Turn corner by the Left (Arm Turn)**...**
Partner Swing...
Promenade home

<u>Singing Call - Figure - No Partner Change</u>

4 men Promenade inside the ring (Single File)**...**
Back home & Swing...
4 ladies Promenade inside the ring (Single File)**...**
Back home & Swing...
Join hands Circle Left halfway around...
Swing your partner...
Promenade home...
Join hands & go Forward & Back

<u>Singing Call - Figure</u>

4 ladies Promenade inside the ring...
Back home & Swing...
4 men Promenade inside the ring...
Back home & Swing...
Corner Left Hand Around (Allemande Left)**...**
Partner Right Hand Around (Arm Turn)**...**
Promenade corner...etc.

DoSaDo

Teaching Tips—Be sure both people are moving around each other. The routines given below are examples and can be inserted into many dance routines.

In addition to being a traditional term closely associated with square dancing, DoSaDo is used to stabilize dance formations. It can be used almost anywhere two people are facing. DoSaDo leaves both hands free for the next movement.

Patter - Big Circle/Square - Easy

Join hands & go Forward & Back...
Circle Right...
DoSaDo your partner...
Swing your partner...
Promenade...etc.

Circle Left...
DoSaDo the corner...
Swing your partner...
Promenade...etc.

Circle Left...
DoSaDo the corner...
Circle Right...
DoSaDo your partner...
Swing your corner...
Join hands & Circle Left...etc.

Circle Right...
Promenade Single File...
All the men turn around (U-turn Back)**...**
Corner DoSaDo
Turn this lady Right Hand Around (Arm Turn)**...**
Bow to your partner...
DoSaDo your partner...
Go back to the corner Left Hand Around (Arm Turn)**...**
Swing your partner...
Join hands & Circle Left...etc.

Patter - Square - Easy

 # 1 couple bow...
 # 2 couple DoSaDo...
 # 3 couple Swing...
 # 4 couple SMILE!...
Everybody Swing awhile...
Promenade...etc.

 # 3 couple bow...
 # 4 couple bow & Swing...
 # 1 couple bow & DoSaDo...
 # 2 couple DoSaDo then Swing...
Everybody Promenade home

1 & 3 men DoSaDo...
2 & 4 men DoSaDo...
1 & 3 ladies DoSaDo...
2 & 4 ladies DoSaDo.

1 & 2 men DoSaDo...
3 & 4 men DoSaDo...
1 & 4 ladies DoSaDo...
2 & 3 ladies DoSaDo.

Heads DoSaDo...
Sides DoSaDo

Patter - Square - Medium

Heads/sides **to center stand back to back** (below)**...**
Sides/heads **Promenade the outside track...**
Turn corner Left Hand Around...
DoSaDo Partner...
Turn corner Left Hand
Around (Arm Turn)**...**
Swing partner...
Promenade home

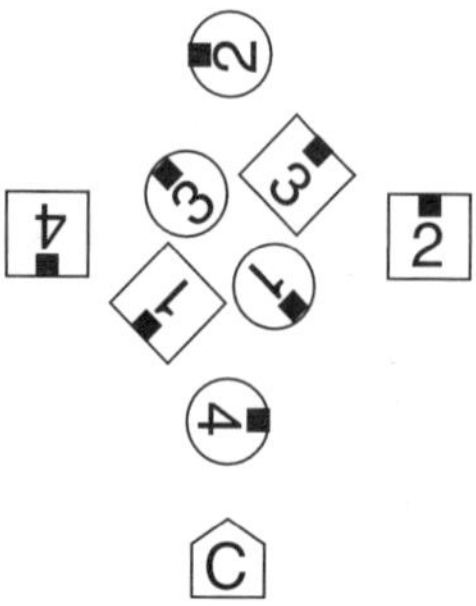

Patter - Square - Unusual

The normal DoSaDo ends with the participants facing each other. DoSaDo once & a half places them back to back.

Head men DoSaDo once & a half...
Swing the opposite...
Side men DoSaDo once & a half...
Swing the opposite...
Head ladies DoSaDo once & a half...
Swing your partner...
Side ladies DoSaDo once & a half...
Swing your partner...
All Circle Left 1/2 back to home

Join hands Circle Left...
Corners DoSaDo once & a half...
Swing the next...
4 ladies/men **Promenade inside the ring...**
Find your partner & Swing...
Promenade home

Singing Call Intro/Brk/End

Join hands & Circle Left...
Turn your corner Left Hand Around (Arm Turn)**...**
Partner DoSaDo...
Corner Left Hand Around (Arm Turn)**...**
Back to your partner DoSaDo...
Promenade around the ring...
Back home & Swing

Singing Call - Figures

4 ladies Promenade inside the ring...
Come back home & DoSaDo...
4 men Promenade inside the ring...
Come back home & DoSaDo...
Turn your corner by the Left (Arm Turn)**...**
DoSaDo Partner...
Promenade the corner home

Allemande Left

Teaching Tips—*Allemande Left* is really another name for a *Left Arm Turn* and is usually done with a corner. It is a traditional part of the terminology people associate with square dancing and can be easily be added to many of the previous routines where a *Left Arm Turn* is used. It is important to be sure the dancers understand that an *Allemande left* is not always followed by a *Right & Left Grand.* The following dance routines, plus a continuing effort on your part, should make that possible.

Patter - Square - Easy

Allemande Left your corner...
DoSaDo your own...
Swing the corner lady...
Promenade her home

(Repeat 4 times to get back the original partner)

Join hands & Circle Left...
Circle Right...
Promenade Single File...
Ladies reach out with your left hand & tap the man in front on the shoulder*...
Left Allemande...etc.

*It's assumed that the man will turn around when they are tapped on the shoulder. In this case, the *Arm Turn* should be once and a half.

Patter - Square - Medium

Heads/sides **Swing the opposite & face the sides...**
Allemande Left...
Swing your partner...
Promenade...etc.

The formation resulting from the *face the sides* is shown to the right and will be seen many times in this book. Notice that everyone is facing their corner and will return to their partner after a *Left Allemande*. The Allemande Left, from this set up, feels different and provides another way of adding variety to the dancing experience.

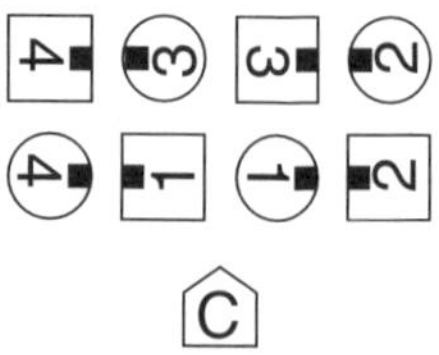

Right & Left Grand

Teaching Tips—*Right & Left Grand* is one of the square dance basics which is not used extensively in other dance forms in this book. It is a traditional movement people associate closely with square dancing and can be added into many of the dance routines after an *Allemande Left* at the end of the routine.

Patter - Square - Easy

Face your partner...
Right & Left Grand...
Meet your partner Promenade...
Come back home & Swing

Allemande Left...
Partner DoSaDo...
Right & Left Grand...etc.

Corners all Left Allemande...
Meet your partner Right & Left Grand...
Meet your partner & DoSaDo...
Step right up & Promeno (Promenade)**...**etc.

Patter - Square - Unusual

1st & 3rd go Forward & Back...
It's forward again turn the opposite lady with a Right Hand Around (Arm Turn)**...**
Partner by the left with a Left Hand Around (Arm Turn)**...**
Now the corner Right Hand Around (Arm Turn)**...**
Partner by the left like a Left Allemande...
The wrong way round* with a Right & Left Grand...
A left & right go round the town meet your partner with a Left Hand Around (Arm Turn)**...**
Turn all the way around to the right hand maid...
And you take that lady & Promenade home

*In a wrong way Right & Left Grand, the ladies will be traveling counterclockwise and the men will be traveling clockwise.

Singing Call - Intro/Brk/End

4 Ladies Promenade Inside (Single File)**...**
Swing your partner...
Join hands Circle Left...
Left Allemande...
Right & Left Grand...
DoSaDo...
Promenade...etc.

Bow to your partner...
Circle Left...
Swing the corner...
Left Allemande new corner & pass by one...
DoSaDo the next...
Left Allemande...
Right & Left Grand...
Promenade...etc.

Singing Call - Figure

1st & 3rd go Forward & Back...
Forward again turn your opposite lady with the Right Hand Around (Arm Turn)**...**
Back to your partner with a Left Hand Around (Arm Turn)**...**
Everybody to the corner with a Right Hand Around (Arm Turn)**...**
Back to your partner with a Left Hand Around (Arm Turn)**...**
All the way round to the right hand lady with a Right & Left Grand...
You're going to get a new lady & give her a Swing...
You Promenade go 'round the ring back to home

Star Right/Left

Teaching Tips—The standard hand position for a *Star* is with palms touching in the middle of the star. *Stars* can be used with almost any combination of people. Mix these figures in with combinations like heads *Circle 4* or ladies or men *Circle 4* for additional dance routines.

Patter - Square - Easy

Join hands & Circle Left...
Reverse back (Circle Right)**...**
All eight Star Left...
All turn around (U-turn Back) **...**
Star Right...
Men turn around (U-turn Back) **...**
Swing partner...etc.

4 men/ladies **make a Right/**left **Hand Star...**
All the way back home & Swing

Head couples make a Right/left **Hand Star...**
All the way back home & Swing...
Side couples make a Right/left **Hand Star...**
All the way back home & Swing

Head/side **couples Circle Left/**right...
Star Left/right...
Swing at home

Patter - Square - Medium

"Triple Allemande"

Allemande Left...
Ladies Star Right...
Men Promenade (Single File)**...**
Allemande Left with a full turn around...
Men Star Right...
Ladies Promenade (Single File)**...**
Allemande Left with a full turn...
Go Right & Left Grand...etc.

The next figure anchors the ladies and the men move around the set. All four men are moving at the same time. The caller needs to time the *Arm Turns* so all the men reach the *Stars* together.

4 men Star Right in the middle of the square...
Turn the opposite lady (Left Arm Turn) **& leave her there...**
Now Star Right back in the center of the square...
Turn your own (Left Arm Turn) **your not thru yet...**
Star by the Right 3/4 around...
Turn right hand lady Left Hand Around (Arm Turn)**...**
Star Right back across the floor...
Turn (Left Arm Turn) **your left hand lady**
she might get sore...
Star Right back 3/4 around...
Turn your partner Left Hand Around (Left Arm Turn)**...**
DoSaDo your corner...
Swing your partner...
Promenade...etc.

In the following figure, both the men and the ladies are moving. It's up to the man to keep track of which person is the opposite and which person is their partner. It is a good idea to walk this figure carefully before dancing it.

Ladies to the center for a Right Hand Star...
Men Promenade (Single File) **1/2 around...**
Turn the opposite lady Left Hand Around (full turn)**...**
The ladies Star Right again...
Men Promenade (Single File) **1/2 again...**
Turn partner by the left (Arm Turn) **go full around...**
4 ladies Star Right one more time...
Men Promenade 1/2 (Single File) **...**
Opposite lady for a left elbow (or Left Arm Turn)
go once & a half...
Men Star Right...
Ladies Promenade 1/2 (Single File) **...**
Partner left for a full turn around (Arm Turn)**...**
Keep her now Promenade the town...etc.

In the figure below, the ladies will need to remember that they will be following their partner into the center of the set for the *Star Left.* Both active couples will need to remember to turn the *Star* far enough to return back to the starting side of the set.

Heads/sides **Swing your opposite & face the sides...**
Corner DoSaDo...
Star Right with the outside two...
Heads/sides **Star Left in the middle...**
DoSaDo the corner...
Swing your partner...
Promenade home

Patter - Square - Difficult

Allemande Left...
Ladies Star Right...
Men Promenade (Single File) **...**
Allemande Left...
Men Star Right...
Ladies Promenade (Single File) **...**
Allemande Left...
Turn partner Right go full around (Arm Turn) **...**
To the right hand lady for a
Left Hand Around (Arm Turn)**...**
Men Star Right once around...
Ladies Promenade (Single File) **...**
Same lady Allemande Left...
Ladies Star...
Men Promenade (Single File) **...**
Allemande left...
Right to the corner step on by...
Left Allemande...
Promenade home...etc.

In the figure above, everyone is moving at the same time. Dancers need to be very comfortable with all the numbered positions in the set before this dance is used.

Singing Call - Intro/Brk/End

Heads Star Right...
Allemande Left your corner...
Swing at home...
Sides Star Right...
Allemande Left your corner...
Swing at home...

Circle Left...
Reverse back & Circle Right...
Single File (Promenade)**...**
Ladies keep walking like you are, men turn in to a Right Hand Star...
Pass her twice & corner Left Allemande...
Right & Left Grand...
Promenade home...
Swing

Singing Call - Figure - Unusual

"On the Trail of the Lonesome Pine"

Head/side **2 men take your corners to the middle & back** (Forward & Back)**...**
Same four Circle Left around that track...
Left Hand Star go back home...
Right Hand Around your own...
Left Hand Around your corner, then you go back home...
DoSaDo...
Then your corner Swing...
Promenade...etc.

The diagram to the right illustrates the action of taking the *corner lady to the middle and back.* The *Forward & Back* is danced on the diagonal. The other people step back a short step to move out of their way if necessary.

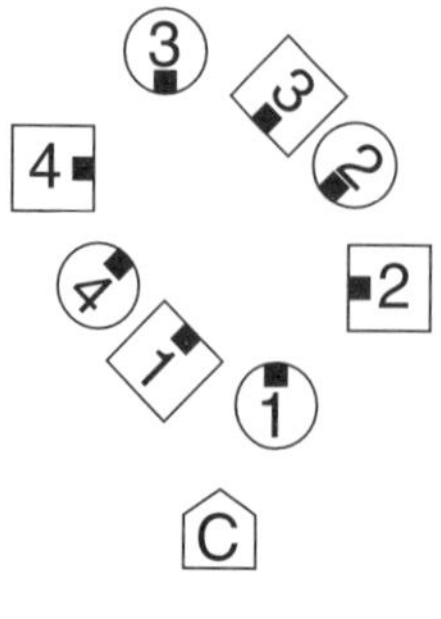

The Great Allemande Left Game

As you probably have noticed, many square dance routines in this manual end with an *Allemande Left*. Over time, the *Allemande Left* has become recognized by dancers as one of the places where one dance routine ends and another begins. From here, the dancers expect to return to home position with their partner and begin another dance routine. The usual calls that follow the (etc.) are *Swing, Promenade, Right & Left Grand* or *Circle* to home

One of the fun aspects of square dance choreography is designing dance routines that place the *Allemande Left* at points where the dancers do not expect it to be called. Then the dancers can't anticipate the end of the routine and feel an enhanced sense of accomplishment when they find they have successfully completed the dance. It is still another way to add variety.

Up to this point in the manual, most of the *Allemande Lefts* have occurred from very predictable formations. The corner was either in front of each dancer or to the man's left (lady's right). There are many other formations where an *Allemande Left* can be called if the dancers are instructed properly (i.e. don't always expect the corner to be in the same old place). In this manual, the corner will almost always be clockwise around the ring for the man and counterclockwise around the ring for the lady.

Here are some examples. In the formation shown to the right, the corner is directly in front of each dancer. In this formation, dancers will almost always select the correct person for an *Allemande Left*.

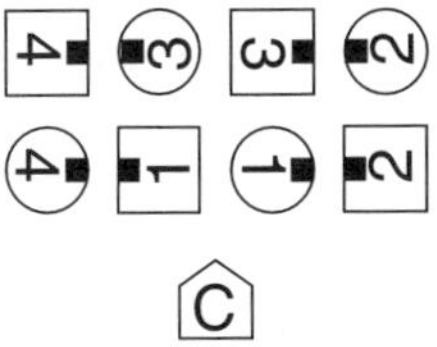

Recognizing the corner in the next two formations is not as obvious. In both formations, the corner is on the man's right (clockwise) and lady's left (counterclockwise). To help leaders recognize when these unusual *Allemande Lefts* are occurring, many of the dance routines in the rest of this manual will include diagrams showing formation prior to the *Allemande Left* when the heads are active. Remember, the set up will be different when sides are active.

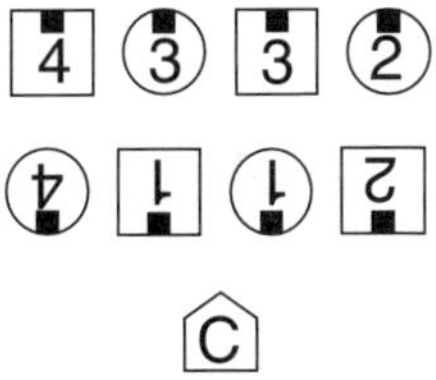

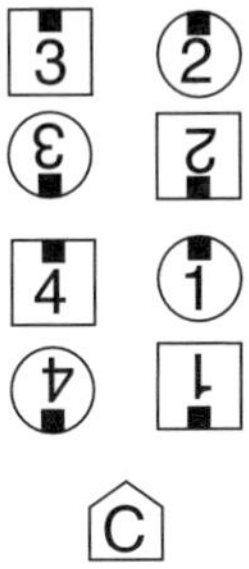

Pass Thru

Teaching Tips— *Pass Thru* is always done right shoulder to right shoulder with someone you are facing. Some people will turn around after a *Pass Thru* and not be in the correct position for the next call.

Up to this point in the manual, each of the calls have been printed on a separate line. Starting with *Pass Thru,* some of the calls take only 2 steps from some formations. For example, *Pass Thru* after a *Right Arm Turn* takes only 2 steps. The two calls will be printed on the same line, when space permits, and will be connected with an (&).

Patter - Square - Easy

Heads/sides **Promenade 1/2...**
Down the middle Pass Thru...
Swing...etc.

Heads/sides **Circle 1/2...**
Pass Thru (2 steps) **& Swing your partner...**etc.

Heads/sides **turn opposite 1/2 by the right** (Arm Turn)
Pass Thru (2 steps) **& Swing your partner...**etc.
Head/sides **Pass Thru...**
Promenade Left/right...
Sides/heads **Pass Thru...**
Promenade left/right...
Turn your corner Left Hand Around...
Swing your partner...
Promenade home

Almost all dance routines require some adjustment by other dancers as the active dancers move. This a called counter-dancing. Each dancer adjusts his/her movements to compliment what is happening with the other dancers.

Sometimes the adjustment needs to be pretty dramatic. In several of the following routines, couples Promenade Single File around two to a line of four. The inactive couples must adjust or slide at least 2 steps to their right in order to keep the two facing lines of four opposite each other.

Patter - Square - Medium

Heads/sides **Circle 1/2…**
DoSaDo…
Turn opposite 1/2 by the Right (Arm Turn)
Pass Thru & both turn right/left
Single File (Promenade)
around 2 to a line (see right)**…**
Circle 4 with the opposite two
halfway around…
Same two DoSaDo…
Turn the opposite 1/2 right (Arm Turn)
Pass Thru & Swing your partner…
Allemande Left…etc.

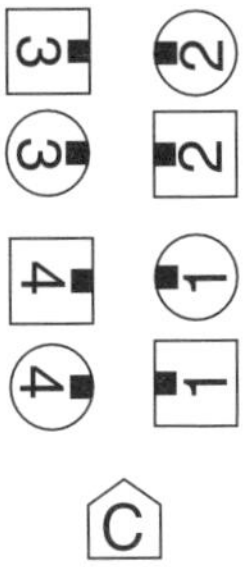

Heads/sides **Promenade 1/2…**
Turn the opposite 1/2 Right (Arm Turn)
Pass Thru & both turn right Single File (Promenade)
around 2 to a line …
Pass Thru…
Swing your partner & face across…
Circle 4 halfway around…
Turn the opposite 1/2 Right (Arm Turn)
Pass Thru & turn your back on your
partner (see right)**…**
Left Allemande

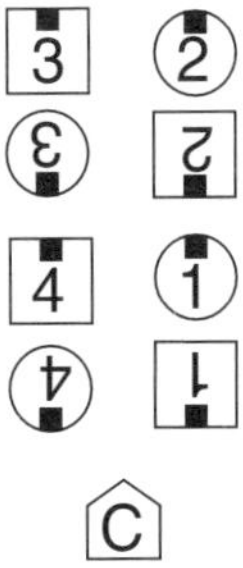

Head/side **ladies DoSaDo once & a half…**
Swing the opposite & face to the middle…
Same 4 Circle Left 3/4 & Pass Thru…
Facing ladies DoSaDo once & a half…
Swing the opposite & face across…
Facing couples Circle Left 3/4
Pass Thru & Left Allemande…etc.

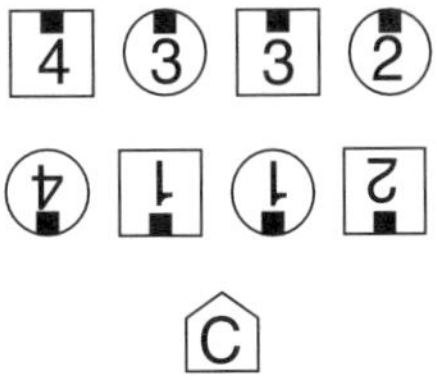

The position for the *Allemande Left* is shown in the diagram to the right. The men must turn to the right and the ladies turn to the left.

Patter - Square - Unusual

In two of the figures below, the inactive couples will have to shift to their right as the active couples *Promenade Single File* around 2. They should move far enough to square up the facing lines of four as shown in the diagrams attached to each figure.

Heads/sides **Pass Thru...**
Both turn left Single File (Promenade) **around 2**
to a line (men on the ends & ladies in the middle as shown below)**...**
Forward & Back...
Same sex DoSaDo...
Face your partner & Pass Thru...
Four men Star Right...
Ladies turn around (U-turn Back)**...**
Men pass by your partner...
Allemande Left with the corner...etc.

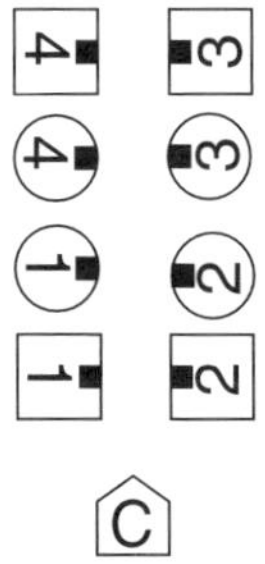

Heads/sides **Pass Thru...**
Both turn right Single File (Promenade) **around 2**
to a line (ladies on the ends & men in the middle as shown)**...**
Forward & Back...
Face your partner & Pass Thru...
Four ladies Star Left...
Men turn around (U-turn Back)**...**
Partner DoSaDo...
Swing...
Promenade...etc.

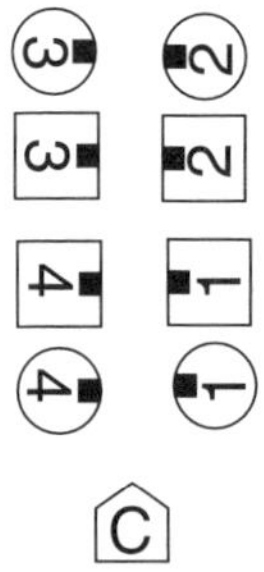

Heads/sides **Pass Thru...**
Both turn left Single File (Promenade) **around 2 to a line...**
Lines Forward & Back...
Turn the opposite 1/2 Right (Arm Turn)
Pass thru & face your partner...
Just the sides Turn 1/2 Right (Arm Turn) **&**
All Pass Thru & Allemande Left...etc.

In the following routines, new dancers will tend to want to turn around after the *Pass Thru* and face back toward the center of the set. When done properly, the four men/ladies should be passing ladies/men facing them.

Head couples Pass Thru, stay facing out...
Sides Pass Thru, stay facing out...
4 ladies Promenade to the right Single File...
Halfway around then Swing that man &
everybody face to the middle...
Side couples Pass Thru, stay facing out...
Heads Pass Thru, stay facing out...
4 men Promenade to the right Single File...
Halfway around then Swing that lady &
everybody face to the middle...
Left Allemande...
Partners all Right & Left Grand...etc.

Singing - Figure - Unusual

See the diagram on page 54 for the diagonal *Forward & Back.* After the *Single File Promenade* to home, the set should be squared up in the standard formation.

Head/side **men & corner lady Forward & Back...**
Pass Thru...
Turn left Single File Promenade around 2 to home...
Side/head **men & corner lady Forward & Back...**
Pass Thru...
Turn left Single File Promenade around 2 to home...
Join hands & Circle Left...
Swing new partner...
Promenade home

Patter - Star Theme

Heads/sides **Star Left to the corner...**
Star Right with the side two...
Heads/sides **Star Left in the middle to the same two...**
Turn the opposite 1/2 Right (Arm Turn) **& Pass Thru...**
Swing & Promenade...etc.

U-turn Back

Teaching Tips— Whenever it is convenient, people should turn toward each other on a *U-turn Back.* Many of the previous dance routines have the men or the ladies turn around. A little note has been added to each of these showing (U-turn Back). All of these routines can now be used again with this new basic term.

Patter - Square - Easy

Heads Pass Thru & U-turn Back...
Sides Pass Thru & U-turn Back*...
Heads Pass Thru & U-turn Back...
Sides Pass Thru & U-turn Back...etc.

*At this point the ladies are on the man's left hand side

Heads/sides **Turn the opposite 1/2 Right** (Arm Turn)**...**
Pass Thru & U-turn Back

Heads Pass Thru & U-turn Back...
Sides Pass Thru & U-turn Back...
Join hands Circle Left...
Swing the corner...
Promenade...etc.

Swing your partner...
Promenade...
Put the ladies in the lead Single File (Promenade)**...**
Ladies U-turn Back & DoSaDo partner...
4 men Star Left once around...
Same lady Right Arm Turn...
Step by & Left Allemande...etc.

Swing your partner...
Promenade...
Put the ladies in the lead Single File (Promenade)**...**
Men U-turn Back & DoSaDo your corner...
4 Ladies Star Left once around...
To the same man & DoSaDo...
Swing your partner...
Promenade...etc.

Patter - Square - Medium

Heads/sides **1/2 Promenade...**
Turn the opposite 1/2 Right (Arm Turn)
Pass Thru & both turn right
Single File (Promenade)
around 2 to a line (see right)**...**
With the opposite two Circle 1/2...
Pass Thru & U-turn Back...
Same two Circle 1/2...
Pass Thru & U-turn Back...
All 8 Circle Left...
Left Allemande...etc.

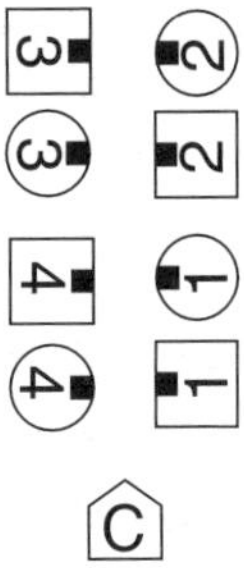

Singing Call - Figures

Head/side **man & corner lady Forward & Back...**
Same two Pass Thru & U-turn Back ...
Side/head **man & corner lady Forward & Back...**
Same two Pass Thru & U-turn Back ...
Join hands & Circle Left to home...
Allemande Left corner...
Promenade home

Heads/sides **Promenade 1/2 outside...**
Pass Thru & U-turn Back...
Sides/heads **Promenade 1/2 outside...**
Pass Thru & U-turn Back...
All eight Circle Left...
Swing Partner...
Promenade home

Heads/sides **Promenade 1/2...**
Sides/heads **Pass Thru & U-turn Back...**
All Circle Left (2 men - 2 ladies)**...**
4 men Forward & Back...
4 ladies Forward & Back...
Ladies DoSaDo...
Ladies Swing the nearest man...
Promenade home

Courtesy Turn

Teaching Tips— The lady's right hand should be placed palm out in the middle of her back where she wants the man to place his right hand. The man then places his right hand in her palm for the *Courtesy Turn.*

Patter - Square - Easy

Heads/sides **Pass Thru...**
Courtesy Turn...
Pass Thru...
Partner Swing...etc.

Heads/sides **Promenade 1/2...**
Down the middle Pass Thru...
Courtesy Turn...etc.

Patter - Square - Medium

Head/side **men Swing the opposite Lady...**
Face the side couples...
Circle 1/2 & Pass Thru...
Courtesy Turn...
Circle 1/2 & Pass Thru...
Face your partner & Pass Thru...
Left Allemande*...etc.

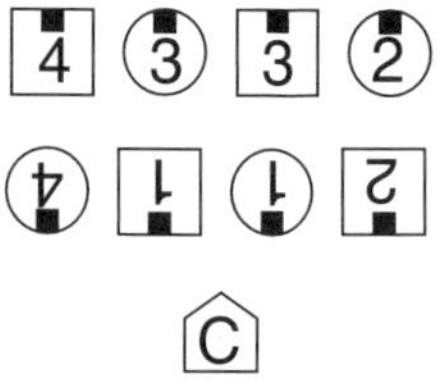

*The position for the *Allemande Left* is illustrated in the above diagram. The men must turn to the right and the ladies turn to the left.

In the following routine, the inactive couples must remember to slide to the right several steps to square up the facing lines as shown below.

Heads/sides **1/2 Promenade...**
Turn the opposite 1/2 Right (Arm Turn)
Pass Thru & both turn right
  Single File (Promenade)
  around 2 to a Line (see right)**...**
Pass Thru...
Courtesy Turn your partner...
Pass Thru...
Courtesy Turn your partner...
Left Allemande...etc.

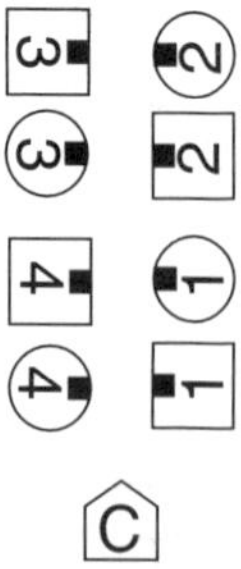

Heads/sides **Turn the opposite 1/2 Right** (Arm Turn)
Pass Thru & both turn right
Single File (Promenade)
around 2 to a Line (see right)**...**
Pass Thru...
Courtesy Turn your partner...
Join hands & Circle Left...
Left Allemande...

Four ladies to the center & Star Right...
To your partner for a Courtesy Turn...
Send them back to a Right Hand Star...
To the corner man for a Courtesy Turn...
Send them back for a Right Hand Star...
To the opposite man for a Courtesy Turn...
Send them back to a Right Hand Star...
To the right hand man for a Courtesy Turn...
Send them back for a Right Hand Star...
To the partner & Swing...etc.

Patter - Square - Unusual

In this dance, the couples are facing each other on a diagonal to the walls of the hall as shown in the diagram. When they *Circle 1/2, Pass Thru and Courtesy Turn,* the lines should still be facing each other on the diagonal. Inexperienced dancers will try to square up the lines of four with the walls.

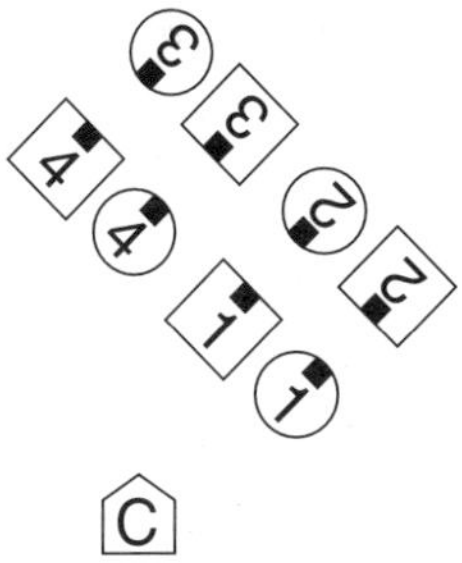

Couple #1 face couple #2...
Couple #3 face couple #4...
Lines of four go Forward & Back...
With the opposite couple Circle 1/2
Pass Thru & Courtesy Turn...
Turn opposite by the Left Hand Around
& back to your partner...
Turn partner Right Hand Around...
To the corner Left Allemande...etc.

Ladies Chain Two/Four

Teaching Tips— As soon as the ladies start across the set, the men should step to the right to meet the oncoming lady for the *Courtesy Turn*.

Patter - Square - Easy

Head/side **2 Ladies Chain...**
Chain back...
All 4 Ladies Chain...etc.

Patter - Square - Medium

Head/side **Ladies Chain...**
Heads/sides **Circle Left 3/4...**
Same two Pass Thru &
Circle Left 3/4...
2 Ladies Chain...
Pass Thru (see right)**...**
Left Allemande...etc.

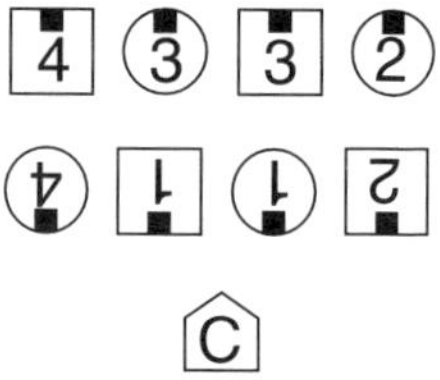

4 Ladies Chain 3/4...
4 Ladies Chain across...
4 Ladies Chain 3/4...
Swing your partner...etc.

The next three dances have the *Ladies Chain* right or *Ladies Chain* left. If the head *Ladies Chain* right then the side couples must turn to the left to face them. At the end of the chain the couples should be facing across the set. If the head *Ladies Chain* left then the side couples must face to the right.

Head/side **Ladies Chain right...**
4 Ladies Chain across...
New head/side **Ladies Chain right...**
4 Ladies Chain home

In the two following dances, the ladies change positional roles and become new head or side ladies when they finish the *2 Ladies Chain.*

Head/side **Ladies Chain right...**
New side/head **Ladies Chain right...**
New side/head **Ladies Chain left...**
New head/side **Ladies Chain left...**
Swing at home

Head Ladies Chain left...
New side Ladies Chain across...
Head couples Pass Thru & U-turn Back...
Side couples Pass Thru & U-turn Back...
Face your partner Right & Left Grand...etc.

The next two routines instruct the dancers to pass right by your own after an *Allemande Left*. Pass right shoulders as in a *Pass Thru*. The dances also contain wording that does not directly refer to anything the dancers should be dancing. This is *filler patter* or words designed to rhyme with the commands. It can be used if the leader chooses or changed to suit individual needs.

Allemande Left your corner girl...
Pass right by your own...
Right Hand Around (Arm Turn) **the right hand lady...**
Allemande Left new corner...
Pass by that new one by without a whirl...
New right hand lady Right Hand Around (Arm Turn)**...**
New corners Left Hand Around...
4 Ladies Chain across...
To a Left Allemande...etc.

Allemande Left the corner maid...
Pass your own right on by...
Right to the next one on the sly (Arm Turn)**...**
Turn all the way around, then step on by...
Go forward left & right, now turn back one
(Right Arm Turn 1/2 & step by the same person)...
It's a Left Hand Around the new corner one...
Put the ladies in the center back to back...
Men Promenade (Single file) **the outside track...**
It's once around & don't be slow same little lady Swing & whirl...
4 Ladies Chain across...
Roll Promenade*, it's home you go

*On a roll *Promenade*, the *Courtesy Turn* is continued until Promenade direction is reached.

Patter - Square - Unusual

Heads/sides **Promenade 1/2...**
Circle four 3/4
Pass Thru & Circle Left 3/4
with the outside two...
Back away to a line of 4...
Pass Thru...
Courtesy Turn...
2 Ladies Chain...
Pass Thru...
Courtesy Turn...
Circle Left 3/4...
Pass Thru (see right) **&**
Left Allemande...etc.

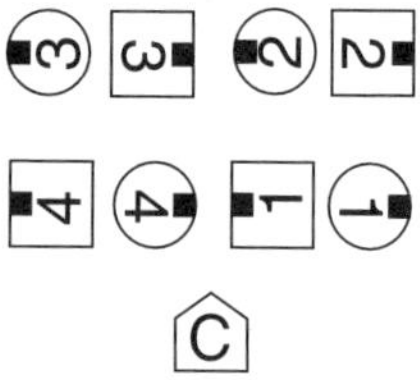

Singing Call - Figure

"Just Because"

Head/side **2 Ladies Chain right on over...**
Same 2 Ladies Chain back again...
Side/head **2 Ladies Chain right on over...**
Same 2 Ladies Chain back again...
Allemande Left the corner...
DoSaDo your own...
Swing the corner...
Promenade...etc.

Head/side **Ladies Chain...**
Head/side **couples Circle Left 3/4**
Pass Thru & DoSaDo outside two...
Same four Star Right once around...
Ladies U-turn Back...
Corner Swing...
Promenade home

Head/side **Ladies Chain across…**
Heads Promenade 1/2…
Into the center DoSaDo…
Circle 4 once & a quarter…
Pass Thru (see right) **& corner Swing…**
Promenade…etc.

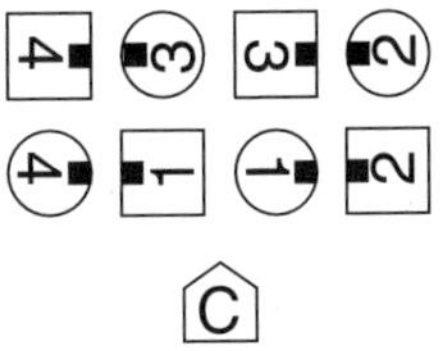

Head/side **Ladies Chain right…**
All Swing your corner…
Head/side **Ladies Chain across…**
Allemande Left corner…
DoSaDo partner…
Swing your corner…
Promenade home

Head/side **two men & corner girl Forward & Back…**
Star Right…
Turn partner Left (Arm Turn)**…**
Corner Right (Arm Turn)**…**
Partner Left (Arm Turn)**…**
4 Ladies Chain 3/4…
Keep this lady & Promenade home

Right & Left Thru

Teaching Tips— The right hand of the *Right & Left Thru* should only be touched lightly and not gripped. The facing dancers should step straight by and *Courtesy Turn* the person beside them.

<u>Patter - Square - Easy</u>

Heads/sides **Right & Left Thru...**
Right & Left back...

Heads/sides **Right & Left Thru...**
Head/side **Ladies Chain...**
Head/side **Ladies Chain back...**
Sides/heads **Right & Left Thru...**
Star Right to the corner...
Left Allemande...etc.

<u>Patter - Square - Medium</u>

The routine below has the couples *Right & Left Thru* with the couple to the right in the square. At the end of the *Right & Left Thru* the couples should be facing across the set.

Couples 1 & 2 Right & Left Thru...
Couples 3 & 4 Right & Left Thru...
Heads/sides **Right & Left Thru...**
Left Allemande...etc.
(Repeat using couples 4 & 1 and couples 2 & 3.)

In the next dance, the center men *U-turn Back, shake right hands and step by*. After the head men step by, the square should look like the diagram to the right

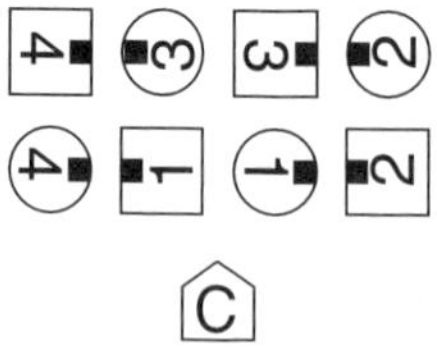

Heads/sides **Right & Left Thru...**
Same Ladies Chain...
Heads/sides **Forward & Back...**
Swing the opposite & face the sides...
Center men U-turn Back...
Shake right hands, step by & Left Allemande...etc.

Heads/sides **Circle Left 3/4...**
Right & Left Thru...
Pass Thru & Circle Left 3/4...
Lines go Forward & Back...
Right & Left Thru...
Pass Thru...
Courtesy Turn...
Same 4 Star Right once around...
Circle Left...
Left Allemande...etc.

Patter - Square - Unusual

The following squares use *Right & Left Thru* with a full turn. The full turn must be taught to the dancers before it is used in a dance. The full turn requires a full 360° turn in the *Courtesy Turn* portion of the *Right & Left Thru* instead of the customary 180° degree turn. The set at the end of the heads *Right & Left Thru* with a full turn should look like the diagram shown to the right.

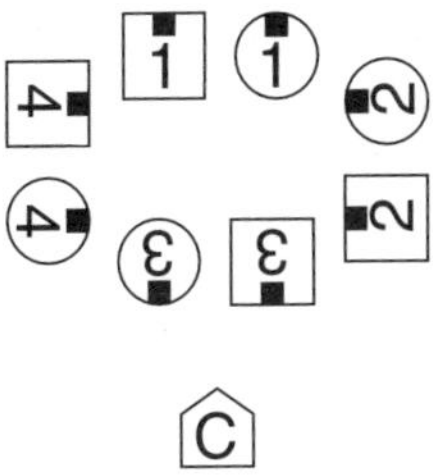

Head/sides **Right & Left Thru with a full turn...**
Promenade Left to home...
Side/heads **Right & Left Thru with a full turn...**
Promenade Left to home...

Heads/sides **Circle Left 3/4...**
Right & Left Thru with a full turn...
DoSaDo the outside two...
Same four Right & Left Thru...
Same four Circle Left 3/4...
Lines Forward & Back...
Right & Left Thru...
2 Ladies Chain...
Same four Circle Left 3/4...
Right & Left Thru with a full turn (see above) **&**
Left Allemande...etc.

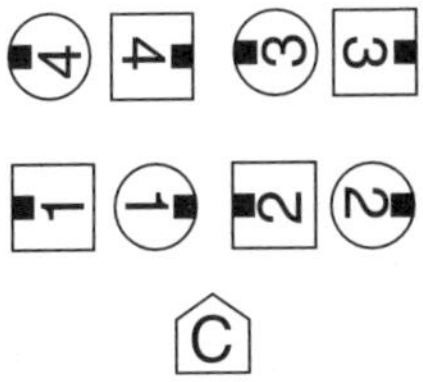

Head/side **Ladies Chain...**
Head/sides **Circle Left 3/4...**
Pass Thru & Right & Left Thru...
2 Ladies Chain...
Circle Right 3/4...
Pass Thru (see right) **&**
Left Allemande...etc.

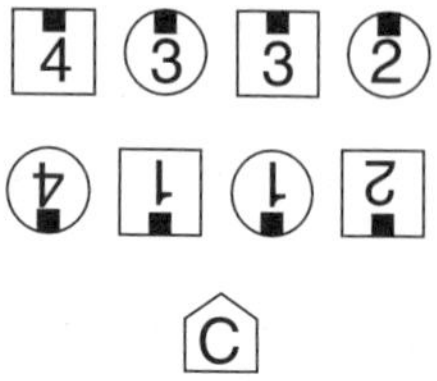

Side Ladies Chain right...
Heads Right & Left Thru...
Heads Promenade outside 3/4* (see right)**...**
Sides Right & Left Thru...
Sides Pass Thru...
Turn the opposite 1/2 Right (Arm Turn)**...**
Pass Thru (see right)**...**
Left Allemande...etc.

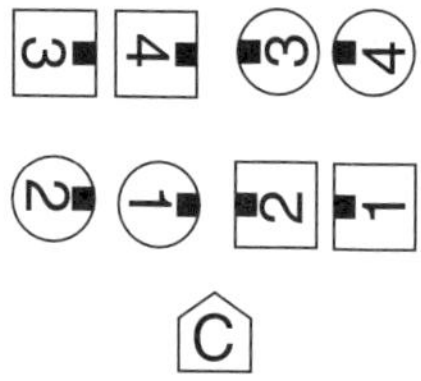

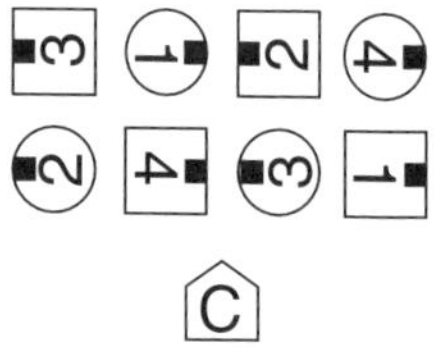

* Notice where the dancers complete the 3/4 Promenade and finish standing behind the side couples.

Patter - Square - Difficult

The following routine requires a very clear understanding of how far to turn each *Star*.

Heads/sides **Right & Left Thru...**
Same two Pass Thru...
U-turn Back...
Star Right 3/4 around
(The #1 man is now facing #2 lady & #1 lady is facing #2 man. The lady is in the lead for the Star with the sides)**...**
Star Left with the sides once around...
Star Right in the center once & a half...
Star Left with the opposites once around...
Heads/sides **to the center & 2 Ladies Chain**
(Head ladies are leading again and the #1 man Courtesy Turns the #3 lady)
Right & Left Thru...
Pass thru & Left Allemande...etc.

Singing Call - Figures

Head two couples Promenade 1/2...
Down the middle Right & Left Thru...
Side two couples Promenade 1/2...
Down the middle Right & Left Thru...
Allemande Left your corner...
Partner DoSaDo...
Swing the corner...
Promenade home

Heads Right & Left Thru...
Side couples Right & Left Thru...
Head Ladies Chain across...
Side Ladies Chain across...
All 4 Ladies Chain 3/4...
Left Allemande...
Promenade home...

4 Ladies Chain across...
Heads Promenade 1/2...
Sides Right & Left Thru...
Join hands & Circle Left...
Allemande Left your corner...
DoSaDo your own...
Swing the corner...
Promenade home

Head two couples Right & Left Thru...
New 3 & 4 Right & Left Thru...
Side two couples Right & Left Thru...
New 2 & 3 Right & Left Thru...
Join hands & Circle Left halfway...
Corner Swing...
Promenade...etc.

Separate

Teaching Tips— On the command of Separate, the designated people move away from each other.

Patter - Square - Easy

First couple stand back to back &
Separate around the outside track...
Pass your partner...
Bow to the corner...
Swing your partner...

(Repeat for couples 2, 3 & 4. You can have the heads or the sides *Separate* and all four *Separate.*)

Heads/sides **Pass Thru...**
Separate around 2...
Swing at home

Heads/sides **Turn the opposite 1/2 Right** (Arm Turn)**...**
Pass Thru & Separate around 2...
Down the middle & Pass Thru...
Swing at home

Patter - Square - Medium

Heads Pass Thru...
Separate around 1...
Into the middle & Circle 1/2...
Pass Thru (see right) **&**
Left Allemande...etc.

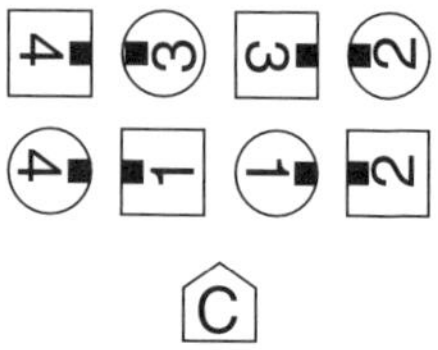

Sides/heads **U-turn Back...**
Separate Around 1...
Into the middle U-turn Back...
Pass Thru & U-turn Back...
Circle 1/2...
Pass Thru & U-turn Back...
Circle 1/2...
Centers U-turn Back...
Star Right to the corner...
Left Allemande...etc.

4 Ladies Chain 3/4...
4 Ladies Chain across...
Sides turn opposite 1/2 Right Hand Around...
Pass Thru & Separate around 1 to a line...
Right & Left Thru...
2 Ladies Chain...
Right & Left Thru...
Same four Circle Left 3/4...
Pass Thru (see right) & Left Allemande

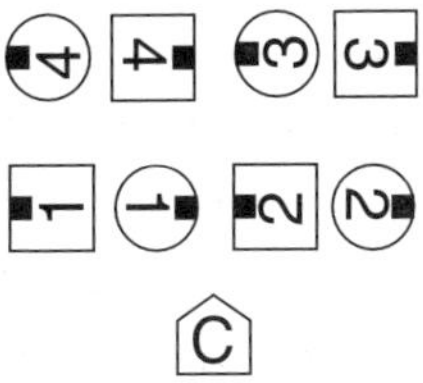

Heads/sides Promenade go half way 'round...
Down the middle & Pass Thru...
Separate go around just 1 into the middle...
Pass Thru & Right & Left Thru the outside two...
Right & Left Back...
Star Right go full around...
Ladies U-turn Back & Left Allemande...etc.

<u>Patter - Square - Unusual</u>

Head/side men & corner go Forward & Back...
Pass Thru & U-turn Back...
Same 4 Right & Left Thru...
Same 4 Pass Thru...
Separate around 1 into the middle...
Same 4 Right & Left Thru...
Same 4 Left Allemande...
Everybody Right & Left Grand...etc.

Head/side men & corner ladies Pass Thru...
Separate around 2 to a line (see right)...
Turn the opposite 1/2 right (Arm Turn)...
Pass Thru & U-turn Back...
Turn the opposite 1/2 right (Arm Turn)...
Pass Thru & face your partner...
Right & Left Grand...etc.

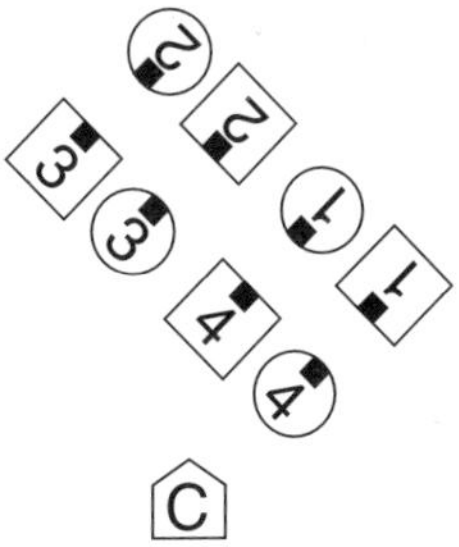

The following square uses *Right and Left Thru* with a full turn as shown to the right. The full turn must be taught to the dancers before it is used. The full turn requires a full 360° turn in the *Courtesy Turn* portion of the *Right & Left Thru* instead of the customary 180° degree turn.

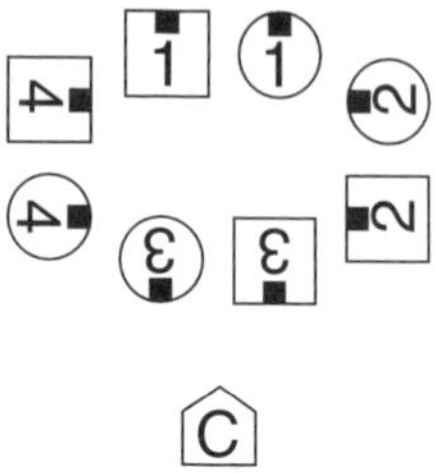

Heads/sides Right & Left Thru
with a full turn...
Separate around 1 into the middle...
Turn the opposite 1/2 Right (Arm Turn)**...**
Star Right...
To the corner Left Allemande...etc.

Patter - Square - Difficult

In the next figure the dancers *Star Left* and then pass by home position and pick up the next person with an arm around the waist. The center dancers back out and the outside dancers walk forward for a full turn & then *Circle Left*.

4 Ladies Chain...
Head/side **men & the corner**
lady go Forward & Back...
Star Left once around...
Pass home take the next (same sex)
back out a full turn...
Circle Left (2 men - 2 ladies, see right)**...**
4 men Pass Thru...
Separate & stand behind the ladies...
Ladies Chain across*...
Everybody Forward & Back...
Pass Thru & face your partner...
Pass Thru & Left Allemande...etc.

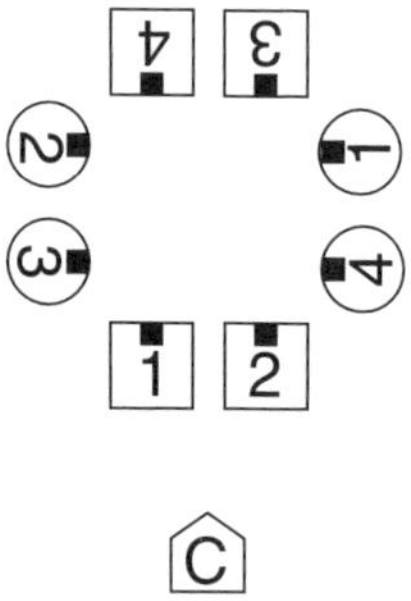

*After the 4 men *Separate* and stand behind the ladies, the four ladies are facing in the center of the square. To *Chain*, the ladies take right hands and step by to the facing man for a Courtesy Turn. The facing man should be the lady's original partner.

Singing Call - Figures

"Solomon Levi"

1st couple Separate go around the outside track...
Pass her going around & pass her coming back...
Bow to the corner...Shake hands with your partner...
Swing partner...Promenade...
(Repeat for couples 2, 3 & 4 and then for heads and sides and all four.)

Head/sides **Forward & Back...**
Pass Thru...
Separate around 2 to a line...
Lines Forward & Back...
All eight Star Right...
Corner Swing...
Promenade home...
Swing

Heads/sides **Pass Thru...**
Separate around 2...
Into the middle & DoSaDo...
Same four Star Right...
Once around & corner Swing...
Allemande Left new corner...
Grand Right & Left...
Promenade...
Home & Swing

Heads/sides **Forward & Back...**
Pass Thru...
Separate around 2 to a line...
Sides/heads **turn opposite Right Hand Around...**
Partners Left Hand Around...
Promenade corner...etc.

Split the Couple/Ring

Teaching Tips— The inactive facing couple should step apart momentarily and then step back together.

Patter - Square - Easy

#1 couple down the middle & Split the Ring...
Separate around 3...
Swing at home

(Repeat for couples #2, #3 & #4)

Heads/sides **Swing the opposite & face the sides...**
Split the outside two...
Separate around 1...
DoSaDo your partner...etc.

Timing the delivery of the calls, in the next several dances, requires some practice and some abbreviation of the commands or calls. When couples are facing and standing face to face, it takes only 2 steps to *Pass Thru* then another 2 steps to *Split* the outside two. *Separate* around one adds a maximum of 4 steps. This means the leader is not going to be able to say all the words in the description of several of the routines listed below. The leader should walk-thru the routine and then call something like *Pass Thru-Split Two-around one* which takes only about 6 beats of music to speak.

Many of these dance figures are classified as "goal post" figures. The goal posts are the inactive dancers. They move enough (counter dance) to allow the active dancers to get around them, but essentially they act as fixed posts. Hence the term "goal posts".

"Goal Post"

Heads/sides **Pass Thru...**
Separate around 1...
Into the middle & Pass Thru...
Split the outside two...
Separate around 1...
Down the middle & Pass Thru...
Swing at home

Patter - Square - Medium

Heads/sides **Circle 1/2...**
Pass Thru & Separate around 1...
In the middle Circle 1/2 & Pass Thru...
Split the outside 2...
Separate around 1...
Down the middle Pass Thru...
Swing at home

Heads/sides **Pass Thru...**
Separate around 1...
Pass Thru in the middle...
Split the outside 2...
Separate around 1...
Down the middle Right & Left Thru...
Swing at home

In the next figure, after the *Pass Thru** two couples will be standing facing out while the center *2 Ladies Chain*. Many dancers will want to turn around to see what is happening. They will have to be cautioned to just wait facing out for 8 beats of music. Then everyone can do the *Left Allemande* from the position shown in the diagram below.

Side Ladies Chain...
Heads Promenade 3/4...
Sides Pass Thru...
Split the outside 2...
Separate around 1...
Pass Thru in the middle...
Separate around 1...
Right & Left Thru in the middle...
Pass Thru & 2 Ladies Chain...
Pass Thru* & don't turn around...
Center 2 Ladies Chain (see right) **...**
Left Allemande

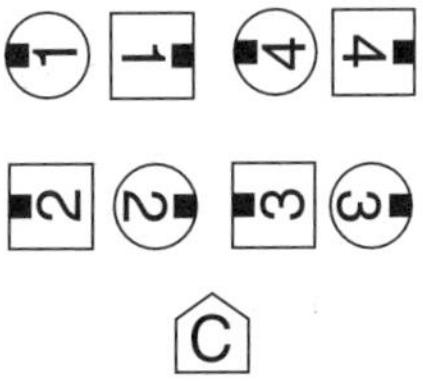

In the next figure, the ladies will be following the man in a *Single File Promenade*. A *Pass Thru* from a *Single File Promenade* is still done by passing right shoulders with the person coming toward you. The active couple is weaving their way *Single File* around the "goal posts".

Sides/heads **Pass Thru...**
Both turn right Single File (Promenade)**...**
Follow that lady & go around 1...
Into the middle Pass Thru & Split Two...
Ladies go left, men go right, around one...
Into the middle Pass Thru...
Both turn right go Single File (Promenade)**...**
Follow that man & go around 1...
Down the middle & Pass Thru & Split two...
Man go left & lady go right, around just 1...
Into the middle & Right & Left Thru...
Star by the Right once around...
Corners all Left Allemande...etc.

Heads/sides **Pass Thru...**
Courtesy Turn your lady...
Pass Thru...
Separate around 1...
In the middle Pass Thru & Split outside 2
Separate around 1...
Down the middle Pass Thru...
Courtesy Turn...
Pass Thru...
Separate around 1...
Pass Thru in the middle &
Split the outside 2...
Separate around 1...
Circle 8 (Left)**...**
Left Allemande...etc.

In both of the following figures, the man will do a *U-turn Back* and then follow their partner in a *Single File Promenade* as shown to the right.

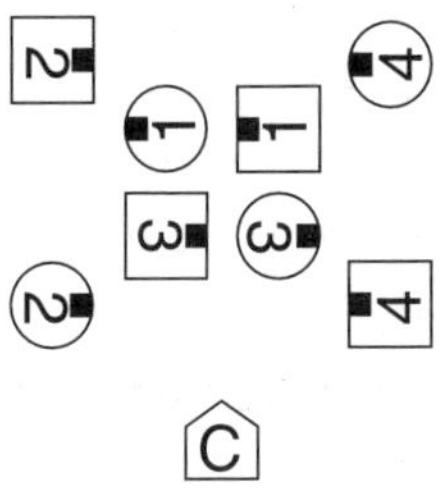

Patter - Square- Unusual

Sides Promenade 1/2...
Head couples Pass Thru...
Separate around just 1...
Into the middle & Pass Thru...
Men U-turn Back & follow that lady*...
Split those two & both go right (Single File Promenade)**...**
Into the middle & 2 Ladies Chain...
Right & Left Thru & turn the lady...
Pass Thru...
Separate around 1...
Into the middle & Pass Thru...
Stop when you meet the sides...
Head ladies U-turn Back & face...
Shake right hands, step by (see right)**...**
Left Allemande...etc.

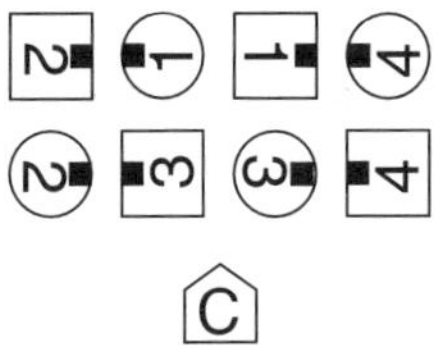

*The head men are looking at the back of their partner. Follow her in a *Single File Promenade.*

Heads Pass Thru...
Head men U-turn Back, follow that lady*...
Both turn right (Promenade Single File)
  around the side lady & into the middle...
Head Ladies Chain...
Pass Thru & Split two...
Separate around 1...
Down the middle & Pass Thru...
Head men U-turn Back & follow that lady...
Both turn right around the side lady...
Into the middle & head Ladies Chain...
Pass Thru & Left Allemande...etc.

*The head man is looking at the back their partner. Follow her in *Single File Promenade*

"H Figure"

1st couple bow & Swing...
Down the center & Split the Ring...
Separate around 1 to a line of 4...
Line of four Forward & Back...
Forward again & stand pat
(The line of four stops in the middle between the side couples)**...**

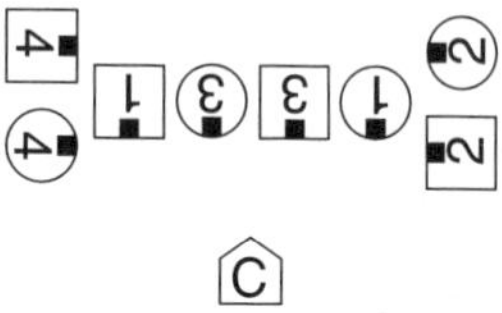

Sides Right & Left Thru down the line
(The man goes down one side & the lady down the other side & *Courtesy Turn* at the end)**...**
Right & Left Thru back...
Center four Circle 4...
Everybody home & everybody Swing...
Promenade...etc.

<u>Singing Call - Figure</u>

1 & 3 bow & Swing...
Forward & Back...
Pass Thru & both turn left...
Single File (Promenade) **around 1 into the middle...**
Pass Thru & Split the outside two...
Both turn right Single File (Promenade) **around 1...**
Star Right in the middle...
Corner Left Hand Around (Arm Turn)**...**
Partner DoSaDo...
Promenade corner home

1 & 3 bow & Swing...
Forward & Back...
Pass Thru & both turn right around 1...
Single File (Promenade) **into the middle...**
Pass Thru & Split the outside two...
Both turn left Single File (Promenade) **around 1...**
Star Left in the middle...
Corner Right Hand Around...
Partner Left Hand Around...
Promenade corner home

Roll Away 1/2 Sashay

Teaching Tips— The lady should roll to face the man and momentarily join both hands with the man before completing the roll. As the lady rolls, the man should take a short step backward as the lady faces him and then step forward as the lady reaches his left side.

Patter- Square- Easy

Circle Left...
Roll Away 1/2 Sashay...
Circle Left...
Roll Away 1/2 Sashay...
4 Ladies Chain across...
Promenade...etc.

4 Ladies Chain 3/4...
Roll Away 1/2 Sashay...
Swing partner...
Promenade...etc.

Heads/sides **Pass Thru...**
Separate around 1 to a line...
Centers Roll Away 1/2 Sashay...
All Roll Away 1/2 Sashay (see right)**...**
Allemande Left...etc.

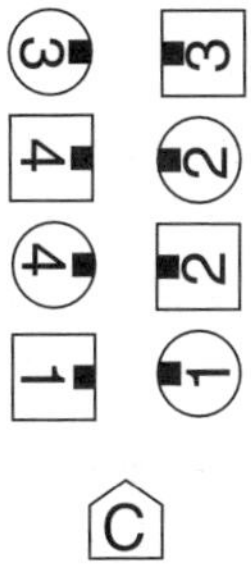

Head/side **couples Forward & Back...**
Roll Away 1/2 Sashay...
Turn the opposite 1/2 by the Right (Arm Turn)**...**
Right & Left Thru...etc.

Patter - Square - Medium

Head/side **couples Roll Away 1/2 Sashay...**
Pass Thru...
Separate around 1...
In the middle Pass Thru & Split Two...
Separate around 1...
Down the middle Pass Thru & U-turn Back...
Allemande Left...etc.

Sides/heads **Right & Left Thru...**
Heads/sides **Roll Away 1/2 Sashay...**
Pass Thru...
Separate around 1 into the middle...
Pass Thru & Split the sides/heads**...**
Separate around 1 come down the middle...
Pass Thru & U-turn Back...
Pass Thru & Separate around 1...
Into the middle Pass Thru & Left Allemande...etc.

In the next figure, the heads stand behind the sides. It should have a walk-thru unless the dancers are very familiar with the concept.

Heads go Forward & Back...
Roll Away 1/2 Sashay...
Pass Thru...
Both turn right go Single File
(Promenade) **stand behind the sides**
(see Right)**...**

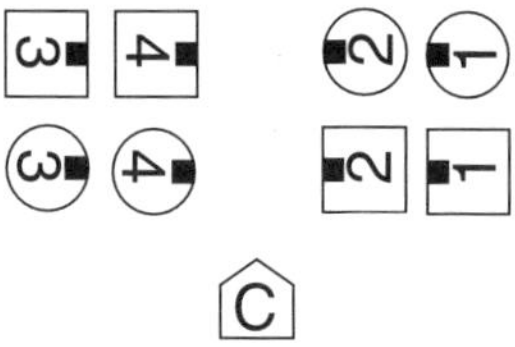

Side 2 Ladies Chain...
Same sides Right & Left Thru...
Pass Thru & Swing the lady coming your way...
Join hands & Circle Left...
Roll Away 1/2 Sashay...
Right & Left Grand...etc.

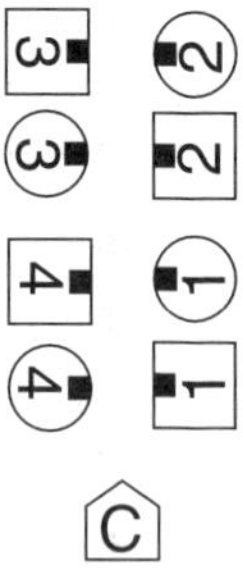

Heads/sides **Roll Away 1/2 Sashay...**
Pass Thru...
Both turn right Single File (Promenade)
around 2 to a line (see right)**...**
Pass Thru...
Courtesy Turn your partner...
Roll Away 1/2 Sashay...
Pass Thru & U-turn Back...
Turn the opposite 1/2 Right Hand Around...
Pass Thru & all turn left...
Promenade Single File...
Men U-turn Back & Allemande Left...etc.

Side Ladies Chain across...
Same sides Roll Away 1/2 Sashay ...
Pass thru & just the men U-turn back...
Now follow that lady* Single File (Promenade)**...**
both turn right Single File (Promenade)**...**
Go around 1 in middle Pass Thru & Split Two...
Lady go left & gent to the right around 1...
Down the middle Pass Thru...
Just the ladies U-turn Back...
Now follow that man Single File (Promenade)**...**
Both turn right & go around 2...
Hook on the ends make lines of 4...
Go Forward & Back with you...
Straight across Right & Left Thru...
Roll Away 1/2 Sashay...
Pass Thru & U-turn Back...
Left Allemande...etc.

*The man will be looking at the back of the opposite lady.

Patter - Square - Unusual

This is the first routine where two men are asked to *Roll Away 1/2 Sashay*. The man on the right side of the pair dances the lady's role. As an alternative, the men can just slide across with the man on the right going in front.

Couples 1 & 2 Two Ladies Chain
Couples 3 & 4 Two Ladies Chain
New side Ladies Chain...
Heads Pass Thru...
Separate around 1 to a line...
Men only Roll Away 1/2 Sashay...
Ladies only Roll Away 1/2 Sashay...
Centers Roll Away 1/2 Sashay...
Everybody Right & Left Thru...
All join hands & Circle Left...
Left Allemande...etc.

Head/sides **Right & Left Thru...**
Same 2 Ladies Chain...
Sides/heads **Roll Away 1/2 Sashay...**
Circle eight while you're that way...
4 ladies Pass Thru...
U-turn Back...
Pass Thru...
Separate & behind the men you stand...
Men Pass Thru (see right)**...**
Left Allemande...etc.

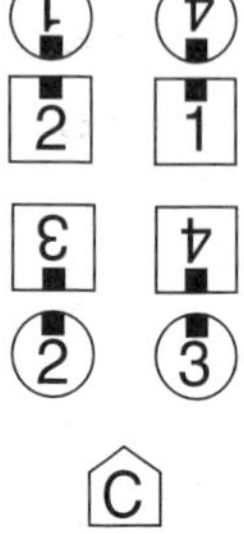

Side/head **Ladies Chain...**
While the heads/sides **Roll Away 1/2 Sashay...**
Sides Pass Thru...
Courtesy Turn...
All eight Circle Left...
4 ladies go Forward & Back...
Now Pass Thru...
U-turn Back & all eight Circle Left...
4 men Forward & Back...
Pass Thru...
Separate &
stand behind the ladies...
Ladies Pass Thru (see right)**...**
Left allemande...etc.

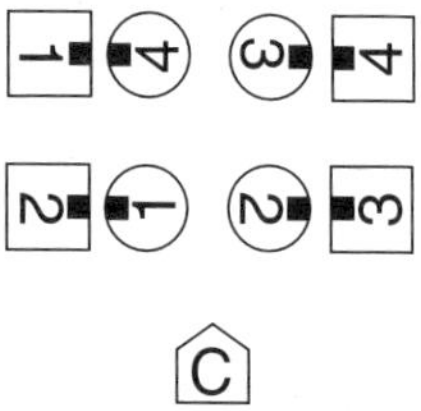

1 & 2 Ladies Chain...
3 & 4 Ladies Chain...
New head Ladies Chain...
Heads Right & Left Thru...
Sides Roll Away 1/2 Sashay...
Heads Pass Thru...
Separate around 1 into the middle...
Centers only Left Allemande...
Everyone Right & Left Grand...etc.

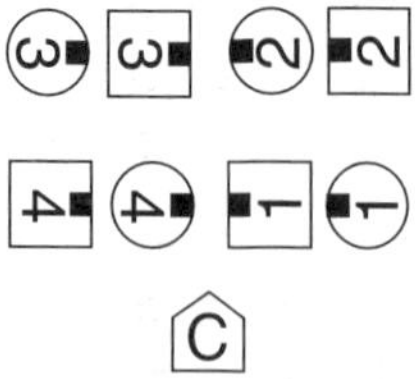

Head/side **Ladies Chain…**
Sides Roll Away 1/2 Sashay…
Circle eight (Left)**…**
4 ladies Forward & Back…
Pass Thru…
Separate go around 1…
Into the middle & Pass Thru…
Both turn left (Single File Promenade)**, keep walking…**
Men U-turn Back…
Swing your own…
Promenade…etc.

The following squares use *Right and Left Thru* with a full turn. The full turn must be taught to the dancers before it is used in a dance. The full turn requires a full 360° turn in the *Courtesy Turn* portion of the *Right & Left Thru* instead of the customary 180° degree turn.

Head/side **couples**
Right & Left Thru
with a full turn around (see right)**…**
Roll Away 1/2 Sashay…
Side/head **couples go Forward & Back…**
Right & Left Thru with a full turn around…
Roll Away 1/2 Sashay…
Everybody Separate…
Left allemande…etc.

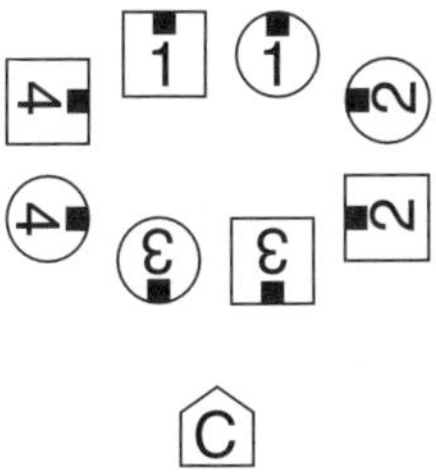

Sides Promenade 1/2…
Into the middle Right & Left Thru…
Courtesy Turn with a full turn around…
Roll Away 1/2 Sashay…
Separate around 1…
Into the middle & Star Right…
To the corner Allemande Left…etc.

Patter - Square - Difficult

After the 1 & 3 *Ladies Chain* and couples 3 & 4 *Right & Left Thru* the square should appear as shown to the right. The whole routine is based around the dancers knowing the positions in the square.

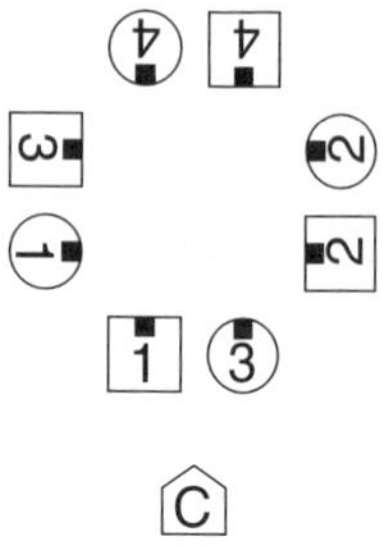

1 & 3 Ladies Chain...
3 & 4 Right & Left Thru...
Sides (old 2 & new 4) **go Forward & Back...**
Right & Left Thru...
Same 2 Ladies Chain...
Same couples
Roll Away 1/2 Sashay...
#1 couple go across the floor &
stand in front of new #3 (see right)**...**
Left allemande...etc.

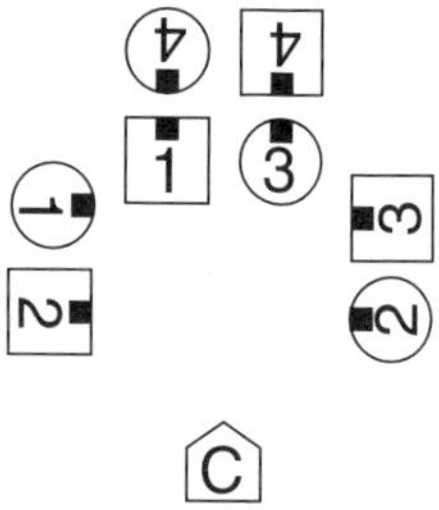

(To change to another position in the square 2 & 4 *Ladies Chain*, 4 & 1 *Right & Left Thru*, Heads *Forward & Back* etc. and #2 position goes across the floor.)

Singing Call - Intro/Brk/End

4 Ladies Chain...
Circle Left...
Roll Away 1/2 Sashay...
Roll Away 1/2 Sashay...
Right & Left Grand...
DoSaDo....
Promenade...etc.

4 Ladies Chain 3/4...
Circle Left...
Roll Away 1/2 Sashay...
Circle Left...
Left Allemande...
Grand Right & Left...
DoSaDo...
Promenade...etc.

Lead Right/Left

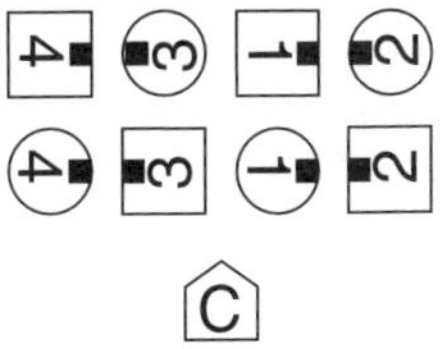

Teaching Tips— The action should finish with the active couple face to face with the inactive couple as shown to the right.

Patter - Square - Easy

Heads/sides **Lead Right...**
DoSaDo...
Circle Left 3/4 (see right)**...**
Left Allemande...etc.

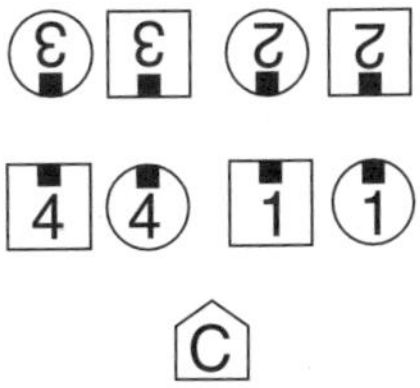

Head/side **couples Promenade half...**
Lead Right...
Right & Left Thru...
Circle Left 3/4...
Side/head **men stretch for the corner** (see below)**...**
Allemande left...etc.

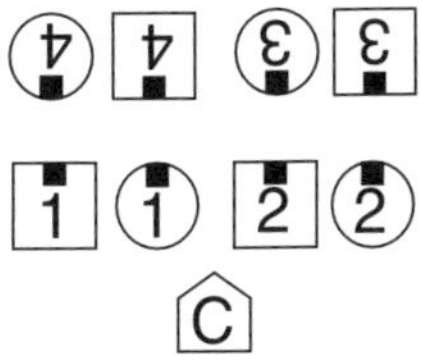

Patter - Square - Medium

Head/side **couples Promenade 1/2...**
2 Ladies Chain...
Same two Promenade 1/2...
Pass Thru...
Courtesy Turn...
Pass Thru...
Promenade 1/2...
Lead Right...
Split 2 & Separate around 1 to a line...
Pass Thru...
U-turn Back & Pass Thru (see right)**...**
Left Allemande...etc.

1st Couple Lead Right...
Circle 4...
Same couple break & pickup 2 more & Circle 6...
Same couple break & pickup 2 more & Circle 8...
Home you go & everybody Swing...etc.

1st couple Lead Right...
Star Right with #2...
Onto the next Star Left (with couple #3)**...**
Onto the next Star Right (with couple #4)**...**
Swing at home
(Repeat for couples 2, 3 & 4)

Heads/sides **Pass Thru...**
Both turn right go Single File (Promenade)**...**
Follow that lady & go around 1...
Down the middle & Pass Thru...
Split two, lady go left, gent go right around 1...
Into the middle Pass Thru...
U-turn Back & Right & Left Thru...
Same couples Lead to the Right...
For a Left Allemande...etc.

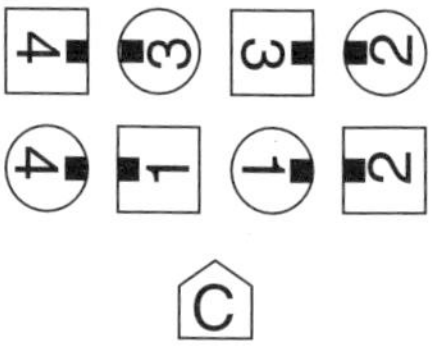

Head 2 Ladies Chain...
Roll Away 1/2 Sashay...
Go up to the middle & back that way (Forward & Back)**...**
Heads Lead Right & Circle 4...
Change the circle to a Right Hand Star...
Back by the Left (Left Hand Star)**...**
Heads to the middle Right & Left Thru...
Pass Thru & Split Two...
Separate around just 1 face to the middle & there you stand...
Side 2 Ladies Chain...
Roll Away 1/2 Sashay...
Go up to the middle & back that way (Forward & Back)**...**
Sides Lead Right & Circle 4...
Change that circle to a Right Hand Star...
Back by the Left (Left Hand Star)...
Sides to the middle Right & Left Thru...
Pass Thru & Split two...
Separate around just 1...
Everybody Left Allemande...etc.

Head/side **couples Lead Right…**
Circle Left with all your might…
Now Circle Right once around…
Stop where you are & opposite Swing…
Send her back & your own partner Swing…
Take her home, make an eight person ring
& Circle Left…
Now partner Swing…
Promenade home

Side/head **two couples Lead to the Right…**
Circle Left go once around…
Now Circle Right & don't fall down…
Two men center, hook left elbows
(or Left Arm Turn) **turn it once around…**
Change those elbows & hook by the right
(or Right Arm Turn)**…**
Go once around & to your partner Swing…
Promenade home you go

<u>Patter - Square - Unusual</u>

Head/side **Couples Promenade 1/2…**
Pass Thru…
Separate around 1…
In the middle Pass Thru & Split the outside 2…
Separate around 1…
Heads/sides **Lead Right…**
Split the outside 2…
Separate around 1…
Heads/sides **Lead Right…**
Split outside 2…
Separate around 1 to a Line…
Lines Forward & Back…
Turn opposite 1/2 Right…
Pass Thru (see right) **& Allemande Left**

4 Ladies Chain 3/4...
Side/head **Ladies Chain across...**
Heads/sides **Promenade half...**
Same two Lead Right...
Pass Thru & U-turn Back (see right)**...**
Go Right & Left Grand...etc.

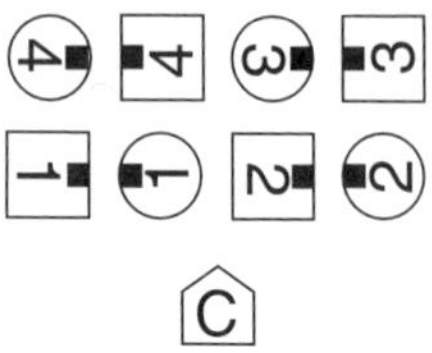

Patter - Square - Difficult

The *Stars* in the following set need to turn exactly once around to place everyone in the correct position for the men to *U-turn Back* and *Swing* the corner.

Head/side **men DoSaDo once & a half...**
Opposite Swing & face across...
Lead Right...
DoSaDo with the sides...
Same four Star Right once around...
Star Left once around...
Men U-turn Back...
Corner Swing...
Promenade home

Singing Call - Figure

"Hurry, Hurry ,Hurry"

1st couple Lead Right...
Circle 4 hands around...
Leave the lady, gent Lead onto the next &
Circle 3 hands round...
Take that couple on with you to the next &
Circle 5 hands round...
#1 gent leave that line & join the line of 3*...
Chain the Ladies across the hall, but don't return...
Chain along the line watch 'em churn...
Turn & Chain across the hall, don't let them roam...
Now chain along the line &...
Swing your honey home
(repeat for couples 2, 3 & 4)

* The man should pass behind the line of three.

Circle to a Line

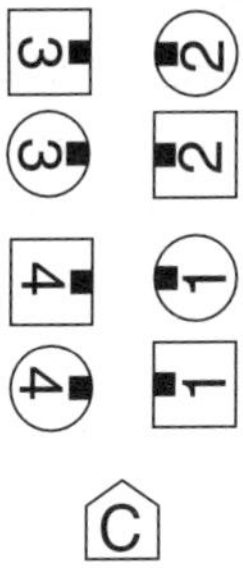

Teaching Tips— When the man breaks to start forming the line, the lady on the opposite end of the line, will find it is much smoother to duck under her partner's arm to finish forming the line.

Patter-Square-Easy

Heads/sides **Lead Right...**
Circle to a Line (see right)**...**
Left Allemande

Side/head **couples Right & Left Thru...**
Head/side **couples Lead Right...**
Circle to a Line...
Pass Thru...
All turn left Single File (Promenade)**...**
Men U-turn Back...
Turn 1/2 by the Right (Arm Turn)**...**
Same one Right & Left Grand...etc.

Patter - Square - Medium

The following routine has the ladies roll back from a *Single File Promenade*. The ladies roll out away from the center and around the man behind them (their partner). The next man will be their corner.

Head/side **two couples Right & Left Thru...**
Heads/sides **Pass Thru...**
Separate around 2...
Swing that lady (partner) **right off the floor...**
Now Lead to the Right...
Circle 4 & Head/side **men break to lines of 4**
(Circle to a Line)...
Go Forward up & Back once more...
Pass Thru...
All turn right go Single File (Promenade)**...**
Ladies roll back to the corner man...
Allemande Left...
Right & Left Grand...etc.

Heads/sides **Lead Right...**
Circle to a Line...
Forward & Back...
Roll Away 1/2 Sashay...
Turn the opposite 1/2 Right (Arm Turn)**...**
Right & Left Thru (see right)**...**
Allemande Left...etc.

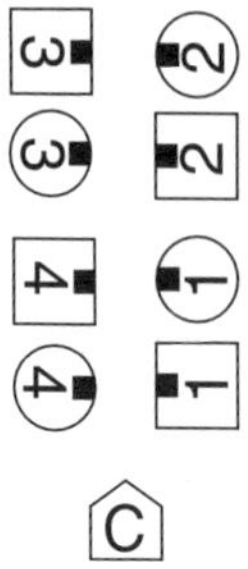

Patter - Square - Unusual

In the following routine, the heads *Lead Right* from a *1/2 Sashay* position (ladies on man's left). The *Circle to a Line* still requires the man to break with the lady on his left to form the facing lines of four.

Head Ladies Chain...
Sides Right & Left Thru...
All 4 couples Roll Away 1/2 Sashay...
Heads Lead Right...
Circle to a line of 4...
Right & Left Thru...
Roll Away to a (Roll Away 1/2 Sashay)(see right)**...**
Right & Left Grand...etc.

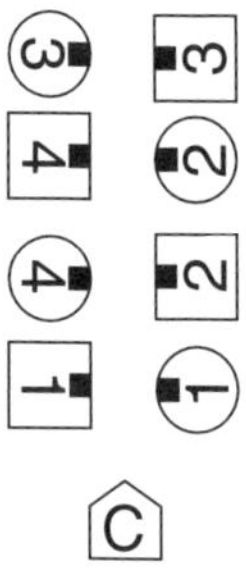

1 & 3 bow & Swing...
Promenade the outside ring...
Go all the way around two by two...
2 & 4 Right & Left Thru...
1 & 3 Lead to the Right...
Circle 4 your doing fine...
Head men break & make two lines...
Forward 8 & Back with you...
Forward again & Pass Thru...
Turn to the left go Single File...
Make a wheel (8 hand Star) **& turn it a while...**
Men reach back with your right hand*...
Now pull them through to a Right & Left Grand...etc.

*The man reaches over his left shoulder with his right hand without turning around. The lady moves to the inside of the set and around in front of the man. Taken from "Runoutanames"

Singing Call - Figure

The next two figures have an interesting theme where either the men or the ladies walk across the set to find their corner. Both figures can be used very effectively in the same tip.

Heads Right & Left Thru...
Same 2 Ladies Chain...
Sides Forward & Back...
Sides Lead Right...
Circle to a Line...
Lines Forward & Back...
Just the men walk across the set &
Swing the corner...
Promenade...etc.

Heads Promenade 1/2...
Right & Left Thru...
Side 2 Ladies Chain...
Sides Lead Right...
Circle to a Line...
Lines Forward & Back...
Just the ladies walk across the set &
Swing that man...
Promenade home

Head/side **Couples Promenade 1/2...**
Lead Right...
Circle 4 to a line...
Pass Thru...
Turn left Single File (Promenade)**...**
Ladies turn around (U-turn Back)**...**
Swing...
Allemande Left new corner...
Promenade...etc.

Bend the Line

Teaching Tips— To Bend the Line, people must be able to 'see' the line. Have the ends walk forward and the centers back up. Then be sure they 'see' the new line.

Patter Square-Easy

Heads/sides **Lead Right...**
Circle to a Line...
Pass Thru...
Bend the Line go onto the next...
Right & Left Thru...
Pass Thru...
Bend the Line...
Right & Left Thru (see right)**...**
Left Allemande...etc.

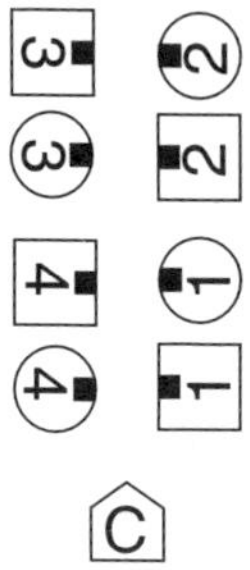

Patter - Square - Medium

Heads/sides **Lead Right...**
Circle Left 3/4...
Pass Thru...
Bend the Line...
Right & Left Thru...
With the same 2 Circle Left 3/4...
Right & Left Thru...
2 Ladies Chain...
Roll Away 1/2 Sashay (see right)**...**
Right & Left Grand...etc.

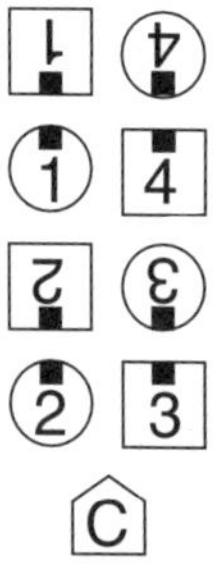

Heads/sides **Pass Thru...**
Separate around 2 to a line...
Pass Thru...
Bend the Line...
Turn the opposite 1/2 Right (Arm Turn)**...**
Pass Thru...
Bend the Line...
Pass Thru (see right)**...**
Left Allemande...etc.

Heads/sides **Pass Thru...**
Separate around 1 to a line (2 men - 2 ladies)**...**
Forward & Back...
Pass Thru...
Bend the Line...
With the opposite two Circle 1/2 (Circle 4)**...**
Pass Thru...
Bend the Line...
With the opposite two Circle 1/2 (Circle 4)**...**
Centers Turn the opposite 1/2 Right (Arm Turn)**...**
Same four Star Right to the corner...
Left Allemande...etc.

Patter - Square - Unusual

Be sure to notice the difference in the lines of four formed in the two following routines.

Couple #1 Swing your own...
Couple #3 Roll Away 1/2 Sashay...
Couple #1 Roll Away 1/2 Sashay...
Now Split #3 around 1 to a line of 4...
Line of 4 go Forward & Back...
Same four to the middle
& stand pat (see right)**...**
Bend the Line...
Pass Thru...
Left Allemande...etc.

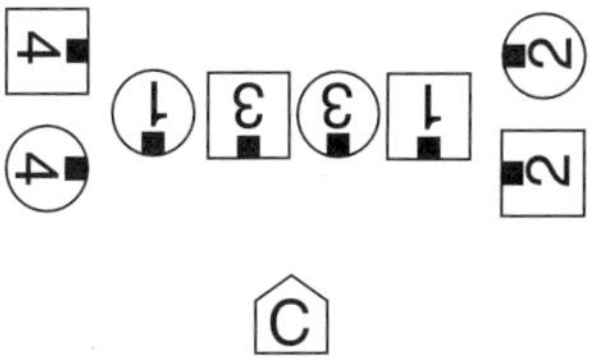

Couple #1 down the middle &
Split the Ring around 1 to a
line of four (see right)**...**
Forward & Back...
Forward & Bend the Line (see right)**...**
Turn opposite 1/2 Right (Arm Turn)**...**
Pass Thru & Left Allemande...etc.
(Repeat for couples 2, 3 & 4)

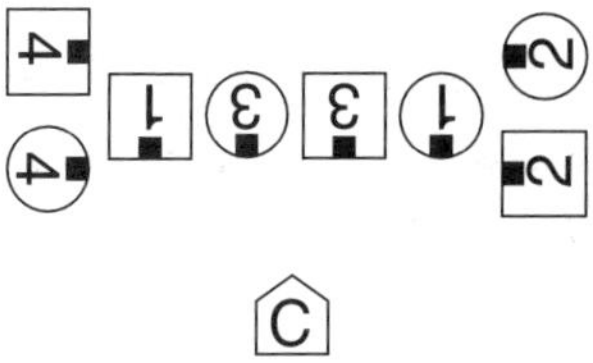

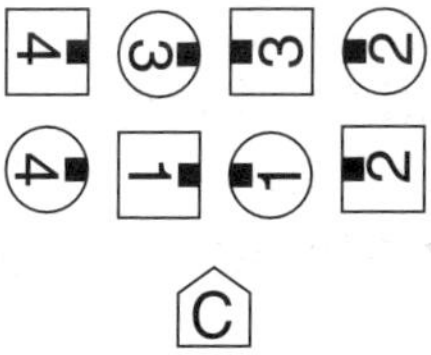

Heads/sides **Pass Thru...**
Both turn left/right **Single File around 2 to a line...**
Lines Forward & Back...
Pass Thru...
Bend the Line...
Turn the opposite 1/2 Right (Arm Turn)**...**
Pass Thru & Bend the Line...
Turn the opposite 1/2 Right (Arm Turn)**...**
Swing your partner...
Promenade home

Heads Pass Thru...
Separate around 1 to a line...
Lines Pass Thru...
Bend the Line...
Center 4 (Heads) **Right & Left Thru**
Pass Thru & Split Two...
Separate around 1 to a line...
Lines Pass Thru...
Bend the Line...
Center 4 (Sides) **Right & Left Thru...**
Pass Thru & Split Two...
Separate around 1 to a line...
Turn the opposite 1/2 Right (Arm Turn)**...**
Center 4 Pass Thru & Split Two...
Separate around 1 to a line...
Ends Turn partner 1/2 Right...
Pass by & Left Allemande...etc.

Singing Call - Figure

Heads/sides **Lead Right...Circle to a Line...**
Forward & Back...
Bend the Line...Right & Left Thru...
Bend the Line...Right & Left Thru...
All Circle Left...
Swing the corner...
Promenade home

Star Promenade

Teaching Tips— On the pickup for the *Star Promenade*, the man places his arm around the waist of the lady. If two men or two ladies are adjacent, the inside person places his/her arm around the waist of the outside person.

Patter - Square - Easy

Allemande Left the corner lady...
DoSaDo your own...
Men Star Left...
Pickup your partner & Star Promenade...
Men back out a full turn*...
Corners DoSaDo...
Swing partner...
Promenade home

* The man has his arm around the lady's waist. When the men back out, the ladies move forward. At the end of the full turn the men release the ladies and go to the corner for a DoSaDo.

Patter - Square - Medium

"Texas Star"

Ladies center & back to the bar*...
Men to the center for a Right Hand Star...
Now, back by the left (Star Left) **but not too far...**
Pass your partner right on by,
pick up the next one on the fly...
Star Promenade...
The hub backs out and the rim goes in...**
Form that "Texas Star" again
(Star Promenade with ladies in the middle)**...**
Hub backs out & everybody Circle Left...
Swing...
Promenade...etc.

(Repeat 3 more times.)

*Keeping hold of right hands with the man, the ladies step to the center and face out and then duck out under the man's arm.

** When the hub backs out and the rim goes in, the man backs up and the ladies move forward pivoting around an imaginary point between the two dancers. The "Texas Star" will reform with the ladies in the middle.

Side men & the corner girl go Forward & Back...
Star Right go once around...
Back by the left (Star Left)**...**
Pass your partner, take the next, Star Promenade
(2 men - 2 ladies)**...**
Back right out & Circle eight (Left)**...**
4 men Pass Thru...
Separate around just 1 & stand behind the ladies...
2 Ladies Chain across...
Roll Away 1/2 Sashay...
Pass Thru...
U-turn Back & Circle eight (Left) **go round the track...**
Left Allemande a new corner...
Go Right & Left Grand...
But only go 3*...Promenade partner home

*On the *Right & Left Grand, Promenade* the 3rd person instead of the 5th person.

Heads/sides **Roll Away 1/2 Sashay...**
Sides/heads **Lead Right...**
Circle to a Line...
Go Forward eight & Back in time...
Pass thru...
Bend the Line...
Go Forward eight & Back once more...
Pass Thru...
Bend the Line...
All 4 ladies Star Right...
Back by the left (Star Left) **don't fall down...**
Pick up the partner with an arm around &
Star Promenade...
Men roll back to the girl behind...
Star Promenade one more time...
Back right out & Circle Left...
Allemande Left...
Promenade home

Singing Call - Intro/Brk/End

Join hands Circle Left...
Allemande Left...
Right Hand Around partner...
Men Star Left...
Star Promenade your partner...
Ladies roll out, turn around (U-turn Back) **&**
Promenade (Single File) **the other way...**
Same two DoSaDo...
Allemande Left...
Promenade home

Singing Call Figures

4 men Star Right inside, let's walk around & then...
Back with a Left Hand Star...
Pickup corner arm around Star Promenade in style...
Back out at home & join hands
you'll circle 'bout a mile...
New corner Left Allemande...
Swing new partner...
Promenade the land...etc.

Corners all Left Allemande...
Partner DoSaDo...
Men Star Left once around...
Partner Star Promenade...
Men back out & ladies in Star Promenade...
Back out at home & corner Swing...
Promenade...

Heads/sides **go Forward & Back...**
Same two Right Hand Star...
Left Hand Star...
Pickup corner arm around Star Promenade...
All back out & Circle Left (2 men - 2 ladies)**...**
Swing the nearest lady...
Promenade...etc.

Wheel Around

Teaching Tips— The left hand person of the pair always backs up and the right hand person of the pair walks forward. The pair rotates half way around (180°) to face the opposite direction.

Patter - Square - Easy

Heads/sides **Pass Thru...**
Wheel Around...
Right & Left Thru...etc.

Heads/sides **Lead Right...**
Circle to a Line...
Pass Thru...
Wheel Around...
Pass Thru...
Wheel Around...etc.

Patter - Square - Medium

Promenade...
Heads Wheel Around...
Right & Left Thru...
Roll Away 1/2 Sashay...
Pass Thru...
Face your partner Right & Left Grand...etc.

In the next figure, men are going to *Wheel Around* with men and ladies are going to *Wheel Around* with ladies.

Heads/sides **Pass Thru...**
Separate around 1 to a line (2 men - 2 ladies)**...**
Lines Pass Thru...
Wheel Around...
Pass Thru
Bend the Line...
Pass Thru...
Wheel Around...
Centers Roll Away 1/2 Sashay...
Star Right to the corner...
Left Allemande...etc.

Promenade...
Heads Wheel Around...
Star Right with the sides...
Heads center Star Left once around...
Star right with the sides...
Head men lead to a line of 4...
Pass Thru...
Face your partner...
Pass Thru (see right) **&**
Left Allemande...etc.

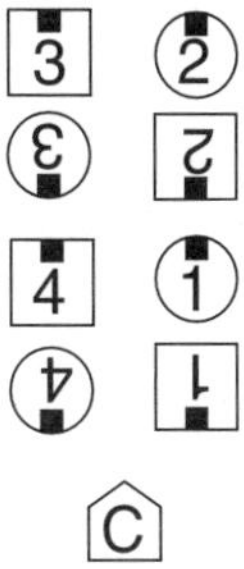

Heads/sides **Lead Right...**
Circle 4 to a Line...
Pass Thru...
Bend the Line...
Pass Thru...
Just the heads Wheel Around...
All Promenade...
Just the sides Wheel Around...
Pass Thru...
Bend the Line...
Right & Left Thru...
Left Allemande...etc.

Promenade...
Heads/sides **Wheel Around*...**
Heads/sides **Split the Sides/**heads**...**
Separate around 1 to a line...
Bend the Line...
Right & Left Grand...etc.

* Any number of calls can be added here such as Right & Left Thru...Right & Left Back or 2 Ladies Chain...Chain Back.

Grand Square Variations

Teaching Tips— Dancers should have a good understanding of the standard Grand Square before any variations are introduced.

In the next dance, only 6 steps of the *Grand Square* are taken. When sides face to start, at the end of 6 steps of the Grand Square, the sides will be approaching their partner and heads will be backing up with their partner .

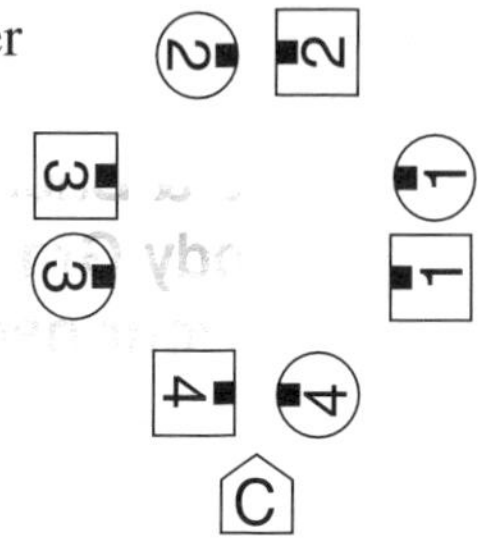

4 Ladies Chain...
Heads/sides **Roll Away 1/2 Sashay...**
Sides/heads **Roll Away 1/2 Sashay...**
Sides/heads **face Grand Square...**
Walk, two, three, turn...
Walk, two, Grand Right & Left...etc.

Another 6 step *Grand Square.* When heads face to start, at the end of the 6 steps, the head men will be walking toward their corner. Side men will be backing away with their corner.

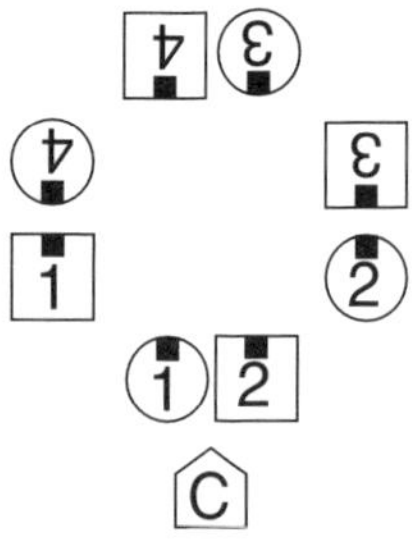

Head/side **Ladies Chain**
to the right...
New side/head **Ladies Chain across...**
Heads/sides **face Grand Square...**
Walk, two, three, turn...
Walk, two, Left Allemande...etc.

Be sure the dancers are confident dancing a *Grand Square* from a *1/2 Sashay* position with the lady on the man's left. When sides face to start, at the end of 16 steps of the *Grand Square*, the head men will be approaching their corner and the side men will be backing away with their corner.

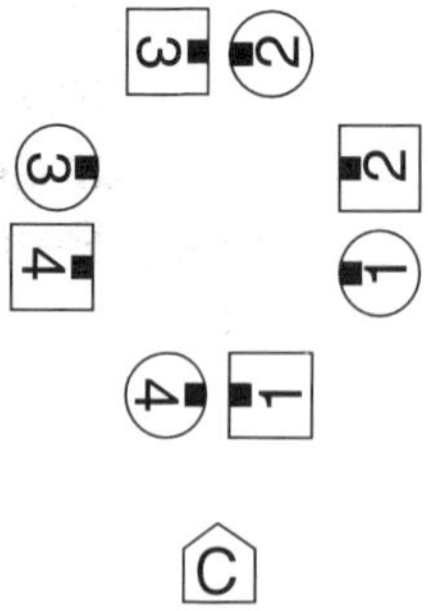

Four Ladies Chain 3/4...
Everybody Roll Away 1/2 Sashay
Sides/heads **face, do a**
1/2 Grand Square (16 steps)**...**
Allemande left

In the following *Grand Square* variation, the lines of four will walk forward 3 steps. Then each person turns as an individual on the 4th step to back away from the center in the formation shown to the right.

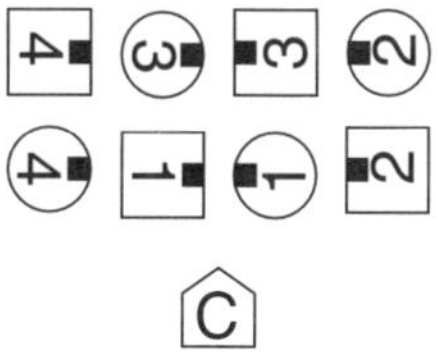

Sides/heads **Pass Thru...**
Separate go around 2 to a line 4...
Forward & Back...
Everybody Grand Square...
Bow to your partner

The following variation is listed in several books as the *"Chinese" Grand Square*. The ladies can also face their partner and everybody *Grand Square* for another variation.

Men face your partner...
Everybody Grand Square
(All ladies go into the center, all men back up)(see right)

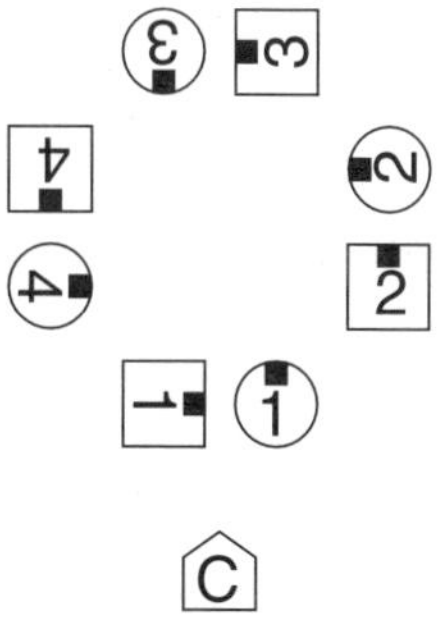

Get home & bow to your partner

An 18 step *Grand Square*. The set will stop in two facing lines of four as shown to the right.

Sides Right & Left Thru...
Everybody Roll Away 1/2 Sashay...
Sides face Grand Square...
One, two, three, turn...
One, two, three, turn...
One, two, three, turn...
One, two, three, reverse...
One, two, stop...
Lines of four go Forward & Back...
Everybody Pass Thru...
Allemande Left (see right)**...etc.**

Star Thru

Star Thru was not one of the 24 square dance basics originally recommended by the CALLERLAB Community Dance Program (CDP) Committee. It is a basic used by many leaders in their programs. Since the term was not part of the original 24 basics, leaders should always expect to teach the term when guests visit or choose to not use *Star Thru* during that program.

Patter - Square - Easy

Heads/sides **Star Thru...**
Right & Left Thru...
Pass Thru & Star Thru the outside two...
Right & Left Thru...
Pass Thru (see right) **&**
Left Allemande...etc.

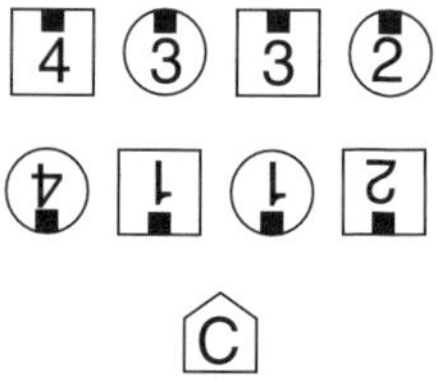

Heads/sides **Star Thru...**
Right & Left Thru...
Pass Thru & Split two...
Separate around 1...
Down the middle Star Thru...
Right & Left Thru...
Pass Thru (see right) **&**
Left Allemande...etc.

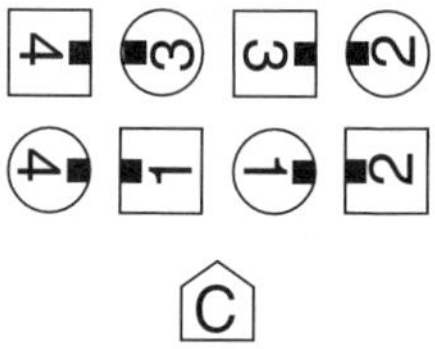

Head/side **couples Right & Left Thru...**
Pass Thru...
Separate around 1...
Into the middle Right & Left Thru...
Pass Thru & Split two...
Separate around 1...
Down the middle Star Thru...
Pass Thru (see above right) **&**
Left allemande...etc.

Promenade...
Heads/sides **Wheel Around...**
Right & Left Thru...
Star Thru...
Pass Thru (see right) **&**
Left allemande...etc.

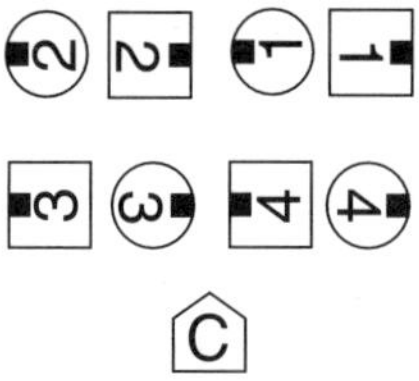

Patter - Square - Medium

Sides/heads **Pass Thru...**
Separate around 1 to lines of 4...
Inside four Right & Left Thru...
Others Star Thru...
Same two Pass Thru...
Separate around 1 to lines of 4...
Inside four Right & Left Thru...
Ends Star Thru...
Left Allemande...etc.

Promenade...
Ladies roll back just one...
Promenade with that new man
Sides/heads **Wheel Around...**
Right & Left Thru...
Star Thru...
Pass Thru...
Give a right to your partner,
Don't ask why, step by (see right)**...**
Left Allemande...etc.

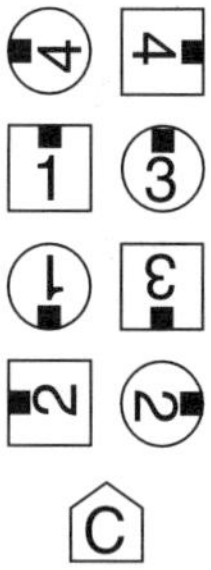

Promenade...
Heads/sides **Wheel Around...**
Right & Left Thru...
Star thru...
Right & Left Thru...
Roll Away 1/2 Sashay...
U-turn Back (see right) **&**
Left Allemande...etc.

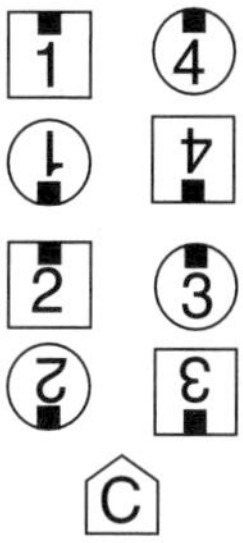

Promenade...
Sides/heads **Wheel Around...**
2 Ladies Chain...
Pass Thru...
Bend the Line...
2 Ladies Chain...
Pass Thru...
Bend the Line...
2 Ladies Chain...
Pass Thru...
Bend the Line...
2 Ladies Chain...
Star Thru...
Pass Thru...
U-turn Back (see above right) **& Right & Left Grand...**etc.

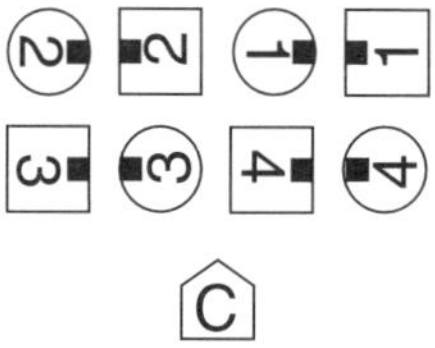

Patter - Square - Unusual

Heads/sides **Lead Right...**
Right & Left Thru...
Circle Left 1/4 (or once & a 1/4)**...**
Face your partner Star Thru,
you're facing out...
Face your partner &
Pass Thru (see right)**...**
Left Allemande...etc.

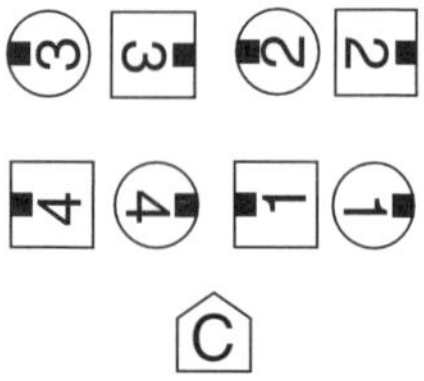

The success of the next figure depends on the head couples continuing to *Single File Promenade* at a normal pace.

Promenade...
Heads/sides **Promenade Single File...**
Keep going don't slow down...
Sides/heads **wheel to the center...**
Right & Left Thru...
Star Thru...
DoSaDo...
Pass Thru...
Left Allemande...etc.

The next two figures are difficult to diagram because the timing of the calls will vary. They both require a lot of space and should not be tried on a crowded floor.

Head/side **men & the corner girl Forward & Back...**
Star by the Right go once around...
Back by the left (Star Left)**...**
Pick your partner Star Promenade...
Outside four roll back one (2 men together, 2 ladies together)**...**
Outside ladies roll back one to a line of six...
Lone ladies roll back one to a line of eight...
Back out & form two lines...
Ends Star Thru...
Same 2 Ladies Chain across...
Face a new corner (original partner) **Star Thru...**
Face that same one, Right & Left Grand...etc.

Head 2 Ladies Chain...
Heads Star Thru...
Roll Away 1/2 Sashay...
Pass Thru & Circle 4...
Ladies break to lines of 4...
Forward eight & Back in time...
Pass Thru...
Bend the Line...
Forward eight & Back once more...
Pass Thru...
Bend the Line...
All four men Star Right...
Now back by the left (Star Left)**...**
Pick up the partner with an arm around
Star Promenade go around the town...
Back right out with a once & a half...
4 Ladies Chain across you go...
Chain them back don't let them stay...
Roll Promenade the partner...etc.

Head 2 Ladies Chain to the right...
New side Ladies Chain across...
Heads Right & Left Thru...
Same two Star Thru...
Pass Thru & Star thru...
Pass Thru...
Bend the Line...
Star Thru...
Pass Thru & Left Allemande...etc.

Side couples Right & Left Thru...
#3 couple Swing...
Other three couples Roll Away 1/2 Sashay...
#1 couple go down the center Split #3...
Separate go around just 3 & stand in line...
Go Forward six & Back away...
Straight across Star Thru...
Left allemande...etc.

Couples 3 & 4 Star Thru...
1 & 2 Right & Left Thru...
3 & 4 Right & Left Thru...
1 & 2 Star Thru...
Everybody Pass Thru...
Left Allemande...etc.

Patter - Square - Difficult

Head couples Right & Left Thru...
Same head Ladies Chain...
Heads Lead to the Right...
Split the sides...
Separate around one to lines of 4...
Go up to the middle & back (Forward & Back)**...**
Star Thru...
Outsiders Promenade to the left 1/4...
Insiders Lead Right...
Left Allemande...etc.

Square Dance Gimmicks

Arch is not really a basic, but a formation. Square dance routines are provided because the arch formation is also used extensively in other dance forms such as contra dances.

All of the figures listed below can be used during beginner parties and taught during the first few sessions of a beginners group. They are fun and help couples identify the numbered positions in a square.

#1 Swing your partner & then make an arch...
Promenade the arch over the other couples...
Back home & Swing
(Repeat for couples 2, 3 & 4)

Couple #1 stand back to back...
Walk away from your partner (Separate)
halfway around the set...
Couple #3 make a 2 hand arch...
#1 duck thru the arch...
Swing at home
(Repeat for couples 2, 3 & 4)

Ladies to the middle & Circle Left/right**...**
Back home & Swing...
Men to the center & Circle Left/right**...**
Back home & Swing...
1 & 3 DoSaDo...
Same two form a 2 hand arch...
2 & 4 ladies tunnel thru the arch...
Swing the opposite man...
Ladies tunnel back...
Swing at home

The same figure can be called with the men tunneling through the arch. If some people have trouble getting though the arch, have the couples forming the arch not touch hands at the top.

Couple #1 stand back to back...
Separate around the outside track...
Pass by six & don't be shy...
Wave at your honey as you go by...
Hook on the ends make lines of 3...
Go Forward & Back you march...
It's forward again & make 3 arches...
Couple #3 duck thru the tunnel...
Then Separate & home you go...
Everybody Swing your own...
Promenade home

"The Bridge"

1 & 3 Forward & Back...
Put the ladies in the center,
make a bridge across the track
(Ladies join right hands in the center to form 3 arches)**...**
Couple #2 duck thru the middle arch...
Couple #4 Separate & duck thru the end arches...
Sides Swing...
Now #4 thru the middle & #2 thru the ends...
Everybody Swing...etc.
(Repeat for the sides. You can also send the ladies thru the middle arch & the men thru the ends, etc.)

The following square dances should only be used after dancers completely trust their caller. Even then, the figure should be walked-thru at least once before attempting any dance.

Couples #3 & #4 Right & Left Thru...
New sides Right & Left Thru...
#1 Lady Chain left...
Same couple Roll Away 1/2 Sashay...
#1 man back out and Promenade around the outside until you find two ladies together...
Squeeze in and everybody Left Allemande...etc.

In the next two dances, a line of four men faces a line of four ladies. It can be done for all four positions in the set with just a little study.

All 4 Ladies Chain…
Couple #1 Split couple #3…
Separate go around 3 to make 2 lines of 3…
Couple #3 walk across the set &
Separate around 2 to a line of 4…
Lines Forward & Back…
Centers Pass Thru & Split 2…
Separate around 1 to a line of 4
(see right)**…**

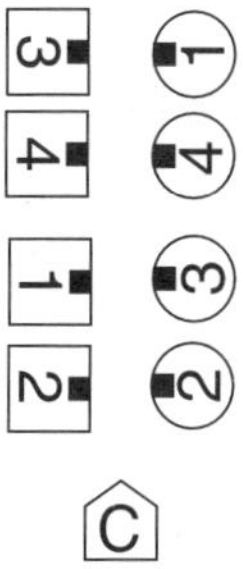

4 men & 4 ladies Forward & Back…
Join hands & Circle Left…
1 man with a lady on his right
Roll Away 1/2 Sashay…
2 men with a lady on the right
Roll Away 1/2 Sashay…
3 men with a lady on the right
Roll Away 1/2 Sashay…
4 men with a lady on the right
Roll Away 1/2 Sashay…
Left Allemande…etc.

A *Couple Promenade* can be substituted for the *Star Promenade* in the following dance. Notice the theme of 4 men facing 4 ladies.

Sides Promenade 3/4...
#1 Roll Away 1/2 Sashay...
Split the Ring thru 2 couples...
U-turn Back...
#2 Roll Away 1/2 Sashay...
Split the Ring thru 3 couples...
U-turn Back...
Everybody face your partner &
make lines of 4 (see right)**...**
Forward eight & Back (4 men - 4 ladies)**...**
Pass Thru...
Bend the Line...
Men Star Left...
Ladies Star Right...
One man first pick up your own* & all
Star Promenade home

*Any one man start the Star Promenade or Couple Promenade with their partner. The rest of the men Star Promenade their partners in rotation.

Head couples Lead Right...
Circle 4 & head men break to lines of four...
Star Right with the opposite pair...
Exactly once & when you're there
Right & Left Thru across the square...
Then Star Right with the same pair
full turn around...
Two head men Star Left between those stars...
Side men fall in behind your man (Side men will join the star behind the head man who was previously in their star)**...**
Men pick up your partner & Star Promenade...
All back out Circle Left...
Allemande Left...
Promenade home

Side 2 Ladies Chain across...
Heads Pass Thru...
Separate around just 1 to lines of 4...
Just the ladies Split the men
around 1 to lines of 4 (see right)**...**
Original heads Pass Thru...
Wheel to the left as a couple &
Star Right with the couple you meet...
Ladies Star Left in the middle...
Men Promenade outside...
Turn partner Right Hand Around (Arm Turn)**...**
Go all the way around to the corner Left
Allemande...etc.

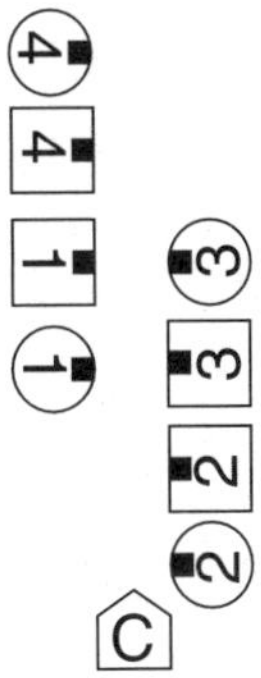

"DR. I. Q."

1st couple bow & Swing...
1st gent out to the center of the ring...
Bow to the girl to the right of you...
Right to the girl in back of you (from there)...
Left to the girl to the left of you (from there)**...**
Right to the girl across from you (from there)**...**
Swing the girl you bowed to &
get out of the center...etc.

(The figure can then be repeated for each gent, head men, side men and\or all four men.)

In the following figure the ladies are on the ends of lines of four as shown below. When the diagonal end *Ladies Chain,* the *Courtesy Turn* at the end of the *Chain* places the lady on the man's right hand side. Everyone should have their partner.

4 Ladies Chain...
Heads/sides **Pass Thru...**
Both turn right Single File (Promenade)
around 2 to a line (see right)**...**
Diagonal head Ladies Chain...
Diagonal side Ladies Chain...
Swing your partner...
Promenade home

"Ocean Sand" was written many years ago and requires very experienced dancers. When done right it is a beautiful dance and fun to do. With the right group, it is well worth the effort to learn.

Head Ladies Chain to the right...
New side Ladies Chain across...
New head Ladies Chain to right...
Side Ladies Chain across...
Head Ladies Chain 3/4 around...
Side gent turn this gal you found...
A full turn round until
you're facing out (see right)**...**

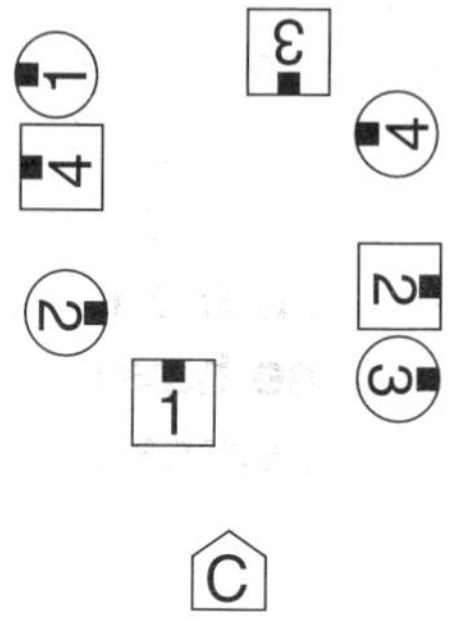

Then Promenade half
outside the square...
While the head men & the corner girl go
Forward & Back...
Pass Thru...
U-turn Back...
Same Ladies Chain 3/4 round...
Side gent turn this girl you found...
A full turn around until
you're facing out (see right)**...**

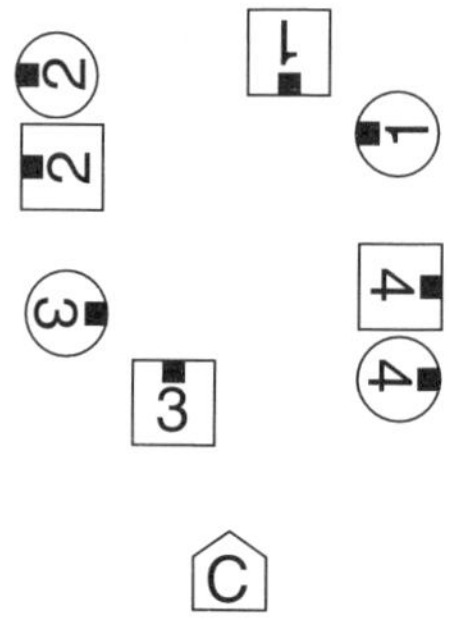

Then Promenade just half
outside the square...
Circle Left when you get there...
Circle eight you're doing fine...
Gentlemen break &
form 2 lines (see right)**...**

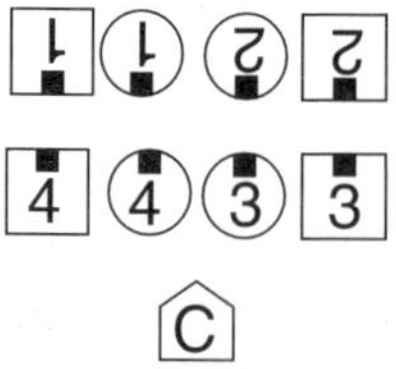

Forward eight & Back with you...
Pass Thru...
Face the girl nearest you...
DoSaDo go all the way around...
Right Hand Turn when you come down ...
All the way around to the corner of the ring...
Allemande left...etc.

Heads dance up to the middle and back (Forward & Back)**...**
Same two Star Right...
Once around, come back by the left (Left Hand Star)**...**
Pick up your corner arm around
Star Promenade around the town...
The inside out & the outside in...
Turn once & a half & you're gone again...
Ladies on the outside roll back one...
Six in line have a little fun...
The lonesome men roll back one...
Eight in line have a little fun...
Bend the big Line...
Bend the little Line...
Bend the itty bitty Line...
Left Allemande...etc.

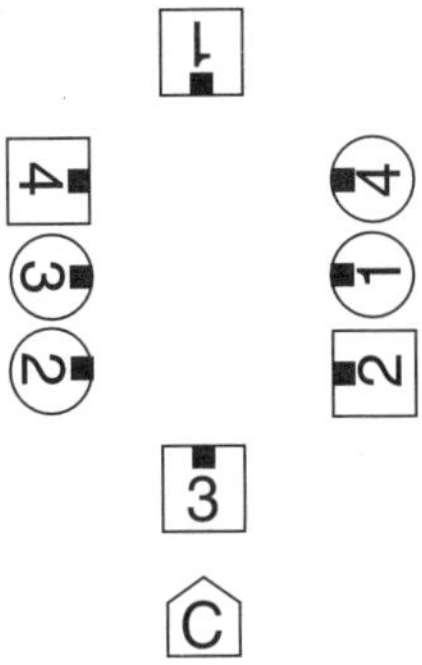

Heads Right & Left Thru...
4 Ladies Chain...
Head Ladies Chain 3/4 (see right)**...**
Just the ends Star Thru...
Right & Left Thru...
2 Ladies Chain...
Pass Thru & Circle 3 once around...
Head men break to a line of 3*(see below right)**...**
Just the ends Star Thru...
Right & Left Thru...
2 Ladies Chain...
Pass Thru & Circle 3...
Head men break to a line of 3...
Just the ends Star Thru...
Right & Left Thru...
2 Ladies Chain...
Pass Thru & Circle 3...
Head men break to a line of 3...
Left Allemande...

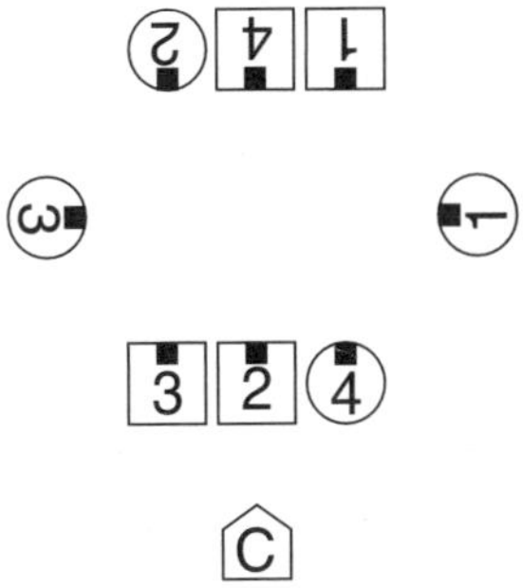

*The head man must break with the lady on the left.

Announcement Routines

The next two routines have all the dancers facing the caller at one point so announcements can be made.

4 Ladies Chain 3/4 round...
Couple #1 go down the middle Split the Ring...
Around #3 & make a line...
Forward six & Back with you...
Lonesome couple walk on thru...
Separate go around 2...
Squeeze right in make a line of 4...
Forward eight & Back with you...
Pass Thru across the track...
All turn left go Single File (Promenade)**...**
Now back right out & Circle Left...
 # 1 man break out and make a line
(Break out to a line of eight facing the caller)**...**
Forward eight & Back...
Break in the middle...
Men face right, ladies face left...
Single File (Promenade) **march straight ahead &**
keep on going until you find your partner...
Swing your partner round & round...
Promenade go round the town...etc.

Head Ladies Chain...
#4 couple Promenade 3/4 & stand behind #3...
#4 Squeeze in between #3 to make a line of 4...
#1 couple Promenade 1/2 & stand behind #4...
Squeeze in between couple #4 to make a line of 6...
#2 couple Promenade 1/4 behind the line of 6...
Squeeze in the middle of the line to make a line of 8
(All facing the caller)**...**
1 man with a lady on his right Roll Away 1/2 Sashay...
2 men with a lady on the right Roll Away 1/2 Sashay...
3 men with a lady on the right Roll Away 1/2 Sashay...
4 men with a lady on the right Roll Away 1/2 Sashay...
Left Allemande...etc.

Those Who Can & If You Want To Routines

In **Those Who Can** routines, the dancers are expected to recognize who is able to execute the call and who is expected to stand still and wait their turn.

Sides Right & Left Thru...
4 Ladies Chain...
Couple #1 Roll Away 1/2 Sashay...
1 & 3 Pass Thru...
Separate around 1 to a line...
<u>Those who can</u>* Right & Left Thru...
Same 4 Roll Away 1/2 Sashay...
<u>Those who can</u> Right & Left Thru...
Same 4 Roll Away 1/2 Sashay...
<u>Those who can</u> Right & Left Thru...
Same 4 Roll Away 1/2 Sashay...
Circle 8...<u>Those who can</u> Right & Left Thru...
Other 4 Swing the opposite & face the outside pair...
Allemande Left...etc.

*Only two couples can. The other 4 people stand in place.

4 Ladies Chain...
Couple #3 Roll Away 1/2 Sashay...
1 & 3 Pass Thru...
Separate around 1 to a line...
All Star Thru...
<u>Those who can</u> Right & Left Thru...Pass Thru...
<u>Those who can</u> Right & Left Thru...Pass Thru...
<u>Those who can</u> Right & Left Thru...Pass Thru...
All face your partner & back away...
All Star Thru...
<u>Those who can</u> Right & Left Thru...Pass Thru...
#4 you're facing out, Courtesy Turn...
<u>Those who can</u> Right & Left Thru...
Pass Thru & Left Allemande...etc.

You can call the same figure for different starting couples. Just remember that if couple #1 does the *Roll Away with a 1/2 Sashay* couple #2 will be facing out for the *Courtesy Turn.*

#1 Couple Lead Right...Circle to a Line...
Just that line of 4 step forward & Bend the Line...
Those who can Circle Four 3/4 around...Pass Thru...
Those who can Circle Four 3/4 around...Pass Thru...
Those who can Circle Four 3/4 around...Pass Thru...
Everybody Courtesy Turn...
Those who can Circle to a Line...
Everybody Circle 8...
Left Allemande...etc.

The interesting thing about this routine is that following any one of the *Pass Thrus* you can jump out of the sequence to the last two lines of the routine. On the other hand, you can add as many lines of *Circle Four 3/4 & Pass Thru* as you think the dancers will enjoy.

If You Want To dance routines give each couple the option of executing the call or standing still. The dancers will find that no matter which choice they make the routine will always come out to a point where they can do a *Left Allemande* with the original corner.

If you want to (but you don't have to) **face your corner & turn them 1/2 Right** (Arm Turn) **square your set that way...**
Any 1 couple Separate & go outside halfway around & squeeze in between the opposite pair...
That line of 4 step forward & Bend the Line...
Circle Four exactly 1/2...
Pass Thru...
Left Allemande...etc.

Quadrilles

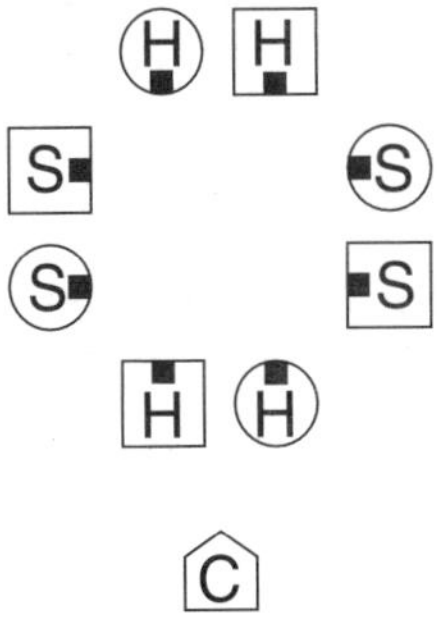

Quadrilles are danced in a four-couple square and preceded square dancing by several hundred years. The dances in this manual are largely taken from more recent material because earlier quadrilles were very formal and required dance knowledge not suitable for this program. Most of the dances address head and side positions only.

Quadrille Music

Quadrilles can be done to many kinds of music. Jigs, Hornpipes and Reels are popular. Singing-call records are often used. Occasionally a waltz is heard. It is really up to the imagination and the skill of the author. The music needs to be strongly phrased and organized into 64-beat tunes unless otherwise noted.

Prompting Quadrilles

In general, all the recommendations for prompting dances apply to prompting quadrilles. The goal is to deliver the commands ahead of when the dancers are expected to dance the figure. However, dancers generally do not expect the timing to be as strict in quadrilles as in contra dancing.

Square dance calling techniques can be used for calling any figures used for quadrilles by simply starting the call on count 1 of each line and filling in the rest of the line with patter as needed. If you choose to use a singing call record, keep in mind that most of these records repeat the tune 7 times. You may want to put in a break (3 times) that does not change partners.

Organization of Quadrilles

The basics used in the quadrilles determined the order the dances are listed in this book. Notice that the routines in the first several quadrilles could easily be used for square dancing. the basics fit well within the scope of material that could be introduced on the first night of dancing.

An additional beginner's quadrille routine is printed in "Programming a Beginner Dance" on page 26. Many other variations can also be constructed. Take a look at the singing call figures in the square dance section and prompt them instead of singing them.

First Night Quadrille

Bob Dalsemer

Formation: Four couples in a square formation.
Record: Jewel 707 "Susie"

Prompts

Intro	*- - - -, Head couples Forward & Back*
1-8	**- - - -, Same 4 Circle Left**
9-16	**- - - -, Same 4 Circle Right**
17-24	**- - - -, Same 4 Star Right**
25-32	**- - - -, - - Allemande Left**
33-40	**- - - -, Grand Right & Left**
41-48	**- - - -, - - Partner DoSaDo**
49-56	**- - - -, - - Promenade home**
57-64	**- - - -, Side couples Forward & Back**

(Alternate head & side couples)

Description

1-8	Head or Side couples Forward & Back.
9-16	Same 4 Circle Left.
17-24	Same 4 Circle Right.
25-32	Same 4 Star Right. Finish at home position.
33-40	Allemande Left with the corner.
41-48	Grand Right & Left to meet partner half way around the set.
49-56	DoSaDo your partner.
57-64	All 4 couples Promenade half way around to home position.

Ladies' Star Turn

Tony Parkes

(Modified slightly by Calvin Campbell)

Formation: Four couples in a square formation.
Record: LS-312 "Fisher's Hornpipe"

Prompts

Intro	*- - - -, 4 ladies Star Right once around*
1-8	**- - - -, Turn partner Left once & a half**
9-16	**- - - -, DoSaDo your corners all**
17-24	**- - - -, 4 ladies Star Left, once around**
25-32	**- - - -, - - Corner DoSaDo**
33-40	**- - - -, - - Corner Swing**
41-48	**- - - -, Promenade around the ring**
49-56	**- - - -, - - - -**
57-64	**- - - -, 4 ladies Star Right**

Description

1-8	4 ladies Star Right once around.
9-16	Left Arm Turn the same person once and a half until everyone can face their corner.
17-24	DoSaDo the corner.
25-32	4 ladies Star Left once around to the same corner person.
33-40	Corner DoSaDo.
41-48	Same corner Swing.
49-64	All 4 couples Promenade once around the set

Note: Tony's original dance has a balance and Swing in place of the DoSaDo and Swing in counts 33-48. The balance can either be a 4 -count balance and a 12-count Swing or a 8-count balance and a 8 -count Swing.

Coronado Quadrille

Don Armstrong

Formation: Four couples in a square formation.
Record: LS E-33 "Coronado Quadrille"

Prompts

Intro	*- - - -, Heads Promenade 1/2* (outside)
1-8	**- - - -, Head Ladies Chain to the right**
9-16	**- - - -, Sides Promenade 1/2** (outside)
17-24	**- - - -, Side Ladies Chain to the right**
25-32	**- - - -, All join hands & Circle 1/2**
33-40	**- - - -, - - 4 Ladies Chain**
41-48	**- - - -, - - All Promenade**
49-56	**- - - -, - - Full around**
57-64	**- - - -, Heads Promenade 1/2**

Description

1-8	Head or side couples Promenade outside the square halfway around and stop in the opposite position.
9-16	From this position the same Ladies Chain with the couple on their right.
17-24	The other couples, sides or head, Promenade outside the square halfway around and stop in the opposite position.
25-32	These same couples Chain the Ladies to their right. Everyone has their own partner back and are halfway across from home.
33-40	All 8 dancers join hands in one circle and Circle Left halfway around the ring to man's original home position.
41-48	4 Ladies Chain across the set.
49-64	All four Couples Promenade once around the set and back to the man's home position. The ladies will end up with their opposite on the first time through the dance and their partner on the second time through the dance and so on.

Note: After 2 times through the routine, repeat 2 more times but begin with the side couples. When the Head Ladies Chain to the right, the Sides should turn to face them as a couple and then finish with all four couples facing back to the center of the square.

Tip Top Quadrille

Don Armstrong

Formation: Four couples in a square formation.
Record: LS E-33 "Tip Top Quadrille"

Prompts

Intro	*- - - -, Men roll out (left) Promenade 1/2*
1-8	**- - - -, Ladies roll out** (right) **Promenade 1/2**
9-16	**- - - -, - - Partner DoSaDo**
17-24	**- - - -, Men Star Left in the middle**
25-32	**- - - -, Pass by partner take the next lady**
33-40	**- - To the man's home, - - 4 Ladies Chain**
41-48	**- - - -, Keep this lady & Promenade**
49-56	**- - - -, - - - -**
57-64	**- - - -, Men roll left, Promenade 1/2**

Description

1-8	All 4 men turn to their left and continue rolling left until they can Promenade Single File counterclockwise around the outside of the square halfway around to the opposite position. It helps if the ladies take a short step toward the center of the set as the men pass by.
9-16	All 4 ladies turn to their right and continue rolling right until they can Promenade Single File clockwise around the outside of the square halfway around to the opposite position. It helps if the men take a short step toward the center of the set as the ladies pass by.
17-24	The men face clockwise around the set and DoSaDo their approaching partner.
25-32	The 4 men Star Left once around.
33-40	The 4 men pass by their partner, release hands in the Star and Promenade with the next lady counterclockwise around the set. (The four men should Promenade shoulder to shoulder.)
41-48	The Couples Promenade to the man's home position and 4 Ladies Chain.
49-64	Finish the Ladies Chain & 4 couples Promenade once around the set.

Note: The timing on this quadrille is very tight. The sets should dance in as small a configuration as is comfortable.

Pretty Baby Quadrille

Jerry Helt

Formation: Four couples in a square formation.
Record: E-Z 725 "Pretty Baby"

Prompts

Intro	*- - - -, Heads to the middle & back*
1-8	**- - - -, Heads Right & Left Thru**
9-16	**- - - -, Sides to the middle & back**
17-24	**- - - -, Sides Right & Left Thru**
25-32	**- - - -, All join hands & Circle Left**
33-40	**- - - -, - - Corner Swing**
41-48	**- - - -, - - - Promenade**
49-56	**- - - -, - - - -**
57-64	**- - - -, Heads to the middle & back**

Description

1-8	Head couples Forward & Back.
9-16	Head couples Right & Left Thru.
17-24	Side couples Forward & Back.
25-32	Side couples Right & Left Thru.
33-40	All join hands and Circle Left.
41-48	Corner Swing.
49-64	Promenade once around the ring.

Note: The music is in two-step rhythm. It has a lazy floating feeling. Suggest to the dancers that they take small steps.

Queen's Quadrille

Jerry Helt

Formation: Four couples in a square formation.
Record: Grenn 12172 "Sweet Georgia Brown" or E-Z 718 "Queen's Quadrille"

Prompts

Intro	*- - - -, Head 2 couples Right & Left Thru*
1-8	**- - - -, Same 2 Ladies Chain**
9-16	**- - - -, Side 2 couples Right & Left Thru**
17-24	**- - - -, Same 2 Ladies Chain**
25-32	**- - - -, All join hands & Circle Left**
33-40	**- - - -, - - Corner Swing**
41-48	**- - - -, - - - Promenade**
49-56	**- - - -, - - - -**
57-64	**- - - -, Side 2 couples Right & Left Thru**

(Alternate head & side couples)

Description

1-8	Head or side couples Right & Left Thru.
9-16	Same 2 Ladies Chain.
17-24	The other facing couples Right & Left Thru.
25-32	Same 2 Ladies Chain.
33-40	All join hands and Circle Left
41-48	Swing the corner.
49-64	4 Couples Promenade once around the ring.

Stars & Stripes Quadrille

Jerry Helt

Formation: Four couples in a square formation.
Record: E-Z 714 or Blue Star 1917 or Grenn 15011 "In The Good Old Summertime"

Prompts

Intro	*- - - -, - - 4 Ladies Chain*
1-8	**- - - -, Heads Right & Left Thru**
9-16	**- - - -, - - 4 Ladies Chain**
17-24	**- - - -, Sides Right & Left Thru**
25-32	**- - - -, Ladies in & sweep hands & back out**
33-40	**- - - -, 4 men Star Right**
41-48	**- - - -, - Turn partner Left**
49-56	**Pick up the corner, Promenade halfway around to home**
57-64	**- - - -, - - 4 Ladies Chain**

Description

1-8	4 Ladies Chain across.
9-16	Head or side couples Right & Left Thru.
17-24	4 Ladies Chain across.
25-32	The other two couple (sides or heads) Right & Left Thru.
33-40	Ladies move to the center of the set 3 steps and stop as they sweep their arms to the center. Then back out with 3 steps and touch.
41-48	4 men Star Right once around.
49-56	Left Arm Turn with the partner and go to the corner.
57-64	Right Arm Turn the corner once around and change to a Couple Promenade and walk halfway around the square to the man's home position.

Quarter Chain Quadrille

Jack Murtha

Formation: Four couples in a square formation.
Record: Square Dancetime SD-006 "Quarter Chain Quadrille"

Prompts

Intro	*- - - -, - - - -*
	- - - -, Head couples Promenade half
1-8	**- - - -, Down the middle Right & Left Thru**
9-16	**- - - -, Side couples Promenade Half**
17-24	**- - - -, Down the middle Right & Left Thru**
25-32	**- - - -, - - 4 Ladies Chain**
33-40	**- - - -, Ladies Chain one quarter**
41-48	**- - - -, - - Promenade**
49-56	**- - - -, - - - -**
57-64	**- - - -, Head couples Promenade Half**

Description

1-8	Head couples Promenade halfway around the outside of the set. The other couples move to the center and back.
9-16	Right & Left Thru across the set to the man's home position.
17-24	Side couples Promenade halfway around the outside of the set.
25-32	Right & Left Thru across the set to the man's home position.
33-40	4 Ladies Chain across the set.
41-48	Chain the Ladies 1/4. In the quarter chain, the Ladies will Chain to their left one quarter of the way or position around the set. Each man will Courtesy Turn his original right hand lady
49-64	All 4 couples Promenade once around.

Note: The recommended music is smooth, but written in 2/4 time. This will necessitate that the dancers use small steps and dance in a tight square.

Gordo's Quadrille

Jack Murtha

Formation: Four couples in a square formation.
Record: Square Dancetime SD-002 "Gordo's Quadrille"

Prompts

Intro	- - - -, - - - -
	- - - -, - - *Heads Lead Right*
1-8	**- Split Two around 1 down the middle Right & Left Thru**
9-16	**- - - -, - - Sides Lead Right**
17-25	**- Split Two around 1 down the middle Right & Left Thru**
25-32	**- - - -, - - Circle Left**
33-40	**- - - -, - - Allemande Left**
41-48	**- Pass your partner- , Take the next & Promenade**
49-56	**- - - -, - - - -**
57-64	**- - - - , - - Heads Lead Right**

Description

1-8	Head or side couples Lead Right and Split the outside two and Separate.
9-16	Around 1 down the middle and Right & Left Thru with the facing couple.
17-24	The other couple (sides or heads) Lead Right and Split the outside two and Separate.
25-32	Around 1 down the middle and Right & Left Thru with the facing couple.
33-40	Circle Left halfway to the man's home position.
41-48	Allemande Left
49-64	Pass by your partner and Promenade the next person 3/4 around to the man's home position.

Note: The intro on the Square Dancetime record is 16 beats of music. If you use another record, the number of lead in counts will need to match the intro of the record.

DoSaDo & Face the Sides Quadrille

Ralph Page

Formation: Four couples in a square formation.
Record: Lloyd Shaw E-32 "Tipperary" or Windsor 4907 "Gal From Arkansas"

Prompts

Intro	*- - - -, Heads Forward & Back*
1-8	**- - - -, Heads DoSaDo & face the sides**
9-16	**- - - -, Circle 4 once around**
17-24	**- - - -, Split Two around 1 to a line**
25-32	**- - - -, - - Forward & Back**
33-40	**- - - -, Center four Star by the Left**
41-48	**- - - -, Turn corner by the Right once & a half**
49-56	**- - - -, Others Star Left back to the corner**
57-64	**- - - -, - - Balance & Swing**
65-72	**- - - -, - - - -**
73-80	**- - - -, - - - Promenade**
81-88	**- - - -, - - - -**
89-96	**- - - -, Heads Forward & Back**

Description

1-8	Head or side couples Forward & Back.
9-16	DoSaDo the opposite person and finish facing the corner person in the set.
17-24	Circle 4 with the outside pair once around
25-32	Inside pair Split the outside pair and Separate around 1 to a line of four.
33-40	Lines of four go Forward & Back
41-48	Center four in the line Star Left once around
49-56	Turn the corner person by the right once and a half
57-64	Send the other four people into the center for a Left Hand Star once around.
65-80	Balance Forward & Back with your corner for 4 or 8 counts and Swing with the corner for the remaining 8 or 12 counts.
81-96	Promenade once around the set.

Notes; If you do not want to use a Balance in your program, a DoSaDo can be substituted for counts 65-72 and then Swing during counts 73-80.

Seeing Stars

Calvin Campbell

Formation: Four couples in a square formation.
Record: Lloyd Shaw LS-330 "Whispering"

Prompts

Intro	*- - - Heads, DoSaDo & face the sides*
1-8	**- - - -, Circle 4 once around**
9-16	**- - - -, Split Two around 1 to a line**
17-24	**- - - -, Center four Star by the Left**
25-32	**- - - -, Turn corner by the Right once & a half**
33-40	**- - - -, Others Star Left back to the corner**
41-48	**- - - -, - - DoSaDo**
49-56	**- - - -, Take her home & Swing**
57-64	**- - - Heads, DoSaDo & face the sides**

Description

1-8	Heads or sides DoSaDo the opposite person and finish facing the corner position in the set.
9-16	Circle 4 with the outside pair once around
17-24	Inside pair Split the outside pair and Separate around one to a line of four.
25-32	Center four in the line Star Left once around
33-40	Turn the corner person by the right once and a half
41-48	Send the other four people (heads or sides) into the center for a Left Hand Star once around.
49-56	DoSaDo the corner
57-64	If you are at home position Swing. If you need to, walk 2 steps to home position and Swing.

Note: This dance is a shortened version of "DoSaDo and Face the Sides Quadrille" adapted to fit the standard 64 beat tune. It is prompted twice for the head position and then twice for the side position. Then return to the head position if needed.

Happy Sounds Quadrille

Ken Kernen

Formation: Four couples in a square formation.
Record: Jewel 706 "Happy Sounds"

Prompts

Intro	*- - - -, Sides face Grand Square*
1-8	**- - - -, - - - -**
9-16	**- - - -, - - - Reverse**
17-24	**- - - -, - - - -**
25-32	**- - - -, Four men Star Right**
33-40	**- - - -, Turn corner by the Left**
41-48	**Keep her & Promenade, - - - -**
49-56	**- - - -, - - - -**
57-64	**- - - -, Sides face Grand Square**

Description

1-32	Sides or heads face and Grand Square.
33-40	Four men Star Right once around in the center.
41-48	Arm Turn the corner lady.
49-64	Men roll in toward the corner left face and Promenade the corner home all the way around the set.

Note: This recording is played 4 times through.

Farmer's Quadrille

Bruce Johnson

Formation: Four couples in a square formation.
Record: MacGregor 2029 "Turkey in the Straw"

Prompts

Intro	*- - - -, Sides face Grand Square*
1-16	**- - - -, - - - -, - - - -, - - - Reverse**
17-32	**- - - -, - - - -, - - - -, Heads Promenade all the way around**
1-16	**- - - -, - - - -, - - - -, Heads face couple on the right & DoSaDo**
17-24	**- - - -, Heads Right & Left Thru across the set**
25-32	**- - Face new, couple to the right & DoSaDo**
1-8	**- - - Heads, Right & Left Thru across the set**
9-16	**- - - -, 4 Ladies Chain across**
17-24	**- - - -, 4 Ladies Chain across**
24-32	**- - - -, Sides Promenade all the way around**
1-16	**- - - -, - - - -, - - - Sides, face couple on the right & DoSaDo**
17-24	**- - - -, Sides straight across Right & Left Thru**
25-32	**- - - -, Sides face to the right & DoSaDo**
1-8	**- - - -, Sides Right & Left Thru across**
9-16	**- - - -, 4 Ladies Chain across**
17-24	**- - - -, 4 Ladies Chain across**
25-32	**- - - -, Sides face Grand Square**

Repeat all the above (except the intro line) one more time

Description

1-32	Sides face & Grand Square
1-16	Head couples Promenade once around the outside of the set.
17-24	Head couples face the side couple to their right and DoSaDo and finish facing across the set.
25-32	Head couples Right & Left Thru across the set.
1-8	Head couples face the new side couple to their right and DoSaDo and finish facing across the set.
9-16	Head couples Right & Left Thru across the set.
17-24	4 Ladies Chain
24-32	4 Ladies Chain
1-16	Side couples Promenade once around the outside of the set.
17-24	Side couples face the head couple to their right and DoSaDo and finish facing across the set.
25-32	Side couples Right & Left Thru across the set.
1-8	Side couples face the new head couple to their right and DoSaDo and finish facing across the set.
9-16	Side couples Right & Left Thru across the set.
17-24	4 Ladies Chain
24-32	4 Ladies Chain

Repeat all the above one more time and finish with a Sides face & Grand Square.

Notes: Bruce does this dance in a style that combines prompting and calling. The dancers should dance on the phrase of the music for maximum enjoyment.

Popcorn Quadrille

Andy Anderson

(Modified slightly by Calvin Campbell)

Formation: Four couples in a square formation.
Record: Collectables 3170B "Popcorn"

Prompts

Intro	*- - - -, Allemande Left with the corner*
	- - - -, DoSaDo your partner
	- - - -, Sides face Grand Square
1-16	**- - - -, - - - -, - - - -, - - - Reverse**
17-32	**- - - -, - - - -, - - - -, 4 Ladies Chain across**
33-40	**- - - -, 4 Ladies Chain back home**
41-48	**- - - -, Roll Away 1/2 Sashay**
49-56	**Promenade the lady that's comin' your way, - - - -**
57-64	**- - - -, Sides face Grand Square**
1-16	**- - - -, - - - -, - - - -, - - - Reverse**
17-32	**- - - -, - - - -, - - - -, 4 Ladies Chain across**
33-40	**- - - -, 4 Ladies Chain back home**
41-48	**- - - -, Roll Away 1/2 Sashay**
49-56	**Promenade the lady that's comin' your way, - - - -**
57-64	**- - - -, Heads face Grand Square**
1-16	**- - - -, - - - -, - - - -, - - - Reverse**
17-32	**- - - -, - - - -, - - - -, 4 Ladies Chain across**
33-40	**- - - -, 4 Ladies Chain back home**
41-48	**- - - -, Roll Away 1/2 Sashay**
49-56	**Promenade the lady that's comin' your way, - - - -**
57-64	**- - - -, Heads face Grand Square**

Continued on next page.

1-16 - - - -, - - - -, - - - -, - - - Reverse
17-32 - - - -, - - - -, - - - -, 4 Ladies Chain across
33-40 - - - -, 4 Ladies Chain back home
41-48 - - - -, Roll Away 1/2 Sashay
49-56 Promenade the lady that's comin' your way, - - - -
57-64 - - - -, Allemande Left on the corner

1-8 - - - -, - - DoSaDo your own
9-16 - - - -, Allemande Left just once again
17-24 - - - -, - - Weave the ring
25-32 - - - -, - - DoSaDo your partner
33-40 - - - -, - - Promenade home
41-48 - - - -, All go Forward 4 slow steps &
48-56 - - - -, Back out 4 slow steps
57-64 - - - -, Bow to your partner

Description

1-32 Sides face Grand Square.
1-8 4 Ladies Chain across the set.
9-16 4 Ladies Chain back across the set.
17-24 All Roll Away 1/2 Sashay and Promenade the right hand lady. The man steps toward the right hand lady as she rolls into the Couple Promenade position. It is not a complete Roll Away 1/2 Sashay. All couples should be Promenading by count 20.
25-32 Couples Promenade with the men almost shoulder to shoulder.

Repeat above three more times.

1-8 Allemande Left with the corner.
9-16 DoSaDo the partner.
17-24 Allemande Left with the corner.
25-32 Weave the ring.
33-40 Couple Promenade home.
41-48 All join hands and walk into the center of the set 4 slow steps.
49-56 Back away from the center 4 slow steps.
57-64 Bow to your partner.

Walkin' in the Black Forest

Chip Hendrickson

(Modified by Calvin Campbell)

Formation: Four couples in a square formation.
Record: Grenn 12237

Prompts

Intro	*- - - -, 4 Ladies Chain across*
1-8	**- - - -, - - Chain Back**
9-16	**- - - -, - - Promenade**
17-24	**- - - -, - - - -**
25-32	**- - - -, Sides face Grand Square**
33-40	**- - - -, - - - -**
41-48	**- - - -, - - - Reverse**
49-56	**- - - -, - - - -**
57-64	**- - - - , Heads Right & Left Thru**
1-8	**- - - -, Pass Thru & Promenade Half**
9-16	**- - - -, Sides Right & Left Thru**
17-24	**- - - -, Pass Thru & Separate around 2**
25-32	**- - - -, All Circle Left half**
33-40	**- - - -, Swing your corner**
41-48	**- - - -, - - Promenade**
49-56	**- - - -, - - - -**
57-64	**- - - -, Head two Right & Left Thru**

Description Intro/Brk/End

1-16	Four Ladies Chain over and back
16-32	Couples Promenade once around
33-64	Sides face and Grand Square

Description Figure (repeat twice for heads and twice for sides)

1-8	Heads or Sides Right & Left Thru.
9-16	Same couples Pass Thru & Promenade half to opposite side.
17-24	The other couple (sides or heads) Right & Left Thru.
25-32	Same couples Pass Thru and Separate around two to opposite position.
33-40	All join hands and Circle Left halfway to home position.
41-48	Swing the corner.
49-64	Promenade once around.

Wheels Quadrille

Author Unknown

Formation: Four couples in a square formation.
Record: Collectables 3819 "Wheels"

Prompts

Intro	*- - - -, Sides face Grand Square*
1-16	**- - - -, - - - -, - - - -, - - Reverse**
17-32	**- - - -, - - - -, - - - -, - - Head Ladies Chain**
33-40	**- - - -, - - Side Ladies Chain**
41-48	**- - - -, - - Head Ladies Chain**
49-56	**- - - -, - - Side Ladies Chain**
57-64	**- - - -, Sides face Grand Square**
1-16	**- - - -, - - - -, - - - -, - - Reverse**
17-32	**- - - -, - - - -, - - - -, Head couples Right & Left Thru**
33-40	**- - - -, Side couples Right & Left Thru**
41-48	**- - - -, Head couples Right & Left Thru**
49-56	**- - - -, Side couples Right & Left Thru**
57-64	**- - - -, Sides face Grand Square**
1-16	**- - - -, - - - -, - - - -, - - Reverse**
17-32	**- - - -, - - - -, - - - -, Head couples Promenade Half**
33-40	**- - - -, Down the middle Right & Left Thru**
41-48	**- - - -, Side couples Promenade Half**
49-56	**- - - -, Down the middle Right & Left Thru**
57-64	**- - - -, Sides face Grand Square**
1-16	**- - - -, - - - -, - - - -, - - Reverse**
17-32	**- - - -, - - - -, - - - -, - - Corner DoSaDo**
33-40	**- - - -, - - Partner DoSaDo**
41-48	**- - - -, Bow**

Grand Square Quadrille

Bob Osgood

Formation: Four couples in a square formation.
Record: LS E-34 or EZ 730 "Grand Square Quadrille"

Prompts

Intro	*- - - -, - - - -, - - - -, - - Grand Square*
1-16	**- - - -, - - - -, - - - -, - - Reverse**
17-32	**- - - -, - - - -, - - - -, 1 & 3 Right & Left Thru**
33-40	**- - - -, Turn her right around & Right & Left back**
41-48	**- - - -, Side two Right & Left Thru**
49-56	**- - - -, Turn her right around & Right & Left back**
57-64	**- - - -, Heads to the right & Right & Left Thru**
1-8	**- - - -, Turn her right around & Right & Left back**
9-16	**- - - -, Sides right & Right & Left Thru**
17-24	**- - - -, Turn her around & Right & Left back**
25-32	**- - - -, - - Grand Square**
33-48	**- - - -, - - - -, - - - -, - - Reverse**
49-64	**- - - -, - - - -, - - - -, 1 & 3 Ladies Chain**
1-8	**- - - -, Turn her around & Chain back**
9-16	**- - - -, Side 2 Ladies Chain**
17-24	**- - - -, Turn her around & Chain back**
25-32	**- - - -, Head Ladies Chain right**
33-40	**- - - -, Turn her around & Chain back**
41-48	**- - - -, Side 2 Ladies Chain right**
49-56	**- - - -, Turn her around & Chain back**
57-64	**- - - -, - - Grand Square**

1-16	**- - - -, - - - -, - - - -, - - Reverse**
17-32	**- - - -, - - - -, - - - -, 1 & 3 Half Promenade**
33-40	**Across the inside with your maid, - - Right & Left home**
41-48	**- - - -, Side couples Half Promenade**
49-56	**- - - -, - - Right & Left home**
57-64	**- - - -, Heads to the right & Half Promenade**
1-8	**- - - -, - - Right & Left home**
9-16	**- - - -, Sides to the right & Half Promenade**
17-24	**- - - -, - - Right & Left home**
25-32	**- - - -, - - Grand Square**
33-48	**- - - -, - - - -, - - - -, - - Reverse**
49-64	**- - - -, - - - -, - - - -, - - - -**

Description

1-32	Side couples face and Grand Square.
33-40	Head couples Right & Left Thru across the set.
41-48	Same couples Right & Left Thru back home.
49-56	Side couples Right & Left Thru across the set.
57-64	Same couples Right & Left Thru back to home.
1-8	Head couples face the side couples to their right and Right & Left Thru.
9-16	Same two couples Right & Left Thru back to home.
17-24	Side couples face the head couples to their right and Right & Left Thru.
25-32	Same two couples Right & Left Thru back to home.
33-64	Heads couples face and Grand Square
1-8	Head two Ladies Chain across the set.
9-16	Same 2 Ladies Chain back to home.
17-24	Side 2 Ladies Chain across the set.
25-32	Same 2 Ladies Chain back to home.
33-40	Head couples face the side couple on their right and 2 Ladies Chain.
41-48	Same 2 Ladies Chain back to home.
49-56	Side couples face the head couples to their right and 2 Ladies Chain.
57-64	Same 2 Ladies Chain back to home.

1-32	Sides couples face and Grand Square.
33-40	Head couples Promenade inside the set halfway around.
41-48	Same head couples Right & Left Thru to home.
49-56	Side couples Promenade inside the set halfway around.
57-64	Same side couples Right & Left Thru to home.

1-8	Head couples face the side couple to their right & Half Promenade.
9-16	Same couple Right & Left Thru to home.
17-24	Side couples face the head couple to their right & 1/2 Promenade.
25-32	Same couples Right & Left Thru to home.
33-64	Head couples face and Grand Square.

Note: Bob Osgood prompts the flip side of the Lloyd Shaw record. Most of the words used in the prompts are the same as used in the recording.

Quebec Quadrille

Jerry Helt

Formation: Four couples in a square formation.
Record: Windsor 4174 (special 96 count music) "Quebec Quadrille"

Prompts

Intro	*- - - -, Heads right with a Right & Left Thru*
1-8	**- - - -, Same heads right with a Right & Left Thru**
9-16	**- - - -, Head Ladies Chain across**
17-24	**- - - -, Side Ladies Chain across**
25-32	**- - - -, Sides right with a Right & Left Thru**
33-40	**- - - -, Same sides right with a Right & Left Thru**
41-48	**- - - -, 4 couples Promenade half the square**
49-56	**- - - -, 4 Ladies Chain 3/4**
57-64	**- - - -, Sides face Grand Square**
65-80	**- - - -, - - - -, - - - -, - - - Reverse**
81-96	**- - - -, - - - -, - - - -, Heads right with a Right & Left Thru**

Description

1-8	Head couples face the side couples to their right and Right & Left Thru.
9-16	Same couples face a new couple to their right & Right & Left Thru. All couples should now be half across from home position.
17-24	Head 2 Ladies Chain across.
25-32	Side 2 Ladies Chain across.
33-40	Same sides face the head couple to their right and Right & Left Thru.
41-48	The same side couple face a new couple to their right and Right & Left Thru.
49-56	All four couples Promenade halfway.
57-64	4 Ladies Chain 3/4.
65-96	Sides face and Grand Square.

Grand Square Six Quadrille

Jack Murtha

Formation: Four couples in a square formation.
Record: SD-009 "Grand Square Six"

Prompts

Intro	*After the opening chord, sides Pass Thru*
1-8	**- - Separate, around two - -**
9-16	**Home you go - -, - - Heads Pass Thru**
17-24	**- - Separate, around two - -**
25-32	**Home you go - -, Sides face Grand Square**
33-40	**Six steps - - , Bow to your partner & Swing**
41-48	**- - - -, - - - Promenade**
49-56	**- - - -, - - - -**
57-64	**- - - -, Side two Pass Thru**

Description

1-8	Side or head couples Pass Thru & Separate.
9-16	Continue walking around the outside of the set to home position.
17-24	The other couple (head or side) Pass Thru & Separate
25-32	Continue walking around the outside of the set to home position.
33-40	Sides face and Grand Square 6 steps and bow for 2 beats of music.
41-48	Swing the person you bowed to.
49-64	Promenade 16 steps to home position.

Note: The recommended record is made up of several jig tunes and works well for contra dances.

Contra Dances

Contra dancing is a very old form of dancing. It has roots extending back over 400 hundred years to dances in early Ireland and Scotland. Thousands of contra dance have been written. The contra dances published in this book use the same dance movements as the square dance section. Many of the dances were adapted from traditional contra dances and simplified. What, hopefully, has been retained is 99.9% of the dancing pleasure.

Contra dancing originally referred to the spacial relationship of the partners in the dance formation. Partners faced each other in long lines composed of 6 to 12 couples or more. The partner was contra as in the opposing line.

Contra Dance Music

Music used for contra dancing should be strongly phrased as described in the discussion "Fundamentals of Calling/Prompting-/Cueing" on page 11. Strongly phrased music is important because contra dancers are expected to execute the dance movements in time with the music. Musical arrangements used for contra dances usually have a strong melody that make it easy for both the leader and the dancers to recognize when each dance routine should begin and end.

The traditional styles of music that have been used for contra dancing include Jigs, Reels and Hornpipes. Each tune and arrangement should be carefully examined before it is used, because not all of them are arranged in blocks suitable for contra dances. Sometimes the count blocking is printed on the jacket or case and sometimes the only way to determine if the tune is useable, is to try and dance to it.

While there are many advantages to using traditional styles of music, there are many other musical styles that work very well for contra dances. For example, during the holiday season a good rendition of "Jingle Bells" could provide a very enjoyable background for a contra dance. Many singing call records can also be used.

You should strive to provide a wide variety in the music you choose. Using all the same style of music for contras as you use for squares will only bore the audience. Give them something with a different feel and fit the dance to the music.

Organization of Dances

The contra dances are divided into several sections organized by formation type. An explanation of each formation precedes the selection of dances. Under some formations, the dances are further divided into sub-groups based on difficulty, etc. Within each grouping, the dances are arranged in a suggested order of teaching based on difficulty or the introduction of new terminology, concepts, etc.

The dance movements (basics) used in the contra dances in this manual are also used in square dancing. The two dance forms compliment each other very well. In square dancing, people learn to dance a varied pattern without knowing the exact dance routine. Contra dances give them the opportunity to dance a repeating dance pattern many times. Contras provide the best place to perfect correct styling and timing. As a rule of thumb, new movements should be first be taught in a square dance formation and then practiced in a contra formation.

Dances specifically for new dancers, are included under each of the four contra formations used in this book. The easier dances are placed at the start of each subsection. Keep in mind that same basic movement danced from a different formation may look entirely new to inexperienced dancers. Be prepared to show them the differences.

Facing Lines Contra Dances

The simplest form of contra dancing places all the men in one line facing all the ladies in the opposite line as shown to the right. In the diagram, the prompter is pictured standing at the head of the hall and looking down the center of the set. All the men (squares) are on the right and ladies (circles) are all on the left. The small black square shows the direction each individual is facing at the beginning of the dance. I.e. facing eachother.

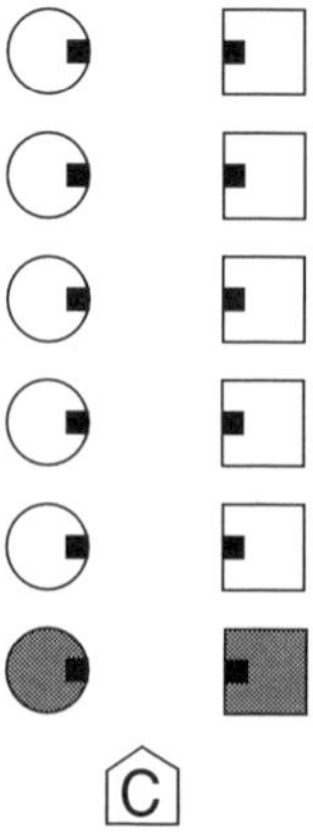

At some point in each dance, the top couple (shaded on the diagram) moves to the foot of the set and the rest of the couples move one place toward the head of the set. This allows each couple, in turn, to dance as the head couple.

Contras danced in this formation are excellent for people who are inexperienced in dancing. **The Virginia NoReel**, **No Name Contra, Tunnel Contra** and **Barley & Oats** (Pgs. 146-149), can also be used in groups where there are more of one gender than the other. For example, two ladies could dance as partners, with one person, of each pair, dancing in the right hand (men's) line. All each individual needs to remember is which line is the home line for them. Even if they occasionally become confused as to who belongs in each line, the commands can still be danced.

All of the dances have a set number of steps recommended for the dance routine. This is based on the normal time it takes to comfortably complete the dance routine in a contra set composed of a reasonable number of couples. In sets containing more that six couples, actions such as, all duck thru an arch and *Promenade* to the head of the set, will take longer than 8 beats of music. When this occurs, the prompter should visually time the next prompt to allow all the dancers to comfortably duck through the arch and march to the head of the set before prompting the dancers to go *Forward & Back.* In long contra lines, the dancers will not be able to complete the entire routine within the 64 beats. While this is not desirable, it is acceptable if the caller is able to prompt the next starting action so it can be danced on the phrase.

Many other factors such as age, altitude, floor conditions, etc. can also result in dancers taking more time to complete a routine than expected. For example, in **NoName Contra,** when people slide down the center of the set and then *Promenade* over both lines, the three movements can often take more than the normal 24 beats of music. Under these circumstances, it is recommended that you provide additional time to complete the three movements by eliminating the 8-beat *Swing*. This gives the dancers a chance to complete the last *Promenade* and start the next routine on the phrase of the music. The notes listed after many of the dance offer suggestions on which basics to eliminate.

Several of the facing line contra dances in this manual require considerable dancing experience. You may want to delay using some of these routines until the dancers become more familiar with contra terminology and how to dance in time with the music. Some of the contra dances in these sections feature unusual movement patterns (gimmicks) that may alter where or when the dance is presented in a teaching sequence. Check the notes list at the bottom of the dance for advice.

Virginia NoReel

Calvin Campbell

Formation: Contra lines. 12 couples or less. All the men in a line on the prompter's right and all the ladies in a line on the prompter's left.
Record: LS 318 "January 7th Jig" or MacGregor 7345 "Virginia Reel"

Prompts

Intro	*- - - -, Everybody Forward & Back*
1-8	**- - - -, Turn your partner Right Hand Around**
9-16	**- - - -, Turn your partner Left Hand Around**
17-24	**- - - -, Turn your partner both hands around**
25-32	**- - - -, Top couple slide to the foot**
33-40	**- - - -, Same two slide back to the head**
41-48	**- - - -, Promenade Single File to the foot**
49-56	**- - - -, Actives make an arch & the others duck thru**
57-64	**- - - -, Everybody Forward & Back**

Description

1-8	Both lines walk Forward & Back.
9-16	Turn your partner with a Right Arm Turn.
17-24	Turn your partner with a Left Arm Turn.
25-32	Join both hands with your partner and walk once around right hip to right hip.
33-40	Keeping both hands joined with your partner, the active couple slide-steps (Sashays) 8 steps toward the foot of the set between the two lines.
41-48	Active couple slide-steps back to the head of the set.
49-56	Everyone should face the head of the set. The active people each lead their line in a Single File Promenade down the outside to the foot of the set. This may take more than 8 beats of music in a set composed of over eight couples.
57-64	Only the active couple face eachother and make a two hand arch. All the other couples duck through the arch and Promenade to the head of the set. When finished, the former head couple is now at the foot of the set and all the other couples have moved one position toward the prompter.

Notes: To add variety to this dance, have 2 to 5 couples slide to the foot of the set and back. These same couples will then all make an arch for the other people to duck through.

NoName Contra

Jerry Helt

Formation: Contra lines. 6 couples or less. All the men in a line on the prompter's right and all the ladies in a line on the prompter's left.
Record: RB 1301 "Love in the Country", Jewel 705 "Show Boat" or LS 193/194 or Folkcraft 1501 "Dashing White Sergeant"

Prompts

Intro	*- - - -, Everybody Forward & Back*
1-8	**- - - -, Forward & Back again**
9-16	**- - - -, Turn the opposite Right Hand Around**
17-24	**- - - -, Turn the opposite Left Hand Around**
25-32	**- - - -, Top couple slide to the foot**
33-40	**- - Same couple, Promenade arch over the lady's Line**
41-48	**- - - - , Promenade arch over the men's line**
49-56	**- - - -, - - Everybody Swing**
57-64	**- - - -, Everybody Forward & Back**

Description

1-8	Long lines Forward & Back.
9-16	Forward & Back again.
17-24	Turn the opposite person (partner) with a Right Arm Turn.
25-32	Turn the opposite person (partner) with a Left Arm Turn.
33-40	The top couple join both hands and slide (Sashay) to the foot of the set.
41-48	The active couple then join inside hands (man's right & lady's left), form an arch and Promenade up the set passing over the lady's line. Lady on the outside and man on the inside.
49-56	The active couple Promenade down the set passing the arch down over the men's line to the foot of the set and then each active person steps back into their home line. The man remains on the inside of the set during the Promenade.
57-64	Everybody Swing their partner (across the set) and then step back into their home line

.

Note: If the active couple has difficulty completing the Promenade over both lines in the 16 beats recommended, eliminate the Swing at the end of the dance (56-64) and wait 8 counts before starting the dance over again.

Tunnel Contra

Herbie Gaudreau

Formation: Contra lines. 6 couples or fewer. All the men in a line on the prompter's right and all the ladies in a line on the prompter's left.
Record: LS E-40 or E-Z 722 "Tunnel Contra" or TNT 271 "Pass Me By"

Prompts

Intro - - - -, Everybody Forward & Back

1-8 - - - -, All Pass Thru & U-turn Back
9-16 - - - -, Everybody Forward & Back
17-24 - - - -, All Pass Thru & U-turn Back
25-32 - - - -, Top couple slide down (others arch)
33-40 - - - -, Lady up inside, man up outside
41-48 - - - -, Man down inside, lady down outside
49-56 - - - -, - - Everybody Swing
57-64 - - - -, Everybody Forward & Back

Description

1-8 Lines walk Forward & Back.
9-16 Pass Thru the opposite line in 4 steps and U-turn Back in 4 steps to end standing where opposite line started.
17-24 Both lines walk Forward & Back.
25-32 Pass Thru the opposite line in 4 steps and U-turn Back in 4 steps to end standing back in the home line.
33-40 The couple nearest the prompter join both hands with the opposite person and slide (sashay) to the foot of the set. The rest of the couples form a two hand arch as the active couple passes by to form a long tunnel.
41-48 The lady walks up through the tunnel as the man walks up the outside of the man's line.
49-56 The man walks down through the tunnel as the lady walks down the outside of the lady's line. The active couple then step into their home line at the foot of the set.
57-64 Everybody Swing their partner and then step back into their home lines.

Note: If you find the active couple cannot go through the tunnel within 16 counts, eliminate the final 8-count Swing and wait the 8 extra beats of music before prompting the Forward & Back. The tunnel can also be eliminated, if needed, for dancers with physical limitations.

Barley & Oats

Ken Kernen

Formation: Contra lines of 4 couples. All the men in a line on the prompter's right and all the ladies in a line on the prompter's left.
Record: Ute UR9 "14 Karot"

Prompts

Intro	*- - - -, Everybody Forward & Back*
1-8	**- - Men arch, Ladies duck thru & U-turn Back**
9-16	**- - - -, Everybody Forward & Back**
17-24	**- - Ladies arch, men duck thru & U-turn Back**
25-32	**- - - -, Top couple slide (sashay) to the foot**
33-40	**- - - -, Slide back to the head of the set**
41-48	**- - - -, Promenade Single File to the foot**
49-56	**- - - -, Actives arch & others duck thru**
57-64	**- - - -, Everybody Forward & Back**

Description

1-8	Everybody go Forward & Back.
9-16	The men join hands along the line & raise their hands & arms to make arches. The ladies duck thru the arches passing to the right of their partner in 4 steps. The foot lady does not have an arch to duck thru and should walk over to the opposite side of the set as the men move over them. Everyone U-turn Back in 4 steps to end standing where the opposite line started.
17-24	Everybody Forward & Back.
25-32	The ladies join hands along the line & raise their hands & arms to make arches. The men duck thru the arches passing to the right of their partner in 4 steps. The foot man will not have an arch to duck thru and should walk over to the opposite side of the set as the ladies move over them. Everyone U-turn Back to end standing in their home line.
33-40	The top couple step to the center, join both hands and slide (sashay) to the foot of the set.
41-48	The same couple slide (sashay) back to the head of the set.
49-56	Everyone face the head of the set. The top couple lead their individual lines in a Single File Promenade down the outside of the set to the foot position and then makes a two hand arch.
57-64	All the other dancers duck thru the arch and Promenade to the head of the set.

OXO Reel

John Tether

Formation: Contra lines of 6 couples. All the men in a line on the prompter's left and all the ladies in a line on the prompter's right.
Record: LS "Major Mackey's Jig"

Prompts

Intro	*- - - -, Everybody Forward & Back*
1-8	**- - - -, First couple slide (sashay) to the foot of the set**
9-16	**- - - -, Everybody Forward & Back**
17-24	**- - - -, New first couple slide to the foot**
25-32	**- - - -, - - Circles & Stars**
33-40	**- - - -, Reverse the Circles & Stars**
41-48	**- - - -, Foot two couples sashay back**
49-56	**- - Same two Promenade, to the foot & others Swing**
57-64	**- - - -, Everybody Forward & Back**

Description

1-8	Long lines Forward & Back.
9-16	First couple join both hands and slide to the foot of the set.
17-24	Everybody Forward & Back.
25-32	The new top couple join both hands and slide to the foot of the set.
33-40	The top two couples Circle Left, the middle two couples Star Left and the bottom two couples Circle Left.
41-48	Everyone reverses direction to Star Right in the middle and Circle Right on the ends.
49-56	The foot two couples slide back to the head of the set.
57-64	The same two couples Separate and Promenade Single File to the foot of the set while the other four couples Swing.

Note: The OXO Reel is a challenging dance because each couple is dancing a different part depending on where they are located within the set. This will require the dancers to have a clear understanding of contra choreography. As such, this dance should not be used until the dancers are competent in dancing the duple contras. This dance is one of several OXO Reels. The dance on the following page is an alternate version of this same dance.

OXO Reel (Alternate)

Unknown

Formation: Contra lines of 6 couples. All the men in a line on the caller's left and all the ladies in a line on the caller's right.
Record: Grenn 12241 "Yankee Doodle Dandy"

Prompts

Intro	*- - - -, Top couple down, bottom couple up*
1-8	**- - - -, New top couple down & bottom couple up**
9-16	**- - - -, Everybody Forward & Back**
17-24	**- - - -, - - Circles & Stars**
25-32	**- - - -, - - Reverse the Circles & Stars**
33-40	**- - All face up, Promenade to the foot**
41-48	**- - First couple arch and others duck thru**
49-54	**Promenade to the head of the set, - - - -**
57-64	**- - - -, Top couple sashay down, bottom couple up**

Description

1-8	First couple joins hands and walk or slide (sashay) to the foot of the set down the inside while the bottom couple Separate and walk or slide (sashay) up the outside to the head of the set.
9-16	The new first couple joins hands and walk or slide (sashay) to the foot of the set down the inside while the new bottom couple Separate and walk or slide (sashay) up the outside to the head of the set.
17-24	Everybody Forward & Back.
25-32	The top two couples Circle Left, the middle two couples Star Left and the bottom two couples Circle Left.
33-40	Everyone reverses direction to a Right Hand Star in the center and Circle Right on the ends.
41-48	Everyone face the head of the set, Separate and Promenade Single File down the outside of the set to the foot position.
49-64	The first couple form an arch and the other couples duck thru the arch and Promenade to the head of the set.

Note: Many people will prefer to walk in this dance rather than slide (sashay). Be sure the dancers understand that either option is acceptable.

Facing Line Contras with a Reel

Thady You Gander and **A Virginia Reel** are both placed at the end of this section because they both contain a reel (described in the notes on the next page.) A reel is a series of *Arm Turns* and can be very confusing for the active couple.

Thady You Gander uses special 80-beat music written specifically for the dance. When danced properly, the 4th couple should complete their reel just as the recording ends. To achieve this, everyone in the set must cooperate to help each active couple. If problems occur with the reel, and the routine is taking longer than 32 beats of music, the new head couple should start down the center of the set at the proper point in the music, the couple reeling-the-set should stop and quickly move to the foot of the set.

A Virginia Reel (Pg. 154) is one version of a large group of dance routines that share the same name. All of these routines have all the couples doing some things as a group and then a head couple or a head and foot couple doing something. Somewhere, the reel is worked in and at the very end of the routine, the head couple moves to the foot of the set. Other than for this rather loose set of conventions, the caller of the dance is allowed to put in any mixture of movements that fit the music and stay with the 64-beat musical structure.

Notice that **A Virginia Reel** is the only dance in the section with variable timing indicated for part of the dance. The reel and the other movements that follow the first 64 beats of music will take a variable amount of time depending on the length of the contra sets. Even if the length of the sets are limited to 6 couples, a reel will normally take more than 32 beats of music. In longer sets, even more time will have to be allowed. The same consideration applies to the other movements. Longer contra lines will have to allow for more time for slides, *Promenades,* etc. Watch the sets and deliver the prompt for the next movement just as the people are finished the prior movement. The ultimate objective is to keep the dancers moving as smoothly as possible.

Thady You Gander

New England

Formation: Contra lines of 4 couples. All the men in a line on the prompter's right and all the ladies in a line on the prompter's left.
Record: LS E-15 or Folkcraft 1167 (Special 80 beat music)
"Thady You Gander"

Prompts

Intro	*...... First couple down the center*
1-8	**- - - -, Cross, come up the outside**
9-16	**- - - -, The woman leads the men around**
17-32	**- - - -, - - - -, - - - -, Men lead women around**
33-48	**- - - -, - - - -, - - - -, 1st couple Reel the set**
49-64	**- - - -, - - - -, - - - -, - - - -**
65-80	**- - - -, - - - -, - - - -, New head couple down the center**

Description

1-8 The couple nearest the prompter face away from the prompter and walk between the lines with inside hands (man's left and lady's right) joined.

9-16 When the active couple reaches the foot of the set, the lady crosses in front of the man and each dancer proceeds up the outside of the opposite line back to the head of the set.

17-32 The lady joins onto the end of the 3-man line, everyone in this line joins hands and then the lady leads the line Single File around the outside of the opposite line.

33-48 The man joins onto the end of the 3-lady line, everyone in this line joins hands and then the man leads the line Single File promenade around the outside of the opposite line.

48-80 The head couple reels the line to the foot of the set and then steps back into the home line and becomes the last couple at the foot of the set.

Reel: The active couple does a Right Arm Turn in the center of the set and then a Left Arm Turn with the person of the opposite sex immediately below. The active couple then does a Right Arm Turn with the partner again. The action is continued by doing a Left Arm Turn with each person in the line followed by a Right Arm Turn with the partner. The inactive dancers should reach for the active dancers as they complete their Right Arm Turns in the center of the set.

A Virginia Reel

Traditional

Formation: Contra lines of 6 to10 couples. All the men in a line on the prompter's right. All the ladies in a line on the prompter's left.
Record: MacGregor 7345 "Virginia Reel"

Prompts

Intro	*- - - -, All go Forward & Back*
1-8	**- - - -, All go Forward & Back again**
9-16	**- - - -, Head man & foot lady DoSaDo**
17-24	**- - - -, Head lady & foot man DoSaDo**
25-32	**- - - -, Turn your partner both hands around**
33-40	**- - - -, All go forward & DoSaDo**
41-48	**- - - -, First couple slide down 8 steps**
49-56	**- - - -, Slide back to place**
57-64	**- - - -, First couple reel the set**
1-?	**See Note - - - -, - - - -, - - - -, - - - - , - - - -, - - - -, - - - -, - - - -**
?-?	**- - - -, Same couple slide to the head**
?-?	**- - - -, Promenade Single File to the foot**
?-?	**- - - -, Active couples arch, others duck thru**
?-?	**- - - -, All go Forward & Back**

Description

1-16	All go Forward & Back twice.
17-32	Head man & foot lady DoSaDo, then head lady & foot man DoSaDo.
33-40	Everyone DoSaDo their partner across the set.
41-56	The top couple slide down the middle & back (See Virginia NoReel on page 146.)
1-32	Top couple reel the set. (see Thady You Gander on page 153)
33-64	The top couple lead each line in a Single File Promenade to the foot & arch. (See Virginia NoReel)

Duple Improper Contras

The instructions describing the formation at the top of each dance in this section state 1, 3, 5, etc. crossed over and active. When a contra dance

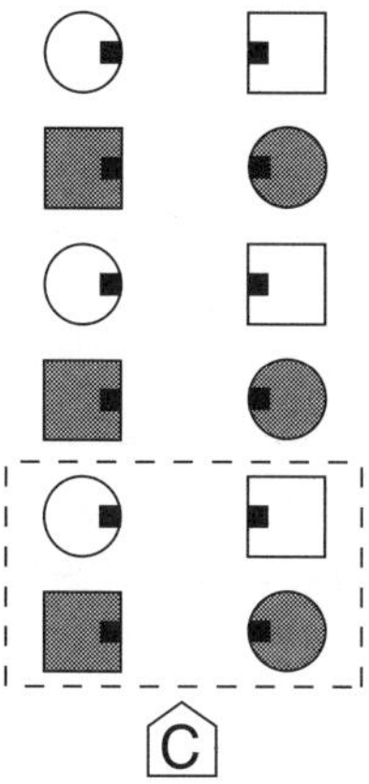

is announced, the dancers should form sets of facing lines with all the men, in each set, on the prompter's right and all the ladies, in each set, on the prompter's left. The caller sets up the desired formation by instructing the odd numbered dancers (1, 3, 5, etc.) to trade places with their partners across the set. These dancers (shaded) are active as long as they remain on the same side of the set, I.e. the men who are on the prompter's left and the ladies who are on the prompter's right. The other dancers (unshaded) are referred to as inactive because the men are on the prompter's right and the ladies are on the prompter's left. Dance instructions are directed to the active or inactive positions.

In duple contras, most of the dance routine is directed to an active couple (shaded) and the couple below (toward the foot of the hall) them in the long set. It is not necessary to tell the dancers this is a duple formation. They only need to understand that they will be primarily working as a foursome composed of two couples. It is also helpful to point out that their partner should be across from them (contra) at the start and at the finish of each 64-beat routine.

At the end of each 64-beat set of movements, the active couples will have moved one or more places toward the foot of the set. The inactive couples will move toward the head of the set at the same time. Each time through the dance, every couple will dance the routine with a new couple.

As the active dancers reach the foot of the set, they cross over, I.e. change positions (side of the set) and become inactive. When the inactive dancers reach the head of the set they exchange places, and thus, change positions (side of the set) and become active. Normally, when the dancers reach the head or the foot of the set, they have to wait one time through the routine as non-participants. These people are referred to as dead-at-the-head or dead-at-the-foot. During this waiting period, the idle people should cross over (trade sides of the set) and change active/inactive roles.

It is critical for the dancers to recognize their role, as active or inactive, will change as they cross over at the head or the foot of the set and stand in the opposite line. They must also recognize that they remain active (as they move toward the head of the set) or inactive (as they move toward the foot of the set) until they cross over at the ends of the set. Understanding how the dancers move or progress in contra sets is the key to becoming a good contra dancer.

Single Progression Contras

Most contras are classified as single progression contras. In these contras, the dancers move one position toward the head or foot of the set each time through the dance routine. Every other time through the routine, a couple is left standing idle at the head and/or the foot of the set for several beats of music. At the head of the set the inactive dancers all cross over at the same time and the prompter can prompt the crossing action. At the foot of the set, the active dancers cross over at different times depending on whether the set has an even or odd number of couples.

Grouping Contras

The contra dances in this manual are divided into several groups arranged more around dance concepts rather than a recommended teaching order or difficulty level. Any dance can be taught independent of any other dance. It is generally recommended that dances for any one event need to be chosen from several different groups to increase the variety of dancing experience. Since most of these dances will be used again, after a set of lessons, the instructor should always provide a walk-thru of the routine prior to doing the dance.

The contra dances within each group are arranged in a progressive order of difficulty. Each subsequent dance incorporates either a new stage of complexity or introduces a new movement (basic.) Each of the basics is coordinated with the teaching order in the square dance section to provide mutual support between the dance forms. Additional teaching hints can also be found included with many of the dance descriptions.

Easy Contras

The contra dances in this group are all suitable for beginner sessions. They all use movements that are common with the square dance section. They all have routines which have couples in the normal lady-on-the-man's-right position. The dances are arranged in the same teaching order as recommended for square dances.

ONS Contra (Pg. 158) places the dancers in a duple improper formation, but the dancers never need to recognize whether they are active or inactive. The dance works very well for learning how to dance in duples and how active dancers progress from the head to the foot of the set and inactive dancers progress from the foot to the head of the set.

Beginner's Luck (Pg. 159), was written to provide a dance to emphasize active and inactive roles and to provide practice in crossing at the head and the foot of the set. **ONS Contra** and **One Horse Reel** (Pg. 160) should solidify learning duple contra progression.

High Five Contra (Pg. 161) adds a hand clap and a foot stomp in the middle of the routine. Audible cues often help the dancers to recognize when they are dancing correctly to the musical phrase.

Contra-action (Pg. 162) and **Homosassa Hornpipe** (Pg.163) both add terminology used extensively in square dancing. Both are excellent dances for polishing timing and styling. They all should be initially taught with an even number of couples in each set so that every one can participate in the action.

Granny's Pearls (Pg. 164) adds a clever use of a *Promenade Half* after a *Left Hand Star.*

Note: In some areas of the country the terminology "neighbor" is used in place of the terminology "corner." The convention in this book is corner which more exactly identifies the dancers relationship.

ONS Contra

Ed Butenhof

Formation: Contra lines. Couples 1, 3, 5, etc., active & crossed over.
Record: LS 342 "Oyster Shucker's Jig" or TNT 138 "Ooga Mooshka"

Prompts

Intro	*- - - -, Everybody Forward & Back*
1-8	**- - - -, With your partner DoSaDo**
9-16	**- - - -, With the corner DoSaDo**
17-24	**- - - -, - - Corner Swing**
25-32	**- - - -, With the couple across Circle Left**
33-40	**- - - -, - - Circle Right**
41-48	**- - - -, Same four Star Right**
49-56	**- - - -, - - Star Left**
57-64	**- - - -, Long lines Forward & Back**

Description

1-8	The long lines go Forward & Back.
9-16	Everybody DoSaDo your partner across the set.
17-24	DoSaDo the corner.
25-32	Swing the corner lady. Finish by placing the lady on the man's right hand side and face across the set as a couple.
33-40	Circle Left with the couple across the set.
41-48	Reverse and Circle Right.
49-56	The same couples Star Right.
57-64	Reverse and Star Left. Return to the home line to face across the set ready to start again.

Note: Every other time through the dance some dancers at the head or the foot of the set will find there is no one in the corner position to DoSaDo and Swing. They are temporarily dead-at-the-head or dead-at-the-foot. At this point, they should cross over to the opposite line and wait. At the start of the next sequence they either become active (at the head) or inactive (at the foot.)

Beginner's Luck

Calvin Campbell

Formation: Contra lines. Couples 1, 3, 5, etc. active and crossed over.
Record: WW-913 "Engine #9" or ESP 185 "Have a Little Faith"

Prompts

Intro	*- - - -, With the corner DoSaDo*
1-8	**- - - -, Corner Swing & put her on your right**
9-16	**- - - -, - - Circle Left**
17-24	**- - - -, - - Circle Right**
25-32	**- - - -, Actives go Forward & Back**
33-40	**- - - -, Actives turn partner Right Hand Around**
41-48	**- - - -, Inactives go Forward & Back**
49-56	**- - - -, Inactives turn partner Left Hand Around**
57-64	**- - - -, With the new corner DoSaDo**

Description

1-8	DoSaDo the corner.
9-16	Swing the same corner and finish facing across the set with the lady on the man's right.
17-24	With the couple across Circle Left
25-32	Same four Circle Right
33-40	Active dancers Forward & Back
41-48	Actives Right Arm Turn their partner (across the set.)
49-56	Inactive dancers go Forward & Back
57-67	Inactives Left Arm Turn with their partner (across the set.)

Note: This is the first contra in the series to identify active and inactive couples. The dance is designed to help the dancers become comfortable with the progression of active dancers toward the foot of the set and inactive dancers toward the head of the set. Every other time through the dance, some people at the head or the foot of the set will find there is no one in the corner position to DoSaDo and Swing. They are temporarily dead-at-the-head or dead-at-the-foot. At this point, they should cross over to the opposite line and wait. At the start of the next sequence they either become active (at the head) or inactive (at the foot.)

One Horse Reel

Bob Howell

Formation: Contra lines. Couples 1, 3, 5, etc. active & crossed over.
Record: Grenn 16017 "One Horse Reel"

Prompts

Intro	*- - - -, Turn Left with the corner*
1-8	**- - - -, Actives to the center for a DoSaDo**
9-16	**- - - -, With the corner DoSaDo**
17-24	**- - - -, - - Corner Swing**
25-32	**- - - -, Put her on your right & Circle Left**
33-40	**- - - -, - - Circle Right**
41-48	**- - - -, Same four Star Left**
49-56	**- - - -, - - Star Right**
57-64	**- - - -, New corner Allemande Left**

Description

1-8	Left ArmTurn with the corner
9-16	Active dancers DoSaDo in the middle of the set
17-24	Active dancers DoSaDo the corner
25-32	Swing the corner and finish by placing the lady on the man's right hand side and face across the set.
33-40	With the couple across Circle Left.
41-48	Same four Circle Right.
49-56	Same four Star Left. The movement continues counterclockwise
56-64	Same four Star Right to the corner.

Note: If the set has an even number of couples, everyone will get to dance the routine the first time through. If the set has an odd number of couples, the foot couple will not start the dance until the second time through the routine. Bob's original description of the dance uses Allemande Left instead of Left Arm Turn.

High Five Contra

Calvin Campbell

Formation: Contra lines. Couples 1, 3, 5, etc. active & crossed over.
Record: Grenn 32054 "Waltzing Matilda" or ESP 717 "Ain't She Sweet"

Prompts

Intro	*- - - -, - - Corner Swing*
1-8	**- - - -, Put her on the right & Promenade Half**
9-16	**- - - -, Ladies DoSaDo once & a half**
17-24	**- - - -, - - Partner Swing**
25-32	**- - - -, Men DoSaDo once & a half**
33-40	**- - - -, Opposite lady Swing -**
41-48	**- - - -, Forward & clap & Backup & stomp**
49-56	**- - - -, Forward & clap & Backup & stomp**
57-64	**- - - -, - - Corner Swing**

Description

1-8	Swing the corner and finish with the lady on the man's right hand side and face across the set in long lines.
9-16	With the same lady, Promenade Half across to the opposite line with the men passing left shoulders.
17-24	Ladies DoSaDo in the middle of the set once and a half to finish back to back and facing their partner.
25-32	Swing your partner and finish facing across the set with the lady on the man's right hand side.
33-40	Men DoSaDo in the middle of the set once and a half to finish back to back and facing their opposite.
41-48	Swing the opposite and finish facing across the set with the lady on the man's right.
49-56	Long lines walk 4 steps forward. On the 4th step clap right hands with the opposite (partner). Then backup 3 steps and stomp your foot on the 4th count.
57-64	Long lines walk 4 steps forward. On the 4th step clap left hands with the opposite. Then backup 3 steps and stomp your foot on the 4th count.

Notes: The Forward & Back with the hand clap and the stomp helps dancers recognize the phrase of the music. Every other time through the dance, some people at the head or the foot of the set will find there is no one in the corner position to Swing. They should cross over to the opposite side of the set.

Contra-action

Ken Kernen

Formation: Contra lines. Couples 1, 3, 5, etc., active & crossed over.
Record: MacGregor 2411 "Pushed in a Corner"

Prompts

Intro	*- - - -, With the corner DoSaDo*
1-8	**- - - -, - - Corner Swing**
9-16	**- - - -, Straight across Right & Left Thru**
17-24	**- - - -, - - Right & Left back**
25-32	**- - - -, - - 2 Ladies Chain**
33-40	**- - - -, - - Chain back**
41-48	**- - - -, Same four Circle Left**
49-56	**- - - -, - - Star Left**
57-64	**- - - -, With the corner DoSaDo**

Description

1-8	All DoSaDo the corner.
9-16	Swing the corner. Place the lady on the man's right hand side and face across the set as a couple.
17-24	Right & Left Thru across the set.
25-32	Right & Left Thru back across the set.
33-40	2 Ladies Chain across the set
41-48	Chain the Ladies back across the set.
49-56	Same two couples Circle 4 to the left.
57-64	Same four Star Left back to the home line.

Note: If the set has an even number of couples, everyone will dance the routine the first time through. If the set has an odd number of couples, the foot couple will not get to dance until the second time through the routine.

Homosassa Hornpipe

Don Armstrong

Formation: Contra lines. Couples 1, 3, 5, etc., active & crossed over.
Record: LS 164 "Homosassa Hornpipe"

Prompts

Intro	*- - - -, Actives DoSaDo in the center*
1-8	**- - - -, - - Corner Swing**
9-16	**- - - -, Put her on the right & Half Promenade**
17-24	**- - - -, Same four Right & Left Thru**
25-32	**- - - -, - - Left Hand Star**
33-40	**- - - -, - - Right Hand Star**
41-48	**- - - -, The men drop out & the Ladies Chain**
49-56	**- - - -, - - Chain back**
57-64	**- - - -, Actives DoSaDo in the center**

Description

1-8	The active couples DoSaDo in the middle of the set.
9-16	Swing the corner and finish by placing the lady on the man's right hand side and face across the set.
17-24	Half Promenade across the set with this same lady. Men pass left shoulders.
25-32	Same four Right & Left Thru across the set.
33-40	With the same couple Star Left.
41-48	Reverse and Star Right
49-56	The men step out of the star, when they reach their home line, and the 2 Ladies Chain. The men will Courtesy Turn their partner.
57-64	The 2 Ladies Chain back across the set

Note: On the Half Promenade, it is acceptable for the man to keep his arm around the ladies waist and not move into the standard hands in front Promenade position. Do what feels the most comfortable.

Granny's Pearls

Lannie McQuaide

Formation: Contra lines. Couples 1, 3, 5, etc., active & crossed over.
Record: LS 323/324 "Miss Thompson's Reel" or Joe Pat 601 "Travel On"

Prompts

Intro	*- - - -, Actives Turn partner Right*
1-8	**- - - -, With the one below Turn by the Left**
9-16	**- - - -, 2 Ladies Chain across the set**
17-24	**- - - -, Same four Right & Left Thru**
25-32	**- - - -, - - Star Right**
33-40	**- - - -, - - Star Left**
41-48	**- - - -, With the lady in front Half Promenade**
49-56	**- - - -, 2 Ladies Chain across the set**
57-64	**- - - -, Actives Turn partner Right**

Description

1-8	The active couples Right Arm Turn each other.
9-16	Left Arm Turn (Allemande Left) the corner lady.
17-24	2 Ladies Chain across the set. The men will Courtesy Turn their partner.
25-32	Same four Right & Left Thru across the set. The men are now in the opposite line with their original partner beside them.
33-40	With the same couple Star Right.
41-48	Reverse and Star Left.
49-56	The men and the lady in front of them (partner) Promenade Half across the set to the home line. Men pass left shoulders.
57-64	2 Ladies Chain back across the set.

Note: On the Half Promenade, it is acceptable for the man to place his right hand on the ladies waist and not move into the standard hands in front Couple Promenade position. Do whatever feels the most comfortable.

Intermediate Contras

Contras in this group are recommended for use with dance groups that have completed a set of lessons or have considerable dance experience. Many of the dances use basics or concepts that need a walk-thru and may cause some confusion the first time they are danced. Plan for extra teaching time and use these dances at points in the program after the dancers have warmed up and before they start to get tired.

Murphy's Helper (Pg. 166) introduces the concept of *Couples Promenading* down the center of the set. The definition for *Promenade* recommends a hands in front position. Dancers will often find that it is easier to just join adjacent hands or to maintain the man's hand at the waist after finishing a *Courtesy Turn* at the end of a *Right & Left Thru* or *2 Ladies Chain.* Any of these options is acceptable in contra dancing. Just do whatever is the most comfortable.

Yucca Jig (Pg. 167) has the dancers traveling down the middle of the set and then moving up the outside of the set back to their starting position. Be aware that the actives can sometimes become confused as to where they should reenter the set for the *DoSaDo.*

Enid's Delight (Pg. 168) features a *Single File Promenade* with both the men and the ladies in the same line. In certain halls this may cause a problem due to the proximity of the walls. The line of dancers can either bend around to the left or to the right or *Promenade* with very short steps.

Broken Sixpence (Pg. 169) & **Fiddle Hill Jig** (Pg. 170) introduce moving down the set four in line. Notice the active couples form the center of the line (shaded) and the inactive dancers are on the ends of the line.

Rutger's Promenade (Pg. 171) has a *Courtesy Turn* and 1/4 more. The normal *Courtesy Turn* will leave couples facing across the set. Turning 1/4 more faces the couples either up or down the set. The *Promenade* should be done with the man's hand behind the ladies back at her waist.

Murphy's Helper

Calvin Campbell

Formation: Contra lines 1, 3, 5, etc. active & crossed over
Record: LS 316 "Flying Scotsmen Hornpipe"

Prompts

Intro	*- - - -, Actives Turn partner Right*
1-8	**- - - -, Actives Turn corner by the Left**
9-16	**- - - -, With your partner DoSaDo**
17-24	**- - - -, - - Same lady Swing**
25-32	**- - - -, Put her on the right & Promenade down in twos**
33-40	**- - U-turn Back, walk back & Separate around 1**
41-48	**- - - -, Just the actives DoSaDo**
49-56	**- - - -, Just the inactives DoSaDo**
57-64	**- - - -, Actives Turn partner Right**

Description

1-8	Active couples turn their partner with a Right Arm Turn.
9-16	Actives turn the corner (one below) with a Left Arm Turn.
17-24	Active couples DoSaDo in the middle.
25-32	Active couples Swing in the middle to finish facing down the set as a couple with the lady on the man's right hand side.
33-40	Promenade down the center of the set with inside hands joined for 6 short steps and U-turn Back.
41-48	Come back up the set Separate and pass between the corner and the person above to the outside of the set. Walk around the one below (corner position) and join hands with a new corner on the left and the previous corner on the right.
49-56	Actives couples only DoSaDo
57-64	Inactive couples DoSaDo

Note: The contra was written to provide practice identifying active and inactive positions within the set. The inactive people should move 2 short side steps towards the head of the set as the actives walk down the center of the set. On counts 41-48 the dancers are instructed to Separate and walk around one. In the traditional contra terminology this is known as Cast Down One. In modern contra dances the Separate Around One would probably be replaced with a Cast Off 3/4. Neither of these terms is used in this manual to reduce the number of terms that the dancers need to learn.

Yucca Jig

Don Armstrong

Formation: Contra lines. Couples 1, 3, 5, etc., active & crossed over.
Record: LS 196 "Major Mackey's Jig"

Prompts

Intro	*- - - -, With the couple below Left Hand Star*
1-8	**- - - -, Same four Star Right**
9-16	**- - - -, Active couples down the center**
17-24	**- - - -, Below 2 then up the outside**
25-32	**- - - -, Actives DoSaDo in the middle**
33-40	**- - - -, With the one below Swing**
41-48	**- - - -, Put her on the right & Half Promenade**
49-56	**- - - -, With the music Right & Left Thru**
57-64	**- - - -, With the couple below Left Hand Star**

Description

1-8	The active couplee and the inactive couplee below Star Left.
9-16	Same four Star Right. The inactive couples return to their home line and the active couples step to the center and face down the set (away from the prompter).
17-24	The active couples Promenade with inside hands joined, down the center of the set past 2 inactive couples.
25-32	Separate and go between the 2nd and 3rd inactive couple. Face up the set (toward the prompter) and return to place on the outside of the line.
33-40	The active couples step back into the center of the set and DoSaDo their partner.
41-48	The active dancers Swing the dancers below (corner position). Finish the Swing with the lady on the man's right hand side and face across the set.
49-56	Same two Half Promenade across the set.
57-64	Right & Left Thru back to the home line.

Note: If the active couple at the foot of the set do not have two inactive couple to pass, they should pretend there is a second inactive couple and move far enough to not be in the way of the next active couple above.

Enid's Delight

Philippe Callens

Formation: Contra lines. Couples 1, 3, 5, etc., active & crossed over.
Record: LS 346 "Enid's Delight" or Rocking M 001 "Dubber Dolly"

Prompts

Intro	*After the chord all Forward & Back*
1-8	**- - - -, Allemande Left & a little bit more**
9-16	**- - - -, - - 2 Ladies Chain**
17-24	**- - - -, Same four Star by the Left**
25-32	**- - - -, Single File Promenade up & down**
33-40	**- - - -, U-turn Back come back to place**
41-48	**- - - -, Same four Star Right**
49-56	**- - - -, Men drop out & 2 Ladies Chain**
57-64	**- - - -, Everybody Forward & Back**

Description

1-8	All Forward & Back.
9-16	Allemande Left with the corner.
17-24	2 Ladies Chain across the set.
25-32	Same couples Star Left.
33-40	When the man reaches his home line, the active dancers (shaded) Promenade Single File up the set (toward the prompter) and the inactive dancers (unshaded) Promenade Single File down the set (away from the prompter) as shown to the right. The lady will be in the lead in each couple.
41-48	All U-turn Back and Promenade Single File back to place.
49-56	Same four Star Right.
57-64	The men step out of the star when they reach their home line and 2 Ladies Chain across the set.

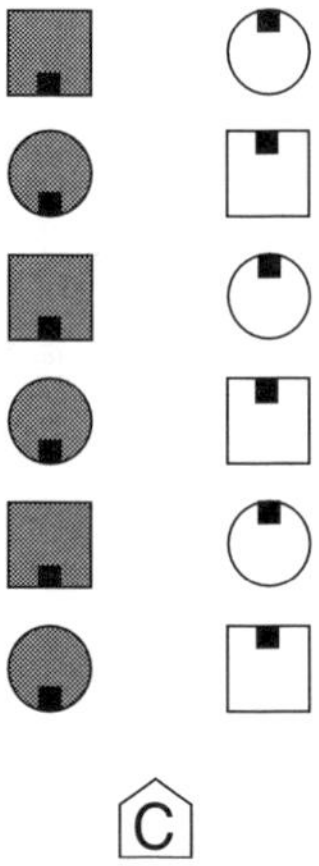

Note: The first recommended piece of music for this dance (LS 346) starts with one single chord. The prompter should tell the dancers to go Forward & Back prior to starting the music.

Broken Sixpence

Don Armstrong

Formation: Contra lines. Couples 1, 3, 5, etc., active & crossed over.
Record: LS 156 "Broken Sixpence" or TNT 173 "Stallion Grey"

Prompts

Intro	*- - - -, With the one below you DoSaDo*
1-8	**- - - -, Now just the men DoSaDo**
9-16	**- - - -, Now just the ladies DoSaDo**
17-24	**- - - -, Active couples Swing in the middle**
25-32	**- - - -, Down the center four in line**
33-40	**- - - -, U-turn Back come back to place**
41-48	**- - Bend the Line, - - Circle Four**
49-56	**- - - -, Star by the Left the other way back**
57-64	**- - - -, With the one below you DoSaDo**

Description

1-8	All DoSaDo their corner (neighbor).
9-16	Men DoSaDo the man diagonally to their right across the set. As the men start the DoSaDo, the ladies face across the set.
17-24	Ladies DoSaDo the lady to their right across the set.
25-32	Active couples Swing in the middle of the set. Finish facing down the set in-between the couple immediately below.
33-40	The inactive couples also face down the set and all four dancers join hands to form a line of four, as shown to the right, and walk down the set (away from the prompter 6 short steps. Each individual does a U-turn Back in 2 steps.
41-48	The line of four walk back toward the head of the set in 4 long steps and Bend the Line in 4 counts. Use the last 2 steps of the Bend the Line to back away from the center of the set to spread the facing lines apart.
49-56	Same four Circle 4 to the left.
57-64	Same four Star Left.

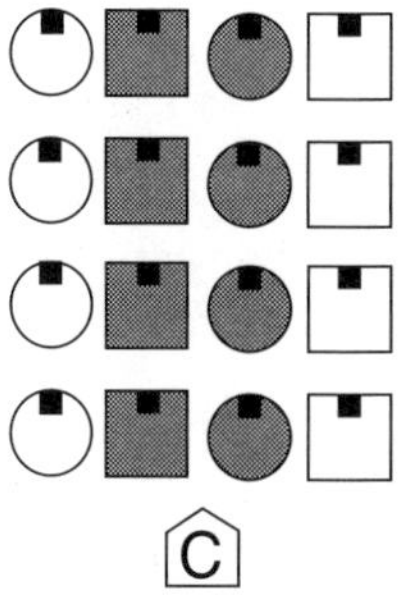

Note: This is the first contra dance in the series to feature lines of four moving down the set. Don's original terminology for the action U-turn Back is Turn Alone which is a more traditional term.

Fiddle Hill Jig

Ralph Page

Formation: Contra lines. Couples 1, 3, 5, etc., active & crossed over
Record: MacGregor C302 "Walkin the Floor Over You"

Prompts

Intro	*- - - -, With the corner DoSaDo*
1-8	**- - - -, With your partner DoSaDo**
9-16	**- - - -, Allemande Left the corner**
17-24	**- - - -, Actives Swing in the middle**
25-32	**- - - -, Walk down the center four in line**
33-40	**- - U-turn Back, - - come back to place**
41-48	**- - Bend the Line, - - Circle Left**
49-56	**- - - -, Same four Star Left**
57-64	**- - - -, With the corner DoSaDo**

Description

1-8	Active couples DoSaDo the corner.
9-16	Active couples DoSaDo their partner (across the set.)
17-24	Allemande Left with the corner.
25-32	Active couples Swing their partner in the middle of the set.
33-40	The active couples (shaded) face down the set and step in between the inactive couples (unshaded) just below. Everyone joins hands four in line as shown to the right and walk away from the prompeter 6 short steps and U-turn Back in 2 steps.
41-48	Line of four walk back toward the prompter 4 steps and Bend the Line in 4 steps. Use the last 2 steps of the Bend the Line to back away from the center of the set to spread the facing lines apart.
49-56	The same four dancers Circle Left.
57-64	Same four Star Left.

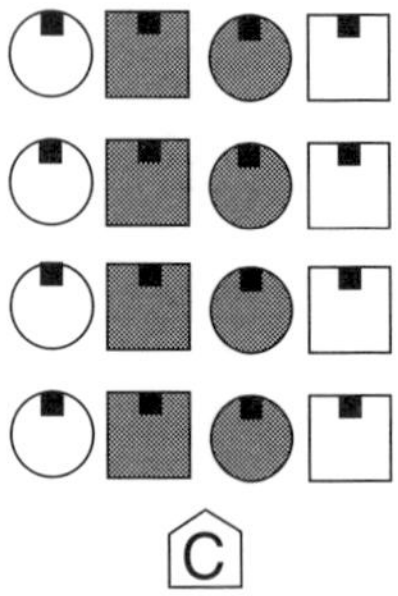

Rutger's Promenade

Art Seele

Formation: Contra lines. Couples 1, 3, 5, etc. active & crossed over.
Record: Jewel 708 "Nobody"

Prompts

Intro	*- - - -, With the corner DoSaDo*
1-8	**- - - -, Same lady Swing -**
9-16	**- - - -, Straight across Right & Left Thru**
17-24	**- - - -, Right & Left back**
25-32	**Courtesy Turn & 1/4 more, Promenade up or down the floor**
33-40	**- - Courtesy Turn, - - Come Back**
41-48	**- - Bend the Line, - - 2 Ladies Chain**
49-56	**- - - -, - - Chain Back**
57-64	**- - - -, With the corner DoSaDo**

Description

1-8	DoSaDo the corner.
9-16	Swing the corner & face across the set.
17-24	Right & Left Thru across the set.
25-32	Right & Left back.
33-40	Courtesy Turn the lady 1/4 more and Couple Promenade the direction each couple is facing. Keep the Courtesy Turn hand position for the Promenade. The active couples (shaded) will be Promenading down the set (away from the prompter) The inactive couples (unshaded) will be Promenading up the set (toward the prompter) as shown to the right. After 4 steps Courtesy Turn.
41-48	Promenade toward the prompter 4 steps. Bend the Line in 4 steps. Use the last 2 steps of the Bend the Line to back away from the center of the set to spread the facing lines apart.
49-56	2 Ladies Chain across the set.
57-64	Chain the Ladies back across the set.

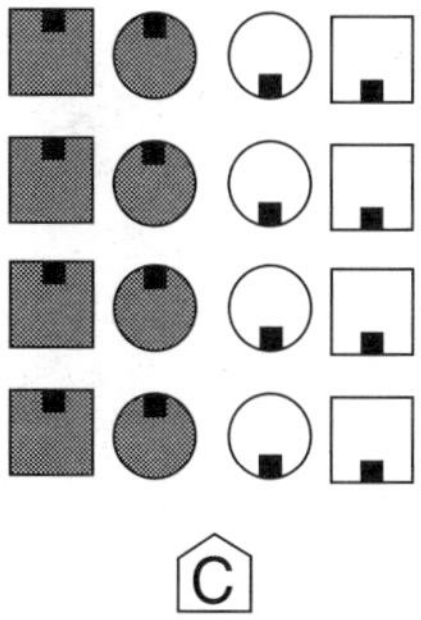

Thinkers Contras

The contra dances, in this group, require experienced contra dancers. Most of them either have movements that are usually taught later in a lesson series or have choreography that challenges the dancers ability. They are recommended for use in dance groups that are very comfortable with contra dancing.

In **Rocky Mountain Hornpiper** the dancers *Separate* around one person prior to the *Circle Four*. The same action is used in **Murphy's Helper** (Pg. 166). In the traditional contra terminology, this is known as Cast Down One. In modern contras the *Separate* around one would probably be replaced with a *Cast Off 3/4*. Neither of these terms is used in this manual in order to reduce the number of terms that the dancers need to learn.

In **Surrey Ridge Reel** (Pg. 174) the actives are expected to dance with both the couple above and the couple below. Once the dancers have mastered this dance, they will have covered one of the most difficult aspects of contra dancing.

Howell's Break (Pg. 175)**, Snow Country Special** (Pg.176)**, A Nice Combination** (Pg. 177) and **Inflation Reel** (Pg 178) all use a basic named *Wheel Around*. A *Courtesy Turn* can be substituted for the Wheel Around. This does require a change of hand positions.

Rocky Mountain Hornpiper

Calvin Campbell

Formation: Contra lines. Couples 1, 3, 5, etc., active & crossed over.
Record: WW-921 "Shindig in the Barn" or Jewel 701 "Coconuts".

Prompts

Intro	*- - - -, With the couple below Right Hand Star*
1-8	**- - - -, Left Hand Star back to place**
9-16	**- - - Actives, down by twos & U-turn Back**
17-24	**- - - -, Come on back & Separate around one**
25-32	**- - - -, - - Circle Left**
33-40	**- - - -, - - Circle Right**
41-48	**- - - -, Same four Right & Left Thru**
49-56	**- - - -, Right & Left Back**
57-64	**- - - -, With the couple below Right Hand Star**

Description

1-8	The active couple and the couple below Star Right
9-16	Same four Star Left.
17-24	The inactive dancers step back into their lines and the active couples Promenade down the center of the set with inside hands joined 6 short steps and U-turn Back.
25-32	The active couples return to place in 4 longer steps and then Separate around one by passing between the corner and the person above, walk around the dancers below to finish facing across the set in long lines.
33-40	Circle 4 with this dancer and the couple across the set. The previous corner has now become part of the new foursome.
41-48	Same four Circle Right to their home lines.
49-56	Same four Right & Left Thru across the set.
57-64	Right & Left Thru back across the set.

Note: In dances where the active couples move down the center of the set, it is very important that the active dancers correctly identify their position within the long line. They need to remember each corner person in turn.

Surrey Ridge Reel

Calvin Campbell

Formation: Contra lines. Couples 1, 3, 5, etc., active & crossed over.
Record: MacGregor 2306 "Everywhere You Go" or Folkcraft 1151B "Devil's Dream"

Prompts

Intro	- - - -, - - - -
	- - - -, - - *Forward & Back*
1-8	**- - - -, Corner Swing**
9-16	**- - - -, Star Right with the couple above**
17-24	**- - - -, Star Left with the couple below**
25-32	**- - - -, Right & Left Thru with the couple above**
33-40	**- - - -, Same two Promenade 1/2**
41-48	**- - - -, 2 Ladies Chain across**
49-56	**- - - -, - - Chain back**
57-64	**- - - -, Everybody Forward & Back**

Description

1-8	Long lines Forward & Back
9-16	Swing the corner. Finish with this lady on the man's right and face across the set in long lines.
17-24	Active couples Star Right with the inactive couples above.
25-32	Active couples Star Left with theinactive couples below.
33-40	Right & Left Thru across the set. This will involve the inactive couple above.
41-48	Same couples Promenade 1/2.
49-56	2 Ladies Chain across the set.
57-64	Chain the Ladies back across the set.

Note: In this contra, the active couples dance with both the couple above and below them. This will require some concentration by the dancers and may require some extra teaching time.

Howell's Break

Bob Howell

(Modified slightly by Calvin Campbell)

Formation: Contra lines. Couples 1, 3, 5, etc., active & crossed over
Record: Grenn 16018 "Auld Lang Syne" is good for seasonal parties or MacGregor C300 "Lamplighting Time" or TNT 148 "Merry Oldsmobile"

Prompts

Intro	*- - - -, With the corner DoSaDo*
1-8	**- - - -, Same lady Swing**
9-16	**- - - -, Walk down four in line**
17-24	**- - Wheel Around, - - come back to place**
25-32	**- - - Bend the Line, - - 2 Ladies Chain**
33-40	**- - - -, - - Chain Back**
41-48	**- - - -, Same four Star Left**
49-56	**- - - -, - - Star Right**
57-64	**- - - -, With the corner DoSaDo**

Description

1-8	Active couples DoSaDo the corner
9-16	Active couples Swing the corner. Finish the Swing by placing the lady on the man's right and face away from the prompter.
17-24	With the couple across form a line of four with the actives (shaded) on the outside and walk down the set 4 steps (see right). Wheel Around in 4 steps.
25-32	Walk back toward the prompter 4 steps. Bend the Line in 4 steps. Use the last 2 steps of the Bend the Line to back away from the center of the set to spread the facing lines apart.
33-40	2 Ladies Chain across the set.
41-48	Chain the Ladies back across the set.
49-56	Same four Star Left.
57-64	Same four Star Right.

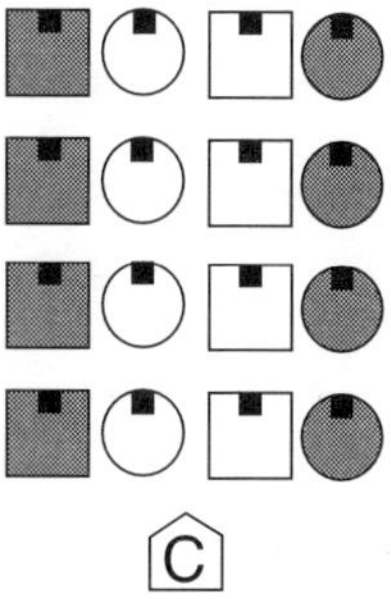

Note: Bob's original figure has a California Twirl instead of the Wheel Around. It dancers very nicely, but does require teaching the California Twirl. You can also substitute a Courtesy Turn if you do not want to use a Wheel Around.

Snow Country Special

Ed Butenhof

(Modified slightly by Calvin Campbell)

Formation: Contra lines 1, 3, 5, etc. active and crossed over.
Record: LS E-52 "Reel St. Sauveur" or Red Boot 1351 "Saturday Night"

Prompts

Intro	*- - - -, Everybody Forward & Back*
1-8	**- - - -, Across the set DoSaDo**
9-16	**- - - -, With the corner DoSaDo**
17-24	**- - - -, - - Corner Swing**
25-32	**- - - -, Promenade down by fours**
33-40	**- - Wheel Around, - - Come back to place**
41-48	**- - Bend the Line, - - Circle Left**
49-56	**- - - -, - - Circle Right**
57-64	**- - - -, Everybody Forward & Back**

Description

1-8	Long lines go Forward & Back.
9-16	Across the set DoSaDo
17-24	DoSaDo the corner.
25-32	Swing the corner.
33-40	As a couple, face away from the prompter and form a line of four with the couple across the set. The line of four walk down the set 4 short steps. Wheel Around in 4 steps.
41-48	Walk back toward the prompter 4 steps. Bend the Line in 4 steps. Use the last 2 steps of the Bend the Line to back away from the center of the set to spread the facing lines apart.
49-56	Circle Left with the opposite couple.
57-64	Same four Circle Right.

A Nice Combination

Don Ward

Formation: Contra lines. Couples 1, 3, 5,etc. active and crossed over.
Record: MacGregor C302 "Walking the Floor Over You"

Prompts

Intro	*- - - -, Face the corner DoSaDo*
1-8	**- - - -, The same one Swing**
9-16	**- - - -, Promenade down in fours**
17-24	**- - - -, Wheel Around & Promenade up**
25-32	**- - - -, Bend the Line & Circle Left 3/4**
33-44	**- - - -, With the one you face Swing**
41-48	**- - - -, Face across & 2 Ladies Chain**
49-56	**- - - -, Same four Star Left**
57-64	**- - - -, Face the corner DoSaDo**

Description

1-8	All face corners and DoSaDo
9-16	Swing the same corner and finish facing down the set in lines of four.
17-24	Promenade away from the prompter 6 steps and Wheel Around as a couple.
25-32	Finish the Wheel Around and Promenade toward the prompter, Bend the Line and finish facing across the set as a couple. Use the last 2 steps of the Bend the Line to back away from the center of the set to spread the facing lines apart.
33-40	Circle Four with the couple across 3/4 around.
41-48	Swing the one you are facing. This is your original partner. Finish facing across the set with your partner.
49-56	2 Ladies Chain across the set.
57-64	Star Left once around to the next corner position.

Note: Don's recording on the flip side of this record uses a Cast Off 3/4 instead of the Bend the Line.

Inflation Reel

Tony Parkes

Formation: Contra lines. Couples 1, 3, 5, etc., active & crossed over.
Record: WW 914 "Hey Li Lee Li Lee" or LS 306 "Ragtime Annie"

Prompts

Intro	*- - - -, With the corner DoSaDo*
1-8	**- - - -, - - Corner Swing**
9-16	**- - - -, Put her on the right go down in fours**
17-24	**- - Wheel Around, - - Come back to place**
25-32	**- - Bend the Line, - - Right & Left Thru**
33-40	**- - - -, Same 2 Ladies Chain**
41-48	**- - - -, - - Circle 4**
49-56	**- - Once &, 1/4 more & Pass Thru**
57-64	**- - - -, With the corner DoSaDo**

Description

1-8	DoSaDo the corner.
9-16	Swing the corner. Finish with the lady on the man's right hand side and facing down the set.
17-24	Line of four walk down the set 4 short steps. Wheel Around in 4 steps.
25-32	Walk back toward the caller 4 steps. Bend the Line in 4 steps. Use the last 2 steps of the Bend the Line to back away from the center of the set to spread the facing lines apart.
33-40	Right & Left Thru across the set.
41-48	Same 2 Ladies Chain across the set.
49-56	Circle 4 to the left once around.
57-64	Circle left 1/4 more and Pass Thru. The active man and his partner will be moving away from the prompter and the inactive man and his partner will be moving toward the prompter as shown to the right.

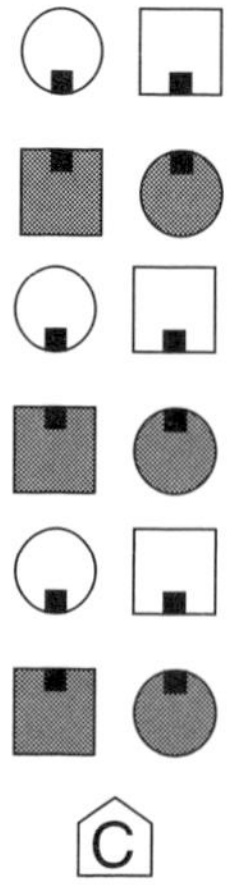

Note: If you do not wish to teach Wheel Around as a basic movement, you can substitute Courtesy Turn. This will require the dancers to shift arm positions. Tony says that the inflation in the name is the 1/4 more in the figure.

Double Progression Contra Dances

In double progression contra dances, the dancers move two positions toward the head or the foot of the set each time through the routine. If the sets have an even number of couples, no one is left dead-at-the-head or dead-at-the-foot for more than half the routine. Dancers typically like double progression contra dances because moving two positions each time enables more dancers to dance both the active and the inactive positions.

The **Caller's Girl Friend** (Pg. 180) is the first dance in the book to use double progression. The dance was designed to introduce double progression early in a series of lessons.

The **Caller's Wife** (Pg. 181) is also suitable for use in a set of beginner lessons. It should be used after the dancers are comfortable with dancing a *Right & Left Thru.*

Constant Contra, Caribbean Contra and **Needham Specia**l (Pgs. 182-184) all use a *Pass Thru* followed by the *U-turn Back* and *Half Promenade* the lady on the right. Almost every time this combination is used, dancers will become confused on which lady to *Half Promenade*. Check the notes at the bottom of each page for suggestions on how to help eliminate the confusion.

The **Snowy Day** (Pg. 185) has the active couples *Star* with both the couple above and the couple below. The inactive dancers will be equally as busy and need to be warned that even though the prompts are given to the actives, the inactive dancers must be prepared to join the *Stars.*

The Caller's Girl Friend

Calvin Campbell

Formation: Contra Lines. Couples 1, 3, 5, etc., active & crossed over. A double progression contra. An even number of couples is recommended.
Record: Chaparral 527 "Kinda Keep it Country" or Red Boot 258 "I Wish I was 18"

Prompts

Intro	*- - - -, With the corner Allemande Left*
1-8	**- - - -, Across the set 2 Ladies Chain**
9-16	**- - - -, Long lines go Forward & Back**
17-24	**- - - -, Circle Four 3/4 around**
25-32	**- - Pass Thru, DoSaDo the next two**
33-40	**- - - -, Same lady Swing -**
41-48	**- - - -, Star Left**
49-56	**- - - -, Star Right**
57-64	**- - - -, With the corner Allemande Left**

Description

1-8	Allemande Left with the corner.
9-16	Across the set 2 Ladies Chain.
17-24	Long lines Forward & Back
25-32	Circle 4 to the left with the opposite couple 3/4 around until the active man and his partner are facing down the set and inactive man and his partner are facing up the set. (See Inflation Reel on page 178 for a diagram.)
33-40	Pass Thru the couple you are facing. Move on to the next couple and DoSaDo.
41-48	Swing the person you are facing at the end of the DoSaDo. Finish the Swing with the lady on the man's right and face across the set.
49-56	With the couple across Star Left
57-64	Same four Star Right.

Note: This contra is a modification of an idea from Ted Sannella's "The Caller's Wife." The routine has been simplified to enable it to be taught earlier in a teaching sequence. The theme is the Circle Four 3/4 around. In this dance, the active dancers will progress two positions toward the foot of the set during each 64-beat routine. The inactive dancers will move two positions toward the head of the set. This is referred to as double progression.

The Caller's Wife

Ted Sannella

Formation: Contra lines. Couples 1, 3, 5, etc., active & crossed over. A double progression contra. An even number of couples is recommended.
Record: Grenn 16005 "The Caller's Wife"

Prompts

Intro	*- - - -, With the corner Allemande Left*
1-8	**- - - -, Across the set 2 Ladies Chain**
9-16	**- - - -, Long lines go Forward & Back**
17-24	**- - - -, Circle Four 3/4 around**
25-32	**- - Pass Thru, next two DoSaDo**
33-40	**- - - -, Same lady Swing -**
41-48	**- - - -, Face across & 1/2 Promenade**
49-56	**- - - -, Right & Left Thru**
57-64	**- - - -, With the corner Allemande Left**

Description

1-8	Allemande Left with the corner.
9-16	2 Ladies Chain across the set.
17-24	Long lines go Forward & Back.
25-32	Circle 4 to the left with the opposite couple 3/4 around until the active man and his partner are facing down the set and inactive man and his partner are facing up the set. (See Inflation Reel on page 178 for a diagram.)
33-40	Pass Thru the couple you are facing. Move on to the next couple and DoSaDo.
41-48	Swing the person you are facing at the end of the DoSaDo. Finish the Swing with the lady on the man's right and face across the set.
49-56	Face across the set and Promenade 1/2 as a couple.
57-64	Right & Left Thru across the set.

Note: If you wish to teach a similar contra using fewer movements, use The Caller's Girl Friend. In this dance the actives dancers will progress two positions toward the foot of the set during each 64-beat routine. The inactive dancers will move two positions toward the head of the set. This is referred to as double progression.

Constant Contra

Mitch Pingel

Formation: Contra lines. Couples 1, 3, 5, etc. active & crossed over. A double progression contra. An even number of couples is recommended.
Record: ESP 412 "Steppin Out"

Prompts

Intro	*- - - -, Face the corner & DoSaDo*
1-8	**- - - -, - - Corner Swing**
9-16	**- - - -, Put her on your right & Star Left**
17-24	**- - - -, Same four Star Right**
25-32	**- - - -, Men drop out & 2 Ladies Chain**
33-40	**- - - -, - - Chain Back**
41-48	**- - - -, All Pass Thru & U-turn Back**
49-56	**- - - -, With the new lady on the right Promenade Half**
57-64	**- - - -, Face a new corner & DoSaDo**

Description

1-8	All DoSaDo their corners.
9-16	Swing the corner. Place the lady on the man's right hand side and face across the set as a couple.
17-24	Star Left with the couple across the set.
25-32	Same four reverse direction and Star Right.
33-40	The men drop out of the Star when they reach their home line. The two ladies continue to hold hands and 2 Ladies Chain across the set. The man will Courtesy Turn their partner.
41-48	Same 2 Ladies Chain back to their home line.
49-56	The two facing lines Pass Thru & U-turn Back.
57-64	The man takes the new right hand lady in Couple Promenade position and Promenade Half back to the home line. (The active couples move down the set two positions. A new couple becomes active at the head of the set and a new couple becomes inactive at the foot of the set.)

Note: The first few times through the dance some people may be confused about which person to Promenade Half in counts 57-64. Have the men look to their right and the ladies look to their left.

Caribbean Contra

Don Armstrong

Formation: Contra lines. Couples 1, 3, 5, etc., active & crossed over. A double progression contra. An even number of couples is recommended.
Record: Grenn 12131 "In the Morning Dew" or Jewel 709 "Whup Whup"

Prompts

Intro	*- - - -, Everybody Forward & Back*
1-8	**- - - -, With the corner DoSaDo**
9-16	**- - - -, - Promenade Single File**
17-24	**- - - -, U-turn Back & return to place**
25-32	**- - - -, Allemande Left & the Ladies Chain**
33-40	**- - - -, - - Chain Back**
41-48	**- - - -, All Pass Thru & U-turn Back**
49-56	**- - - -, With the new lady on the right Promenade 1/2**
57-64	**- - - -, Long lines Forward & Back**

Description

1-8	The long lines go Forward & Back.
9-16	Face the Corner & DoSaDo. Be sure to finish the DoSaDo facing the corner.
17-24	Promenade Single File by the corner, passing right shoulders. All the men, on each side, will Promenade Single File. All the ladies, on each side, will Promenade Single File.
25-32	All U-turn Back and return Single File back to the corner.
33-40	Do a quick Allemande Left with the corner and then 2 Ladies Chain across the set. The man will Courtesy Turn his partner.
41-48	Chain the Ladies back across the set.
49-56	The two facing lines Pass Thru and U-turn Back.
57-64	The man takes the new lady on the right in Couple Promenade position and Promenade Half across back to the home line. (The active couples have moved down the set two positions. A new couple becomes active at the head of the set and a new couple becomes inactive at the foot of the set.)

Note: The first few times through the dance some people may be confused about which person to Promenade Half in counts 57-64. Have the men look to their right and the ladies look to their left. Don's original terminology for the action U-Turn Back is Turn Alone .

Needham Special

Herbie Gaudreau

Formation: Contra lines. Couples 1, 3, 5, etc. active & crossed over. A double progression contra. An even number of couples is recommended.
Record: LS 302 "Sherbrooke"

Prompts

Intro	*- - - -, Everybody Forward & Back*
1-8	**- - - -, - - Corner Swing**
9-16	**- - - -, Promenade down in lines of four**
17-24	**- - Wheel Around, - - Come back to place**
25-32	**- - Bend the Line, - - 2 Ladies Chain**
33-40	**- - - -, - - Chain Back**
41-48	**- - - -, Pass Thru & U-turn Back**
49-56	**- - - -, With the lady on the right Promenade Half**
57-64	**- - - -, Everybody Forward & Back**

Description

1-8	Long lines Forward & Back.
9-16	Actives Swing the corner. Finish the Swing facing down the set away from the caller with the lady on the man's right.
17-24	With the couple across, form a line of four & walk down the set 4 short steps. Wheel Around as a couple in 4 steps.
25-32	Walk back toward the prompter 4 steps. Bend the Line in 4 steps. Use the last 4 steps of the Bend the Line to back away from the center of the set to spread the facing lines apart.
33-40	2 Ladies Chain across the set. The man will Courtesy Turn his partner.
41-48	Chain the Ladies back across the set.
49-56	Pass Thru and U-turn Back.
57-64	With the new lady on the right Half Promenade.

Note: If you do not choose to use Wheel Around as a basic term, you can substitute Courtesy Turn. This will require the dancers to shift arm positions, but it does set up for a 2 Ladies Chain. The first few times through the dance some people may be confused about which person is the partner for the Promenade Half in counts 57-64. Have the men look to their right and the ladies look to their left.

The Snowy Day

Tony Parkes

Formation: Contra lines. Couples 1, 3, 5, etc., active & crossed over. A double progression contra. An even number of couples is recommended.
Record: MacGregor C303 "More Chords"

Prompts

Intro	*- - - -, With the corner DoSaDo*
1-8	**- - - -, - - Same lady Swing**
9-16	**- - Face across, put the lady on the right & Circle 4**
17-24	**- - - -, With the couple below Star Left**
25-32	**- - - -, With the couple above Star Right**
33-40	**- - - -, With the one below Allemande Left**
41-48	**- - - -, Same Lady Chain across**
49-56	**- - - -, - - Chain Back**
57-64	**- - - -, With the corner DoSaDo**

Description

1-8	All DoSaDo their corners.
9-16	Swing the corner. Finish with the lady on the man's right hand side and face across the set.
17-24	Circle 4 with the couple across the set.
25-32	Actives Star Left with the couple below them.
33-40	Actives Star Right with the couple above them.
41-48	Allemande Left with the new corner.
49-56	Chain the same Lady across the set.
57-64	Chain the Ladies back across the set.

Note: In this contra, the active couples work with both the couple above and below them. This may require some concentration for the dancers and may require some extra teaching time.

Gimmick Contras

The contra dances, in this group, all contain choreography which sets them apart from the average contra dance. They all have a gimmick that makes them unusual. As with all gimmicks used in dancing, they should be used carefully. Don't use too many of them during any one program. Save them for the special times when the dance program needs a boost.

In **Jefferson's Reel**, the dance begins with the active couples facing down the set and the inactives facing up the set. The dancers never face across the set in the usual contra dance configuration. The dance also has the foursomes (duples) backing toward the head of the hall.

Thru the White and Drifted Snow, Aston Polka and **Callison Hall Jig** (Pgs. 188-190) feature a heel & toe step combined with a slide step to the side. The steps are not hard, but a quick demonstration is helpful. Several dances in the section on mixers use this same step. The use of a heel and toe step does limit the music suitable for these dances.

Aw Shucks (Pg. 191) has a very nice hand clapping sequence which adds variety to the dance. This is an excellent way to emphasize timing to the dancers.

Who's in the Middle (Pg. 192) can get pretty wild. The dancers have 8 beats of music for a *Right Arm Turn*. Some couples will be able to turn around several times.

Lighted Sconce (Pg. 193) has both very unusual music and a gimmick with the arch and the ends duck thru.

Jefferson's Reel

Dud Briggs

Formation: Contra lines. Couples 1, 3 ,5, etc., active & crossed over & facing the foot of the set. Others inactive & facing the head of the set.
Record: LS E-18 or Grenn 15008 "Jefferson's Reel" or TNT 271 "Pass Me By"

Prompts

Intro - - - -, - - Circle 4

1-8 - - - -, - - Circle Right
9-16 - - - -, - - Right Hand Star
17-24 - - - -, - - Left Hand Star
25-32 - - - -, Active couples down the outside
33-40 - - - -, Come back up the outside
41-48 - - - -, Four in line go down the set
49-56 - - - -, Actives arch & ends duck thru
57-64 - - Up the set, - - Circle 4

Description

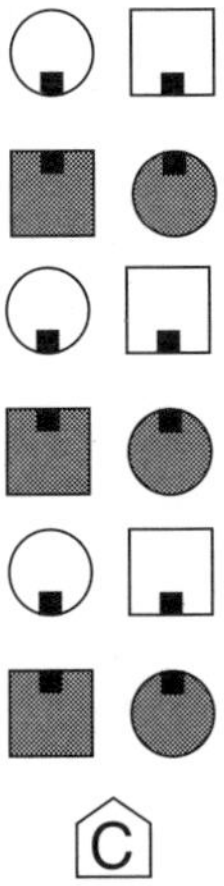

1-8 The dance starts in the formation shown to the right. Active couples are shaded, inactive couples are unshaded. The facing four dancers Circle Left.
9-16 Same four Circle Right back to their original facing position.
17-24 Same four Star Right.
25-32 Same four Star Left back to their original position facing up or down the set.
33-40 Active dancers walk down the outside of the set for 6 short steps and U-turn Back.
41-48 The active dancers walk back up the outside of the set to their original position & step into the center of the set to form a line of four with the couple below them. All should be facing down the set with the actives in the middle of the line of four.
49-56 The line of four walk down the set 6 short steps and the active couples make an arch between them.
57-64 The inactive couples duck through this arch dropping hand holds with the actives. As the inactive couples move forward to the next active couple, the active couples back up 4 steps toward the head of the set.

Thru The White & Drifted Snow

Bob Howell

Formation: Contra lines. Couples 1, 3, 5, etc., active and crossed over.
Record: Grenn 16021 "Thru The White & Drifted Show"

Prompts

Intro	*With the music heel & toe out*
1-8	**- - Heel & toe in, - - Heel & toe out**
9-16	**- - - -, Same lady DoSaDo**
17-24	**- - - -, Same lady Swing -**
25-32	**- - - -, Put her on the right & 2 Ladies Chain**
33-40	**- - - -, - - Chain Back**
41-48	**- - - -, - - Star Left**
49-56	**- - - -, - - Star Right**
57-64	**- - - -, With a new corner heel & toe**

Description

1-8	Begin the dance facing the corner with arms extended to the side with elbows bent and palms touching about shoulder level (butterfly dance position). With the man's left foot and the lady's right foot do a heel & toe step (touch heel of foot to the floor slightly to the side and then touch the same toe to the floor next to the other foot) and then slide away from the center of the set with a quick side-close-side-touch. Change lead foot and do a heel & toe step and then slide back toward the center of the set with a side-close-side-touch.
9-16	Repeat 1-8.
17-24	Same lady DoSaDo.
25-32	Same lady Swing and finish the Swing with the lady on the man's right side and facing across the set.
33-40	2 Ladies Chain across the set.
41-48	Chain the Ladies back across the set.
49-56	Same four make a Left Hand Star.
57-64	Reverse the star to a Right Hand Star and end facing the corner in butterfly position.

Note: Teach the heel & toe movements by demonstration, or teach it in a mixer such as "Patty Cake Polka" (Pg. 259).

Aston Polka

Herbie Gaudreau

Formation: Contra lines. Couples 1, 3, 5, etc., active & crossed over.
Record: LS 187 or Grenn 12272 "Sweet Georgia Brown" or Jewel 710 "Charlie's Polka"

Prompts

Intro	*With the music heel & toe out*
1-8	**- - Heel & toe in, - - Heel & toe out**
9-16	**- - Ladies in, - Promenade Single File**
17-24	**- - - -, U-turn Back come back to place**
25-32	**- - - -, Allemande Left & 2 Ladies Chain**
33-40	**- - - -, - - Chain Back**
41-48	**- - - -, - - Star Left**
49-56	**- - - -, - - Star Right**
57-64	**- - - -, With a new corner heel & toe**

Description

1-8 See description on **Thru The White & Drifted Snow** *(Pg.188).*

9-16 Repeat the heel & toe and slide out. On the second heel & toe, the man remains in place and only the ladies slide back in to form 2 Single File lines on each side of the set.

17-24 All Promenade Single File in the direction each line is facing, as shown to the right, for 6 short steps. U-turn Back in 2 steps. Men will be following men and ladies will be following ladies. Active dancers (shaded) will be moving away from the prompter. Inactive dancers (unshaded) will be moving toward the prompter.

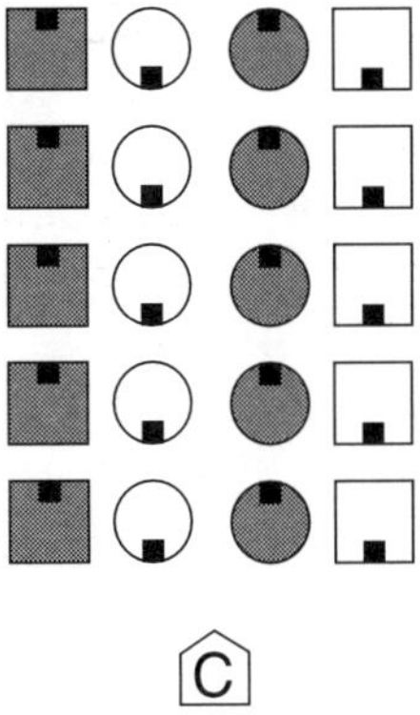

25-32 Return to the corner in longer steps and Allemande Left with this corner.

33-40 2 Ladies Chain across the set.

41-48 Chain the Ladies back across the set.

49-56 Same four Star Left

57-64 Reverse to a Right Hand Star and end facing a new corner in butterfly position.

Note: Teach the heel & toe step by demonstration.

Callison Hall Jig

Don Armstrong

Formation: Contra lines. Couples 1, 3, 5, etc., active & crossed over. A double progression contra. An even number of couples is recommended.
Record: LS 320 "Callison Hall Jig" or Jewel 710 "Charlie's Polka"

Prompts

Intro - - Face below, with the music heel & toe out

1-8 - - - In, - - Heel & toe out
9-16 - - Heel & toe in, - - DoSaDo
17-24 - - Pass Thru, - - Swing the next
25-32 - - - -, Put her on the right & Half Promenade
33-40 - - - -, - - Right & Left Thru
41-48 - - - -, Same four Circle Left
49-56 - - - -, Same four Star Left
57-64 - - - -, New corners heel & toe

Description

1-8 See description on **Thru The White & Drifted Snow** *(Pg. 188)*
9-16 Repeat 1-8
17-24 DoSaDo the same dancer and Pass Thru.
25-32 Swing the next dancer and finish the Swing by facing across the set with the lady on the man's right hand side.
33-40 1/2 Promenade across the set
41-48 Right & Left Thru across the set.
49-56 Same four Circle Left
57-64 Same four Star Left. Finish facing a new corner in butterfly dance position.

Notes: This contra routine can simplified with the following modifications. The lines walk forward 3 steps and clap their hands and back into place. Cross over in 6 steps and turn alone. Repeat both actions.

25-32 - - - -, Long lines Forward & Back
33-40 - - - -, Pass Thru & U-turn Back
41-48 - - - -, Long lines Forward & Back
49-56 - - - -, Pass Thru & face new corners
57-64 - - - -, New corners heel & toe

Aw Shucks

Carol Kopp

Formation: Contra lines. Couples 1, 3, 5, etc., active & crossed over.
Record: LS 343/344 "Combination Rag"

Prompts

Intro	*- - - -, Actives in & slide down*
1-8	**- - Slide up ,- - Slide down**
9-16	**- - Slide up, between the couple below & clap**
17-24	**Together right together left turn half, together right together left & Swing**
25-32	**- - - with, Lady on the right go down in fours**
33-40	**- - Wheel as a couple, - - come on back**
41-48	**- - - Bend the Line, - - 2 Ladies Chain**
49-56	**- - - -, - - Chain Back**
57-64	**- - - -, Actives in & slide down**

Description

1-8	Active couples step to the center of the set, join both hands with their partner and slide down toward the foot of the set with a side-close-side-touch in 4 counts. Slide up the set with side-close-side-touch in 4 counts.
9-16	Active couples slide down toward the foot of the set with a side-close-side-touch in 4 counts. Slide up the set with a side-close-side-close and stop in the middle of the set between the inactive couple below.
17-24	Actives clap their own hands together on 1, clap right hands with their partner on 2, clap own hands together on 3, clap left hands with partner on 4, and turn quickly to face the inactive person behind them. Repeat the same clap sequence with own hands-opposite right-own hands-opposite left.
25-32	Actives Swing the inactives.
33-40	Men place the lady on the right hand side, form a line of four and walk down the set 4 short steps and Wheel Around in 4 steps.
41-48	Walk back toward the head of the set 4 long steps. Bend the Line in 4 steps. Use the last 2 steps of the Bend the Line to back away from the center of the set to spread the facing lines.
49-56	2 Ladies Chain across the set.
57-64	Chain the Ladies back across the set.

Who's In The Middle

Al Olsen

Formation: Contra lines. Couples 1, 3, 5, etc., active & crossed over.
Record: Cardinal 16 "Old Cold Tater"

Prompts

Intro	*- - - -, Turn your corner Right Hand Around*
1-8	**Put someone in the middle &, centers Turn Left Arm full around**
9-16	**- - - -, - - Corner Swing**
17-24	**- - - -, - - Half Promenade**
25-32	**- - - -, - - Right & Left Thru**
33-40	**- - - -, Straight across 2 Ladies Chain**
41-48	**- - - -, - - Chain back**
49-56	**- - - -, Circle 4 once around**
57-64	**- - - -, Turn your corner Right Hand Around**

Description

1-8 Turn the corner with a Right Arm Turn and finish with either dancer of the pair with left hands joined with the opposite dancer to form a four person line across the center of the set. Two dancers will be facing up the set, alternating with two dancers facing down the set. It can be any combination shown to the right.

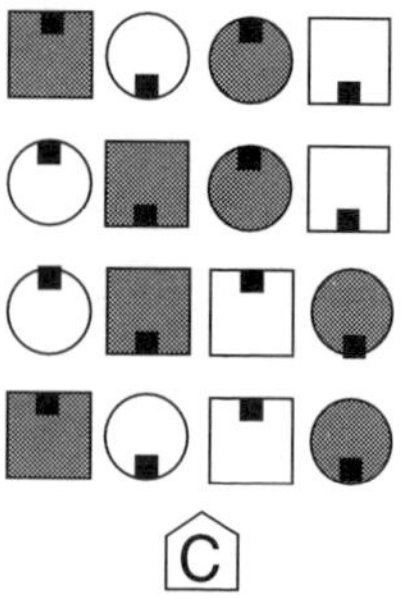

9 -16 Center dancers Left Arm Turn full around.
17-24 Swing your corner and finish with the lady on the man's right and facing across the set.
25-32 Half Promenade with this lady.
33-40 Right & Left Thru back to home lines.
41-48 2 Ladies Chain across.
49-56 Chain the ladies back across the set.
57-64 Same couples Circle 4 once around.

Lighted Sconce

Glen Morningstar

Formation: Contra lines. Couples 1, 3, 5, etc., active & crossed over.
Record: LS 337/338 "Lighted Sconce"

Prompts

Intro	*- - - -, Two ladies Turn opposite Right*
1-8	**- - - -, - - Swing your partners**
9-16	**- - - -, - - Circle Four 3/4 around**
17-24	**- - Arch below, actives duck thru to a line of four**
25-32	**- - - -, Four In line come up the set**
33-40	**- - U-turn Back, - - Go back down**
41-48	**- - Bend the Line, - - 2 Ladies Chain**
49-56	**- - - -, Chain the Ladies back again**
57-64	**- - - -, Two ladies Turn opposite Right**

Description

1-8	Facing ladies Right Arm Turn the opposite lady.
9-16	The ladies Swing their partner. Finsh the Swing facing across the set on the man's side of the set.
17-24	The foursome Circle Left 3/4 until the active couples are facing down the set and the inactive couples are facing up the set.
25-32	The inactive couples form an arch between them. The active couples duck thru the arch and Separate to face the head of the set while continuing to hold hands with the inactive couple. The inactive couples turn under their joined hands and all four face up the set in a line of four.
33-40	The line of four walk 4 short steps toward the head of the hall and all U-turn Back.
41-48	The line of four walk toward the foot of the hall 4 steps and Bend the Line in 4 steps. Use the last 2 steps of the Bend the Line to back away from the center of the set to spread the facing lines apart.
49-56	2 Ladies Chain across the set.
57-64	Chain the Ladies back across the set.

Couple Facing Couple Contras

Several contras have been written that have the partners side by side as shown below. In a way, it could be argued that they are not really contra dances because the partner is not across the set, but common usage of the term has placed them in the contra dance category anyway.

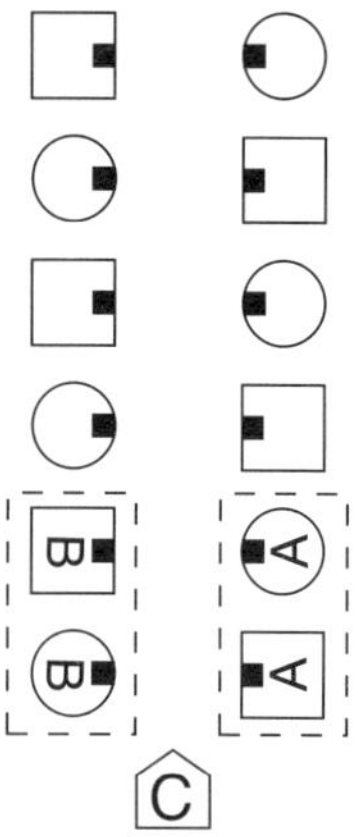

There are no active or inactive couples. The partners will be beside each other at the start and at the end of each 64-beat routine. Each set should have an even number of couples.

Skontra, Beckett Reel, and **Slant Pretoria** (Pgs 195-197) have the directional reference to slant left and *Right & Left Thru*. Each couple faces the couple diagonally to their left as shown in the diagram in **Skontra**.

The dances in this section should not be used until the dancers are comfortable with contra dancing. If they are introduced too quickly, new dancers will have more difficulty with understanding how contra dances progress and where their partner is normally located in the majority of contra dances.

Allynn's Mountain Reel (Pg. 198) has a slant right *Right & Left Thru.* Once people understand how to slant left then a slant right is usually no problem.

In **Chain Reaction** (Pg. 199) the couples move one position clockwise in the formation. In **Rightway Reel** (Pg. 200) the dancers move counterclockwise one position in the formation. It all adds spice to the dances.

Many facing couple contras can also be done as a large double circle with the couple in the outside circle facing the center of the hall and the couples in the inside circle each facing an outside couple and the wall. When this alternate formation is used, 26 to 30 couples are needed to make the circle large enough for comfortable dancing.

Skontra

Ken Kernen

Formation: Contra lines. Couple facing couple across the set. An even number of couples is needed.
Record: Silver Sounds 155 or Mustang 179 "Columbus Stockade Blues"

Prompts

Intro	*- - - -, Everybody Forward & Back*
1-8	**- - - -, With the couple across Circle Left**
9-16	**- - - -, Same four Star Left**
17-24	**- - - -, - - Star Right**
25-32	**- - - -, Men drop out & 2 Ladies Chain**
33-40	**- - - -, - - Chain Back**
41-48	**- - - -, Slant left & Right & Left Thru**
49-56	**- - - -, Straight across Right & Left Thru**
57-64	**- - - -. Everybody Forward & Back**

Description

1-8	Long lines Forward & Back.
9-16	Circle Left with the couple across
17-24	Same four Star Left
25-32	Same four Star Right
33-40	When the men reach their home line they step out of the star and 2 Ladies Chain across the set.
41-48	The 2 Ladies Chain back across the set.
49-56	As a couple, face diagonally to the left and Right & Left Thru with the facing couple. Two couples, one on each end of the set, will have no couple diagonally to the left. They wait in place for 8 beats of music.
56-64	Right & Left Thru with the couple across the set. The two couples left idle, during the previous move, will change sides of the set during the Right & Left Thru and have a new home line.

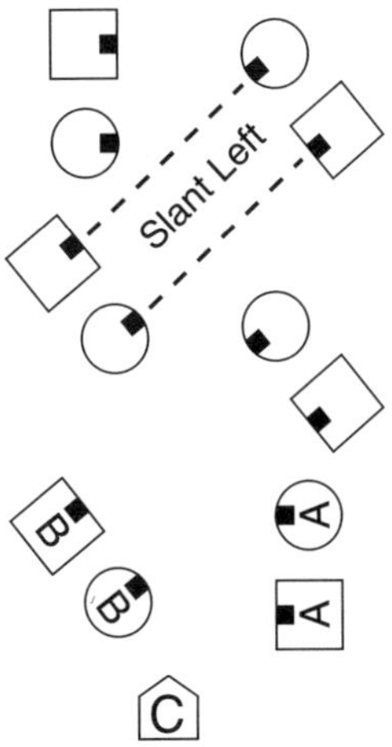

Beckett Reel

Herbie Gaudreau

Formation: Contra lines. Couple facing couple across the set. The dance requires an even number of couples.
Record: LS 190 or Grenn 12239 "Back to Donegal"

Prompts

Intro	*- - - -, With the corner Allemande Left*
1-8	**- - - -, - - Partner Swing**
9-16	**- - - -, Slant left & Right & Left Thru**
17-24	**- - - -, Straight across Right & Left Thru**
25-32	**- - - -, Same 2 Ladies Chain**
33-40	**- - - -, - - Chain Back**
41-48	**- - - -, Same four Star Left**
49-56	**- - - -, - - Star Right**
57-64	**- - - -, With the corner Allemande Left**

Description

1-8	Allemande Left with the corner.
9-16	Swing your partner and finish facing across the set.
17-24	As a couple, face diagonally (see page 195) to the left and Right & Left Thru with the facing couple. Two couples, one on each end of the set, will have no couple diagonally to the left. They face across the set and wait in place for 8 beats of music.
25-32	Right & Left Thru with the couple across the set. The two couples left idle, during the previous move, will change sides of the set during the Right & Left Thru and have a new home line.
33-40	2 Ladies Chain across the set.
41-48	Chain the ladies back across the set.
49-56	Same four Star Left.
57-64	Same four Star Right back to the home lines.

Slant Pretoria

Don Armstrong

Formation: Contra lines. Couple facing couple across the set. An even number of couples is needed.
Record: LS 183/184 "Marching to Pretoria"

Prompts

Intro	*- - - -, Slant left & Right & Left Thru*
1-8	**- - - -, Straight across Right & Left Thru**
9-16	**- - - -, Same four Star Left**
17-24	**- - - -, - - Star Right**
25-32	**- - - -, Promenade Single File**
33-40	**- - - -, U-turn Back come back to place**
41-48	**- - - -, Straight across 2 Ladies Chain**
49-56	**- - - -, - - Chain Back**
57-64	**- - - -, Slant left & Right & Left Thru**

Description

1-8	As a couple, face diagonally to the left (see page 195) and Right & Left Thru with the facing couple. Two couples, one on each end of the set, will have no couple diagonally to the left. They wait in place for 8 beats of music.
9-16	Right & Left Thru with the couple across the set. The two couples left idle, during the previous move, will change sides of the set and have a new home line.
17-24	With the couple across the set Star Left.
25-32	Same four Star Right.
33-40	When you reach your home lines, Promenade Single File. The man will be in the lead. The line on the caller's left will be promenading away from the caller. The line on the caller's right will be promenading toward the caller.
41-48	Each individual U-turn Back and Promenade Single File until they can face the same couple across the set.
49-56	The 2 Ladies Chain across the set.
57-64	The 2 Ladies Chain back across the set.

*Note: **Slant Pretoria** is a modification of **Marching to Pretoria** found on page 286.*

Allynn's Mountain Reel

Allynn Riggs

Formation: Contra lines. Couple facing couple across the set. The formation requires an even number of couples.
Record: TNT 228 "Merry Christmas Polka" or Blue Ribbon BR 257 "Me and My Shadow"

Prompts

Intro	*- - - - , Across 2 Ladies Chain*
1-8	**- - - -, - - Ladies DoSaDo**
9-16	**- - - -, - - Men DoSaDo**
17-24	**- - - -, 2 Ladies Chain & turn a quarter more**
25-32	**- - - -, Promenade go up & down**
33-40	**- - Wheel Around, - - come back**
41-48	**- - - - , Find those two & Half Promenade**
49-56	**- - - -, Slant right & Right & Left Thru**
57-64	**- - - -, Straight across 2 Ladies Chain**

Description

1-8	2 Ladies Chain across the set.
9-16	Same two ladies DoSaDo.
17-24	Opposite men DoSaDo.
25-32	2 Ladies Chain and the men Courtesy Turn the ladies 1/4 more to face up or down the floor. The couples on the prompter's left will be facing down the set and the couples on the prompter's right will be facing up the set.
33-40	Couples Promenade the direction they are facing for 4 short steps and Wheel Around as a couple in 4 steps.
41-48	Couples Promenade the opposite direction.
49-56	When each couple is across from the original opposite couple in the foursome, the two couples Half Promenade across, men passing left shoulders.
57-64	Each couple face the couple diagonally to the right and Right & Left Thru. Two couples, one at each end of the set, will have no couple diagonally to their right. They should face across the set and wait in place for 8 beats of music.

Note: *A point of confusion in this dance may occur after the slant right and Right & Left Thru. Be sure new couples are facing across the set before the 2 Ladies Chain.*

Chain Reaction

Calvin Campbell

Formation: Contra lines with couples facing couples. An even number of couples is required.
Record: Folkcraft 1151 "Paddy on the Turnpike" or ESP 141 " I'm Confessin"

Prompts

Intro	*- - - -, Ladies Chain diagonally left*
1-8	**- - - -, Ladies Chain diagonally right**
9-16	**- - - -, Facing couples Promenade Half**
17-24	**- - - -, 2 Ladies Chain across**
25-32	**- - - -, Circle Left once & a quarter more**
33-40	**- - - -, Weave by two**
41-48	**- - - -, Swing your partner**
49-56	**- - - -, Everybody Forward & Back**
57-64	**- - - -, Ladies Chain diagonally left**

Description

1-8	Ladies that can, Chain with the lady diagonally to their left in the opposite line. Two ladies on the ends of the lines will not be able to Chain
9-16	Ladies that can, Chain with the lady diagonally to their right in the opposite line. Two ladies on the ends of the lines will not be able to Chain
17-24	Facing couples Promenade Half across to the opposite side of the set. Men pass left shoulders.
25-32	2 Ladies Chain across the set.
33-40	The same two couples Circle Left once around and then circle 1/4 more to finish facing up or down the set.
41-48	Weave by two people by passing right shoulder with the first person and left shoulders with the next. As couples reach the end of the lines they should exchange sides of the line & face the opposite direction.
49-56	Swing with your original partner and finish facing across the set. At this point each couple has moved one place to the left in the formation.
57-64	Long lines go Forward & Back

Rightway Reel

Calvin Campbell

Formation: Contra lines. Couples facing couples. An even number of couples is required

Record: 4 Bar B "Good Old Country Song"

Prompts

Intro	*- - - -, With the corner Allemande Left*
1-8	**- - - -, - - Partner Swing**
9-16	**- - - -, Straight across Right & Left Thru**
17-24	**- - - -, - - Right & Left back**
25-32	**- - - -, Circle Right 3/4 then Pass Thru**
33-40	**- - - -, DoSaDo the next two**
41-48	**- - - -, Pass Thru & Circle Left 3/4**
49-56	**- - - -, Long lines Forward & Back**
57-64	**- - - -, With the corner Allemande Left**

Description

1-8	Allemande Left with the corner. The people at the top and foot of the set wait 8 beats of music.
9-16	Swing your partner and finish facing across the set.
17-24	Right & Left Thru with the couple across the set.
25-32	Right & Left Thru back across the set.
33-40	Same four Circle Right 3/4 (6 steps) and Pass Thru (2 steps)
41-48	DoSaDo with the next couple.
49-56	Pass Thru this couple (2 steps) and Circle Left 3/4 with the next couple (6 steps.) Each couple has now progressed right one position in the formation.
57-64	Long lines Forward & Back

Triple Contras Improper

Triple improper contras are dance routines that have an active couple and two couples below them in as shown in the diagram. As usual, when a contra dance is announced, the sets should form with the men in a long line on the prompter's right facing their partners in a long line on the caller's left. The prompter then directs the 1st, 4th, 7th, etc. couples to cross over and become active. At this point it is a good idea to have the groups of six join hands in a circle so everyone recognizes the group of six people that will be dancing the first time through the routine. Point out that only the top couple in each threesome is active.

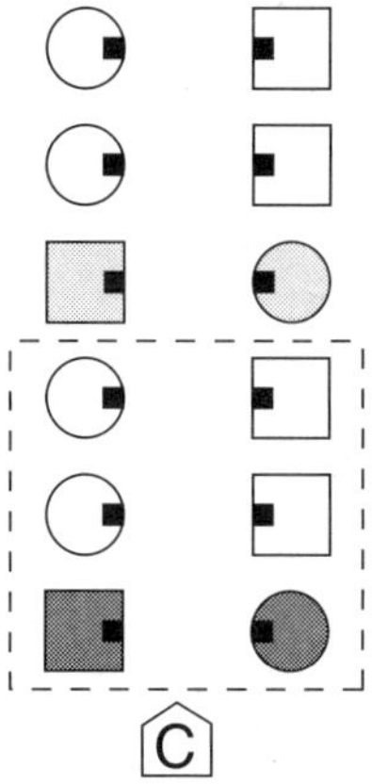

In **Third Trip Special** (Pg. 202) and **La Semilla Hornpipe** (Pg. 203) another aid is used to help teach the concept of dancing in groups of three couples. Early in each dance, the two sets of threesomes *Circle Left 3/4* to the position shown in the diagram on page 202. This movement isolates the threesomes away from the long lines and makes it easier for the dancers to visualize the dance pattern.

Each dance also has the active couple move to the center position in the line of three and a *Circle Right 3/4* to return the set to the long line configuration. At this point, the dancers should recognize that the active couple has moved down one position. The new threesome now picks up a new person on the end of each triple.

In sets with all complete groups of threesomes, the first time through the routine, one top couple is left dead-at-the-head and two bottom couples are dead-at-the-foot. The bottom two couples should dance the routine with a third 'ghost' couple. The top couple just stands in place.

The second time through the routine, there are two couples dead-at-the-head and one couple dead-at-the-foot. During this time through the routine the top couple and the foot couple cross over and change active/inactive roles.

Lonesome Shepherd Special, **Six on a Merry-Go-Round**, **Kitchen Hornpipe**, **April's Hornpipe** and **Market Lass Crossed** (Pgs. 204-208) all keep the threesomes in long lines. When these dances are used, the people will need to be reminded when the new threesome forms.

Third Trip Special

Jerry Helt

(Modified slightly by Calvin Campbell)

Formation: Contra lines. Couples 1, 4, 7, etc., active & crossed over.
Record: Grenn 12271 "Island In The Sun"

Prompts

Intro - - - -, Lines of three Forward & Back

1-8 - - - -, Circle Left 3/4 -
9-16 - - - Actives, down the middle & U-turn Back
17-24 - - - -, Come back & Separate around one
25-32 - - - -, Actives DoSaDo while ends Star Right
33-40 - - - - , Ends DoSaDo & actives Star Right
41-48 - - - -, Lines of three Forward & Back
49-56 - - - -, Circle Right 3/4 around
57-64 - - - -, New lines of three Forward & Back

Description

1-8 The active people and the two people below them form a line of three and walk Forward & Back.

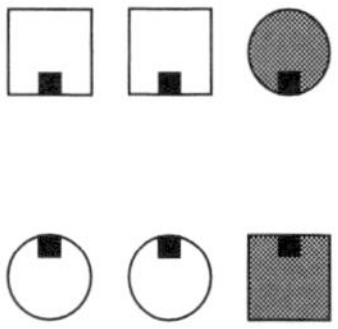

9-16 The threesomes join hands and Circle Six to the left 3/4. The active man and two inactive ladies are facing down the set. The active lady and two inactive men are facing up the set as shown to the right.

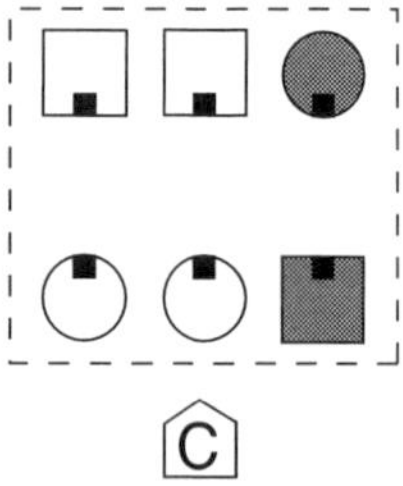

17-24 The active couple walk between the inactive couples to the end of these lines in six short steps & U-turn Back

25-32 Actives return to place in longer steps. Separate and walk around one person to stand between the inactive dancers.

33-40 The end dancers (inactives) DoSaDo with their partner. The center dancers (actives) form a two hand Right Hand Star.

41-48 The end dancers form a two hand Right Hand Star while the center dancers DoSaDo.

49-56 The lines of three go Forward & Back.

57-64 The lines of three Circle Right 3/4 and the active couples join hands with two new people below them to form new mini-sets of three.

La Semilla Hornpipe

Don Armstrong

(Modified slightly by Calvin Campbell)

Formation: Contra lines 1, 4, 7, etc., active and crossed over.
Record: LS 310 "Here's to the Fiddler" or Jewel 702 "Wild About Harry"

Prompts

Intro	*- - - -, Everybody Forward & Back*
1-8	**- - - -, Lines of three Circle Left 3/4**
9-16	**- - Active couples, walk thru the middle then U-turn Back**
17-24	**- - - -, Come back & Separate around one**
25-32	**- - - -, Those that can Right & Left Thru**
33-40	**- - - -, Same four Right & Left back**
41-48	**- - - -, Lines of three Forward & Back**
49-56	**- - - -, Circle Right 3/4 around**
57-64	**- - - -, New lines of three Forward & Back**

Description

1-8	The active dancers and the two dancers below them in the same line form a line of three and walk Forward & Back.
9-16	The threesomes across the set join hands and Circle Left 3/4. The active man and two inactive ladies are facing down the set. The active lady and two inactive men are facing up the set.
17-24	The active couple walk between the inactive couples to the end of the lines in 6 short steps & U-turn Back
25-32	Actives return to place in longer steps. Actives Separate at the end of the lines and walk around one dancer to end standing between the inactive dancers.
33-40	The active couple and the inactive dancers above them Right & Left Thru across the set.
41-48	The same four Right & Left Thru back across the set.
49-56	The lines of three go Forward & Back.
57-64	The lines of three Circle Right 3/4 and the active dancers and two new inactive dancers below them join hands to form new mini-sets of three.

Notes: The original "Third Trip Special" & "La Semilla Hornpipe" uses the movement Cast Off in counts 25-32. The Separate Around One is an unassisted Cast Off in traditional terminology.

Six On A Merry-Go-Round

Calvin Campbell

Formation: Contra lines. Couples 1, 4, 7, etc., active & crossed over
Record: TNT 211 "Music Box Dancer"

Prompts

Intro	*- - - -, Lines of three go Forward & Back*
1-8	**- - - -, Circle Left full around**
9-16	**- - - -, - - - -**
17-24	**Bow to partner, actives down center then U-turn Back**
25-32	**- - - -, Come back & Separate around one**
33-40	**- - - -, Active couples DoSaDo**
41-48	**- - - -, Those that can Right & Left Thru**
49-56	**- - - -, Same two Right & Left Back**
57-64	**- - - -, New lines of three go Forward & Back**

Description

1-8	The active persons and the two dancers below them form a line of three and walk Forward & Back.
9-24	The threesomes across the set join hands and Circle Left full around. Bow to partner at home.
25-32	The active couples walk down the center in 6 short steps & U-turn Back
33-40	Actives return to place in longer steps. Actives Separate and pass between the corner and the person above and walk around the person below (corner position) to stand between the inactive dancers in the threesome.
41-48	The active couples DoSaDo.
49-56	The active couple and the inactive people above them Right & Left Thru across the set.
57-64	The same four Right and Left Thru back across the set and then the active dancers and two new inactive people below them join hands to form new mini-sets of three.

Kleen Kitchen Hornpipe

Calvin Campbell

(Modified from a dance by Ralph Page)

Formation: Contra lines. Couples 1, 4, 7, etc., active & crossed over.
Record: LS 168 "Come Under My Pladie"

Prompts

Intro	*- - - -, With the Corner DoSaDo*
1-8	**- - - -, - - Corner Swing**
9-16	**- - - -, Circle Left full around**
17-24	**- - - -, - - - -**
25-32	**- - - -, With the couple above Star Right**
33-40	**- - - - , With the couple below Star Left**
41-48	**- - - With the, couple above Right & Left Thru**
49-56	**- - - -, Same four Right & Left back**
57-64	**- - - -, With the corner DoSaDo**

Description

1-8	All DoSaDo the corner.
9-16	Swing the corner and put her on the man's right and face across the set. The active couple is now between the two inactive people in the threesome.
17-32	The six people (the actives and the dancers on either side) Circle Left once around.
33-40	The active couples Star Right with the couple above.
41-48	The active couples Star Left with the couple below.
49-56	The active couple and the inactive people above them Right & Left Thru across the set.
57-64	Same four Right & Left back and then the active dancers form new threesomes with the two below.

April's Hornpipe

Ralph Page

Formation: Contra lines. Couples 1, 4, 7, etc., active & crossed over.
Record: LS 348 "The Spider Bit The Baby"

Prompts

Intro	*- - - -, Allemande Left once & a half*
1-8	**- - - -, Next one below DoSaDo**
9-16	**- - - -, Face the center & Circle 6**
17-24	**- - - -, - - - -**
25-32	**- - - -, Actives Star Left with the couple below**
33-40	**- - - -, Swing with the couple above**
41-48	**- - - -, Face across Right & Left Thru**
49-56	**- - - -, - - Right & Left back**
57-64	**- - - -, Allemande Left once & a half**

Description

1-8	Left Arm Turn the corner once & a half to finish facing the next dancer below in the same line.
9-16	DoSaDo this third person and everyone finish by facing across the set.
17-32	Actives join hands with the person on either side of them and Circle 6 to the left full around
33-40	Actives Star Left with the couple below.
41-48	Actives Swing the person above and finish facing across the set.
49-56	The active people and the inactive people above them Right & Left Thru across the set.
57-64	Right & Left back across the set.

Lonesome Shepherd

Ernie Johnson

(Modified slightly by Calvin Campbell)

Formation: Contra lines. Couples 1, 4, 7, etc., active & crossed over
Record: Folkcraft 745 "FLK Progression"

Prompts

Intro	*Active ladies lead the men, around the opposite three -*
1-8	**- - - -, - - - -**
9-16	**Active men lead the ladies, around the opposite three -**
17-24	**- - - -, - - - -**
25-32	**- - - -, Actives down center then U-turn Back**
33-40	**- - - -, Come back to place Separate around one**
41-48	**- - - -, Those that can Right & Left Thru**
49-56	**- - - -, Same four Right & Left Back**
57-64	**Active ladies lead the men, around the opposite three**

Description

1-16	The active ladies and the two inactive men below join hands in a line of three. The active ladies lead their lines around the opposite threesome.
17-32	The active men and the two inactive ladies below join hands in a line of three. The men lead their lines around the opposite three-some.
33-40	The active couples Promenade down the center of the set in 6 short steps & U-turn Back in 2 steps.
41-48	The active couples walk back up the set to place in longer steps. The active couples then Separate and each active person passes between the corner and the one above, walk around the person below (corner position) to stand between the two inactive people in the threesome.
49-56	The active people and the inactive people above them Right & Left Thru across the set.
57-64	Same four Right & Left back and then the active people form new threesomes with the two below.

Market Lass Crossed

Traditional

Researched by Ralph Page & modified for CDP by Cal Campbell

Formation: Contra lines. Couples 1, 4, 7, etc., active & crossed over
Record: LS 1008

Prompts

Intro	*Actives down the outside*
1-8	**- - Below two couples, - - Cross over**
9-16	**Up the outside past one couple, Step in & Forward six & Back**
17-24	**- - - -, Partners Right Hand Turn 3/4**
25-32	**- - - -, Forward six & Back again**
33-40	**- - - - Partners Right Hand Turn 3/4**
41-48	**- - - -, Couple above Right & Left Thru**
49-56	**- - - -, - - Right & Left back**
57-64	**- - - -, Actives down the outside**

Description

1-8	The active couples (1, 4, 7, etc.) walk down the outside of the their line past two people. Come in to the center of the set and cross over to the opposite side of the set
9-16	The same actives proceed up the outside of the set and up toward the prompter past one person and take the hands of the adjacent person on each side.
17-24	The actives and the person on each side go Forward six & Back.
25-32	The actives Turn partner Right 3/4 as the inactives turn 1/4 to face each other. At the end of the 3/4 turn, the actives join adjacent hands with the inactives to form lines of three across the set.
33-40	The lines of three go Forward & Back.
41-48	The actives Turn partner Right 3/4 as the inactives turn 1/4 to face across the set. The actives finish the 3/4 turn back in their home lines.
49-56	Actives and the couple above Right & Left Thru across the set.
57-64	Same four Right & Left back.

Note: This is a really elegant dance to elegant music. The original version is uncrossed and requires a Right & Left Thru with the same sex.

The 3/4 Arm Turns can be done in the old style with the man holding the lady's hand at shoulder level with his arm bent at the elbow.

Trios

Trios are very useful in dance groups where there are more of one gender than the other. They are also excellent to use at beginner parties. Many of the dances on the following pages have hand clapping sequences which are fun and help teach new dancers the correct timing associated with certain dance movements such as *Forward & Back*

Trios are danced in groups of three people standing in a line. The combination of people can be all men or all ladies or any combination of men and ladies. When the line of three is composed of two men and one lady, the lady is usually the center person in the line. When the line consists of two ladies and one man, the man is normally in the center of the line. This can change as the dance progresses

Trios can be arranged in a variety of formations. If the number of dancers is large and the hall size permits, the dancers usually form a large circle with lines of three arranged in a wagon spoke arrangement. All the dancers can be facing one direction around the hall (counterclockwise) or alternate sets of three can face clockwise to form the pattern shown above.

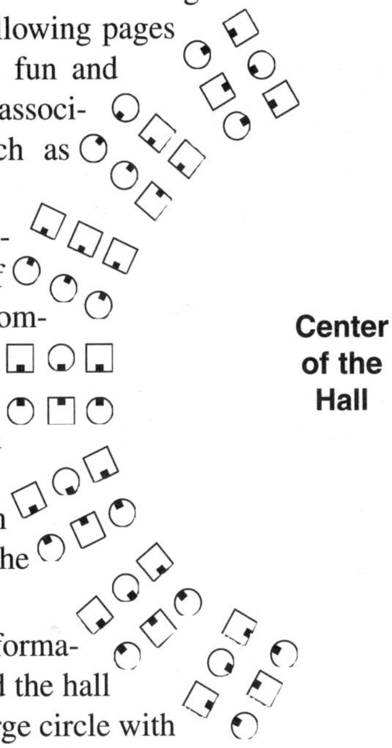

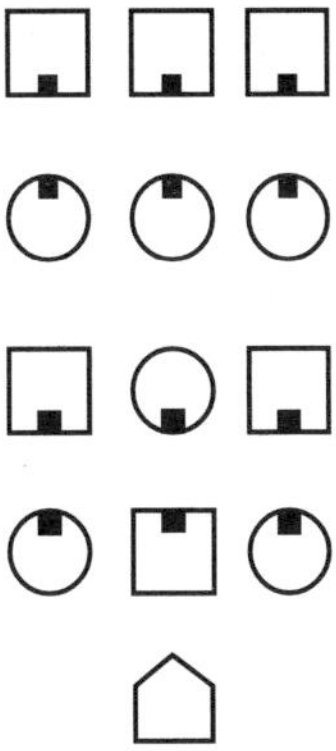

There will be occasions when the number of dancers will be too small to utilize the wagon spoke arrangement. When this occurs, Trios can be danced with the facing lines of three arranged the length of the hall as shown to the left. Keep in mind that the arrangement of men and ladies in each line is still arbitrary. When each line of three reaches the head or foot of the hall, they will have no facing line of three for one time through the dance. These dancers simply turn around and wait for someone to come to dance with them.

The first two dances in this section, **Wild Turkey** and **Theil's Trio** (Pg. 211) have all of the lines of three facing in the same direction around the hall. Both of these dances are excellent to use in situations where the time for starting the dance has arrived, but people are still coming in the door. Start the dance and have someone at the door organize the people in groups of three as they come in and route them on to the floor. The dance routines are so easy that simple observation will tell them what to do.

Wild Turkey

Bob Howell

Formation: Lines of three facing counterclockwise around the room.
Record: Grenn 15008 "Sherbrooke"

Prompts

Intro	*- - All Walk*
1-8	**- - - -, - - - -**
9-16	**- - - -, Right hand person Right Hand Around**
17-24	**- - - -, Left hand person Left Hand Around**
25-32	**- - - -, Centers forward & all Walk**

Description

1-8	The lines of three Walk 16 steps counterclockwise around the hall.
9-16	The center person on the line of three (the Wild Turkey) turns the person on their right with an Arm Turn or a hooked right elbow turn.
17-24	The same center person turns the person on the other end of the line with a Left Arm Turn or a left hooked elbow turn.
25-32	The center person then moves forward (counterclockwise) around the room to a new pair to join hands with them in a line of three and prepare to walk forward.

Theil's Trio

Jack Theil

Formation: Lines of three facing counterclockwise around the room.
Record: Lloyd Shaw LS E-17 or LS 3323 "Phrase Craze"

Prompts

Intro	*- - - -, Walk forward 8 steps*
1-8	**- - - -, - - Back up 4 &**
9-16	**Clap your hands, stamp your feet, turn the right hand person Right Hand Around**
17-24	**- - - -, Turn left hand person Left Hand Around**
25-32	**- - On to the next, walk forward 8 steps**

Description

1-8	The lines of three people walk forward 8 steps counterclockwise around the hall.
9-16	The lines of three back up 4 steps, clap your own hands 3 times quickly in 2 beats of music and then stamp your feet 3 times quickly in 2 beats of music.
17-24	The center dancers will Arm Turn the dancer on their right with a Right Hand Around.
25-32	The center dancer will turn the dancer on the left end of the line with a Left Hand Around and then move forward to join the next line.

Note: In this dance everyone is facing the same direction (counterclockwise) around the hall. On the Left Arm Turn and move onto the next (counts 25-32), the end dancers need to take short steps to allow the center dancers to easily catch up with them and join the new line of three.

A fun variation is to have the two outside people join inside hands as the center person moves up to the next trio. The previous center person must then choose to join one end or the other of the new line. The result will be a new center person each time through the routine.

Do-Ci-Dizzy

Bob Howell

Formation: Lines of three dancers facing lines of three dancers in a wagon spoke formation around the hall.
Record: Kalox 1112 "Colonel Bogie March"

Prompts

Intro	*- - - -, All six Circle Left 8 steps*
1-8	**- - - -, Circle Right to home**
9-16	**- - - -, DoSaDo the opposite**
17-24	**- - - -, Right ends DoSaDo**
25-32	**- - - -, Left ends DoSaDo**
33-40	**- - - -, Lines of three DoSaDo**
41-48	**- - - -, - - - -**
49-56	**- - - -, Half way more & onto the next**
57-64	**- - - -, All six Circle Left**

Description

1-8	The six people in the two lines of three join hands and Circle Left.
9-16	Circle Right back to home position.
17-24	The people in each line DoSaDo the person in the opposite line.
25-32	The right end dancers in the two facing lines DoSaDo.
33-40	The left end dancers in the two facing lines DoSaDo
41-56	The dancers in each line of three hook adjacent elbows with each other and the entire line of three DoSaDo the opposite line of three.
57-64	Continue the DoSaDo until the lines of three are back to back once more and then move on to the next line of three.

Note: The three person DoSaDo is a real crowd pleaser. This dance is a good example of how people can be entertained with very few basic moves. The entire dance uses only two basics.

Tres

Ken Kernen

Formation: Lines of three dancers facing lines of three dancers in a wagon spoke formation around the hall.
Record: TNT 189 "If I Were A Rich Man"

Prompts

Intro	*- - - -, All six Circle Left once around*
1-8	**- - - -, - - - -**
9-16	**- - - -, - - Ends DoSaDo**
17-24	**- - - -, - - Centers DoSaDo**
25-32	**- - - -, Centers face right & DoSaDo**
33-40	**- - - -, Centers face left & DoSaDo**
41-48	**- - - -, - - Forward & Back**
49-56	**- - - -, Pass Thru to a new three**
57-64	**- - - -, All six Circle Left once around**

Description

1-16	The six people in the two lines of three join hands and Circle Left once around.
17-24	The end four people in each line of three DoSaDo the facing person in the opposite line.
25-32	The center people in each line DoSaDo the center person in the opposite line.
33-40	The center people face to the right and DoSaDo the right end person in their own line.
41-48	The center people face to the left and DoSaDo the left end person in their own line.
49-56	Lines of three walk Forward & Back.
57-64	Pass Thru the facing line of three and move onto a new line of three.

Alternate Trios

Ken Kernen

Formation: Lines of three dancers facing lines of three dancers in a wagon spoke formation around the hall.
Record: Lloyd Shaw LS 194 or Folkcraft 1501 "Dashing White Sergeant"

Prompts

Intro	*- - - -, Circle to the Left*
1-8	**- - - -, - - Circle Right**
9-16	**- - - -, - Centers only DoSaDo**
17-24	**- - - -, - Ends only DoSaDo**
25-32	**- - - Centers, Turn one on the right by the Right**
33-40	**- - - Centers, Turn one on the left by the Left**
41-48	**- - - -, Lines of three go Forward & Back**
49-56	**- - - -, Pass Thru go onto the next**
57-64	**- - - -, Join hands & Circle to the Left**

Description

1-8	The two lines of three join hands for a circle of six and Circle Left eight steps
9-16	All Circle Right to original facing positions.
17-24	The center dancer in each line of three will DoSaDo the center person in the opposite line.
25-32	The end dancers in the lines of three will DoSaDo the facing dancers in the opposite line.
33-40	The center dancers in the line of three turn the dancer on their right with a Right Hand Around.
41-48	The center dancer will turn the dancer on the left end of their threesome with a Left Hand Around.
49-56	Facing lines of three go Forward & Back.
57-64	Pass Thru the facing line of three and walk forward to the next line of three.

Three Legged Stool

Calvin Campbell

Formation: Lines of three dancers facing lines of three dancers in a wagon spoke formation around the hall.
Record: Rockin M MR-001 "Carnival"

Prompts

Intro	*- - - -, All six Circle Left once around*
1-8	**- - - -, - - - -**
9-16	**- - - -, - - Centers DoSaDo**
17-24	**- - - -, Diagonal right ends turn Right Hand Around**
25-32	**- - - -, Diagonal left ends turn Left Hand Around**
33-40	**- - - -, Centers turn both hands around**
41-48	**- - - -, - - Forward & Back**
49-56	**- - - -, Pass Thru to a new three**
57-64	**- - - -, All six Circle Left once around**

Description

1-16	The six people in the two lines of three join hands in one circle of six and Circle Left once around.
17-24	Center dancers DoSaDo the center dancer in the opposite line.
25-32	The two dancers on the right end of each line face the corresponding end dancer in the opposite line, Right Arm Turn and back into their home line.
33-40	The two dancers on the left end of each line face the corresponding end dancer in the opposite line, Left Arm Turn and back into their home line.
41-48	The center dancers join both hands with the opposite person and two hand turn (right hip to right hip) once around and step back into their home line.
49-56	Lines of three walk Forward & Back.
57-64	Pass Thru the facing line of three and move on to a new line of three.

Mason's Apron Trio

modified by Ken Kernen

Formation: Lines of three dancers facing lines of three dancers in a wagon spoke formation around the hall.
Record: Folkcraft 1512 "Mason's Apron"

Prompts

Intro	*- - - -, All six Circle Left once around*
1-8	**- - - -, - - - -**
9-16	**- - - -, - - Centers DoSaDo**
17-24	**- - - -, - - Ends DoSaDo**
25-32	**- - - -, Centers Star Right with the right hand two**
33-40	**- - - -, Centers Star Left with the left hand two**
41-48	**- - - -, - - Forward & Back**
49-56	**- - - -, - - Pass Thru & bow**
57-64	**- - - -, All six Circle Left once around**

Description

1-16	The six dancers in the two facing lines of three join hands and Circle Left once around.
17-24	The center dancer in each line DoSaDo the facing center dancer in the opposite line.
25-32	The end dancers DoSaDo the facing end dancers in the opposite line.
33-40	The center dancers face to the right and Star Right with two dancers on that end of the line. One person will be in the same line and one person will be in the opposite line.
41-48	The center dancers then cross to the opposite end of the line and Star Left with the two dancers on the opposite end of the line who change direction and put left hands into the star.
49-56	Lines of three walk Forward & Back.
57-64	Pass Thru the facing line of three and move on to a new line of three.

T.B.C. Trio

Bob Howell

Formation: Lines of three people facing lines of three people in a wagon spoke formation around the hall.
Record: Grenn 16018 "Auld Lang Syne" or Gold Star 715 "America the Beautiful"

Prompts

Intro	*- - Leader #1, lead lines around the opposite three*
1-8	**- - - -, - - - -**
9-16	**- - Leader #2, lead lines around the opposite three**
17-24	**- - - -, - - - -**
25-32	**- - - -, The four corners Star Right**
33-40	**- - - -, Centers DoSaDo**
41-48	**- - - -, - - Forward & Back**
49-56	**- - - -, - - Pass Thru & bow**
57-64	**- - Leader #1, lead lines around the opposite three**

Description

1-16	The outside person in the lines facing counter-clockwise around the hall is leader #1. They lead their lines around the opposite three.
17-32	The outside person in the lines facing clockwise around the hall is leader #2. They lead their lines around the opposite three.
33-40	The end four people make a Right Hand Star. The center people will have to step back out of the way a little.
41-48	The center people DoSaDo the facing center person in the opposite line.
49-56	Lines of three walk Forward & Back.
57-64	Pass Thru the facing line of three and move onto a new line of three.

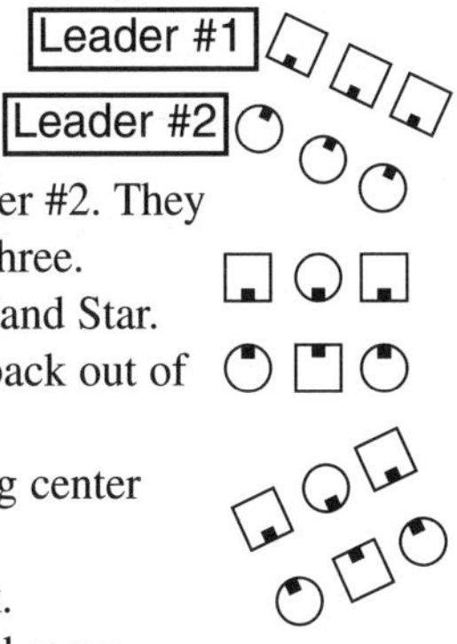

Three's Greet

Bob Howell

Formation: Lines of three dancers facing lines of three dancers in a wagon spoke formation around the hall.
Record: Grenn 15010 "When You & I Were Young Maggie"

Prompts

Intro	*- - - -, Walk forward & stamp your feet*
1-8	**- - Back away & stamp, - - Walk forward & stamp**
9-16	**- - Back away & stamp, all six Circle Left**
17-24	**- - - -, - - Circle Right**
25-32	**- - - -, Center people DoSaDo**
33-40	**- - - -, End people DoSaDo**
41-48	**- - - -, Everybody Forward & Back**
49-56	**- - - -, Pass Thru onto the next**
57-64	**- - - -, Walk Forward & stamp your Feet**

Description

1-8	The lines of three walk towards each other 2 steps. Every one stamp their feet quickly 3 times in 2 beats of music. Back away from each other 2 steps. Everyone stamp their feet quickly 3 times in 2 beats of music.
9-16	Repeat 1-8
17-24	All six dancers Circle Left 8 steps.
25-32	Circle Right back to the original place.
33-40	Center dancers DoSaDo the center dancer in the opposite line.
41-48	End dancers DoSaDo the end person in the opposite line.
49-56	Everyone walk Forward & Back
57-64	Pass Thru the opposite three and move on to the next three

Note: The gimmick in this dance is the walk and stamp sequence. The rhythm is step and step and stamp, stamp, stamp and step and step and stamp, stamp, stamp and.

General Bradford's Charge

Mary Jo Bradford

Formation: Lines of three dancers facing lines of three dancers in a wagon spoke formation around the hall.
Record: Blue Star 2260 "Schatzie" or LS 335/336 "Doc Boyd's Jig & Beaver Hat"

Prompts

Intro	*- - - -, Circle 6 to the Left*
1-8	**- - - -, Circle 6 to the Right**
9-16	**- - - -, Turn right hand dancer Right Hand Around**
17-24	**- - - -, Turn left hand dancer Left Hand Around**
25-32	**- - - -, All six Star Right**
33-40	**- - - -, Star Left back to place**
41-48	**- - - -, Face the opposite and clap hands**
49-56	**- - - -, - - Pass Thru & bow**
57-64	**- - - -, Circle 6 to the Left**

Description

1-8	The two lines of three join hands and Circle Left 8 steps.
9-16	Circle Right 8 steps back to the original facing position
17-24	Center dancers turn the dancer on their right in the same line with a Right Hand Around
25-32	Center dancers turn the dancer on the left end of the same line with a Left Hand Around.
33-40	Form a six hand Right Hand Star.
41-48	Star Left back to the original place.
49-56	Facing the person in the opposite line. Clap own hands together on 1. Clap right hands with the opposite on 2. Clap own hands together on 3. Clap left hands with the opposite on 4. Clap own hands together on 5. Clap both hands with the opposite on 6. Clap own hand together 3 quick times on 7 and 8.
57-64	Pass Thru the facing line of three and move on to a new line of three.

Hand Maze

Calvin Campbell

Formation: Lines of three dancers facing lines of three dancers in a wagon spoke formation around the hall.
Record: LS 344 "Combination Rag"

Prompts

Intro	*- - - -, Circle 6 to the Left*
1-8	**- - - -, Circle 6 to the Right**
9-16	**- - - -, Clap hands with opposite & left**
17-24	**- - - -, DoSaDo the left hand person**
25-32	**- - - -, Clap hands with opposite & right**
33-40	**- - - -, DoSaDo the right hand person.**
41-48	**- - - -, Lines of three Forward & Back**
49-56	**- - - -, - - Pass Thru to the next & bow**
57-64	**- - - -, Circle 6 to the Left**

Description

1-8	The two lines of three join hands and Circle Left 8 steps.
9-16	Circle Right back to original facing positions.
17-24	With everyone face a dancer in the opposite line of three, clap their own hands together on 1. Clap the right hand of the opposite dancer on 2. Clap both hands together on 3. Clap the opposite dancer's left hand on 4. The center person and the left hand person in same line turn quickly toward each other and repeat the above 4 count clapping sequence with this person.
25-32	The center person DoSaDo with the same left hand person.
33-40	The lines of three clap their own hands together on 1. Clap the right hand of the opposite person on 2. Clap both hands together on 3. Clap the left hand of the opposite person on 4. The center person and the right hand person in the same line turn quickly toward each other and repeat the above 4 count clapping sequence with this person.
41-48	The center person DoSaDo with the same right hand person and finsh facing the opposite line of three.
49-56	Lines of three go Forward & Back.
57-64	Pass Thru the facing line of three and move on to a new line of three.

Dos Plus One

Ken Kernen

Formation: Lines of three dancers facing lines of three dancers in a wagon spoke formation around the hall.
Record: TNT "Reel Madrid"

Prompts

Intro	*- - - -, Circle 6 to the Left*
1-8	**- - - -, Circle 6 to the Right**
9-16	**- - - -, Inside ends sashay over & back**
17-24	**- - - -, Outside ends sashay over & back**
25-32	**- - - -, In your own lines Star Right**
33-40	**- - - -, Star Left back to lines**
41-48	**- - - -, - - Forward & Back**
49-56	**- - - -, - - Pass Thru & bow**
57-64	**- - - -, Circle six to the Left**

Description

1-8	The two lines of three join hands and Circle Left 8 steps.
9-16	Circle Right back to original facing positions.
17-24	The two dancers on the end of the lines toward the inside of the big circle step forward, join both hands, and sashay (slide) 3 steps toward the outside between the two lines and return back to place with 3 sashay (slide) steps.
25-32	The two dancers on the ends of the line toward the outside of the circle step forward, join both hands, and sashay (slide) 3 steps toward the inside of the big circle between the two lines and return back to place with 3 sashay (slide) steps.
33-40	The lines of three Right Hand Star with the dancers in their own line.
41-48	Star Left back to the original facing lines
49-56	Lines of three Forward & Back
57-64	Pass Thru the facing line of three and move onto a new line of three.

Taos Trio

Ken Kernen

Formation: Lines of three dancers facing lines of three dancers in a wagon spoke formation around the hall.
Record: TNT 271 "Pass Me By" or Red Boot 1325 "Susanna/Turkey"

Prompts

Intro *- - - -, - - Ends DoSaDo*

1-8 **- - - -, - - Centers DoSaDo**
9-16 **- - - -, Centers Lead Right & Circle to a line**
17-24 **- - - -, - - Forward & Back**
25-32 **- - - -, New centers Lead Right & Circle to a line**
33-40 **- - - -, - - Forward & Back**
41-48 **- - - -, New centers Star Right with the right hand two**
49-56 **Lead your line home, Pass Thru to a new three**
57-64 **- - - -, - - Ends DoSaDo**

Description

1-8 The end dancers DoSaDo the facing dancer in the opposite line.
9-16 The center dancer in each line DoSaDo the center dancer in the opposite line.
17-24 The center dancer in each line Lead to the Right and Circle three with the two people on that end of the line. One person will be in the same line and one person will be in the opposite line. The centers will break with the person on the left and lead to line of three facing another line of three. One line will now have their backs to the center of the hall and one line will have their backs to the wall.
25-32 Lines of three go Forward & Back.
33-40 The new center of each line Lead Right and Circle to a Line.
41-48 The lines of three go Forward & Back.
49-56 The new centers of each line face to the right and Star Right with the two people there.
57-64 These new centers, lead out of the Stars and lead their line home to their original facing position. Everyone will be back to their orginal position in the line of three. The lines then Pass Thru to the next line of three.

Rio Trio

Ken Kernen

Formation: Lines of three dancers facing lines of three dancers in a wagon spoke formation around the hall.
Record: Hi-Hat 457 "Paloma Blanca"

Prompts

Intro	*- - - -, - - Ends Star Left*
1-8	**- - - -, - - Star Right**
9-16	**- - Centers Turn, Right & right opposite Left**
17-24	**- - - -, Centers Right & left opposite Left**
25-32	**- - - -, Centers Right & left corner Left**
33-40	**- - - -, Centers Right & right corner Left**
41-48	**- - - -, Circle six half way**
49-56	**- - - -, All U-turn Back**
57-64	**- - Bow, - - Ends Star Left**

Description

1-8	Ends of each threesome step to the center and form a four person Left Hand Star.
9-16	Same four Star Right. Finish in original facing lines.
17-24	The center dancer in each threesome take right hands and step by to the dancer in the opposite line diagonally to the right. Left Arm Turn once around.
25-32	Center people Right Arm Turn in the center to the dancer in the opposite line diagonally to the left. Left Arm Turn once around.
33-40	Center dancers Right Arm Turn in the center to the dancer on the left end of their original line. Left Arm Turn once around.
41-48	Center people Right Arm Turn in the center to the dancer on the right end of their original line. Left Arm Turn once around and quickly step back into the center of their original line.
49-56	Circle Six half around.
57-64	All U-turn Back and proceed to the next line of three and bow.

Notes: Have the center people identify each of the people in the Arm Turn sequence by pointing to each of them. Notice that the center person does a Left Arm Turn with each of the corner people starting with the opposite left and proceeding counterclockwise. Between each of the Left Arm Turns they Right Arm Turn the opposite center person. This is a fun dance, but it requires practice and should be walked-thru completely.

Toots' Trio

Bob Howell

Formation: Lines of three dancers facing lines of three dancers in a wagon spoke formation around the hall.
Record: TNT 107 "Freight Train"

Prompts

Intro	*- - - -, Circle 6 to the Left*
1-8	**- - - -, - - - -**
9-16	**- - - -, Center people DoSaDo**
17-24	**- - - -, With the diagonal right DoSaDo**
25-32	**- - - -, With the diagonal left DoSaDo**
33-40	**Left end slide right, everybody Forward & Back**
41-48	**- - - -, Single File Promenade to the right**
49-56	**- - On to the next, face right & Forward and Back**
57-64	**- - - -, Circle 6 to the Left**

Description

1-16	The two lines of three join hands and Circle Left all the way back to the original facing position.
17-24	The center dancers DoSaDo the center dancer in the opposite line.
25-32	The center dancer DoSaDo the end dancer diagonally to the right and in the opposite line
33-40	The center dancers DoSaDo the end dancer diagonally to the left and in the opposite line. The left end person slides to the right to become the center person in the line as the previous center person backs up into the left hand person's vacated slot.
41-48	The lines of three go Forward & Back
49-56	Each line of three face right and Single File Promenade around the opposite three and onto a new line of three to finish with another right face turn to face the new line of three. This move swaps the ends of the lines.
57-64	Lines go Forward and Back

Note: This dance was adapted by Bob Howell from a dance used by Irvin "Toots" Tousignant. The rotation of the dancers gives each person the opportunity to be the center person as the dance sequence repeats.

Sicilian Circles

A Sicilian Circle is formed by couples facing couples like spokes of a wheel in a large circle around the hall as shown to the right. They require a large group of people to be danced comfortably. At least 24 couples are needed to keep the radius of the circle large enough to permit couples to quickly identify the next couple in the ring.

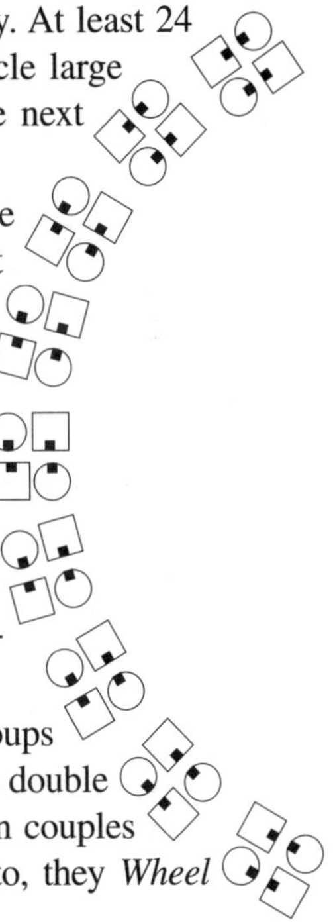

Dances in a Sicilian Circle formation can be called in the same style as square dances. Almost any combination of figures done by facing couples can be used. In most dances, you should attempt to keep original partners together when they move on to a new couple. This is an excellent formation to use to teach new basics which involve facing couples. Everyone gets to participate and the facing couples are isolated away from the confusion of the rest of the square formation.

The same dances can also be done in small groups or small halls by having the facing couples in one double line the length of the hall as shown below. When couples have no facing couple to move on to, they *Wheel Around* and wait.

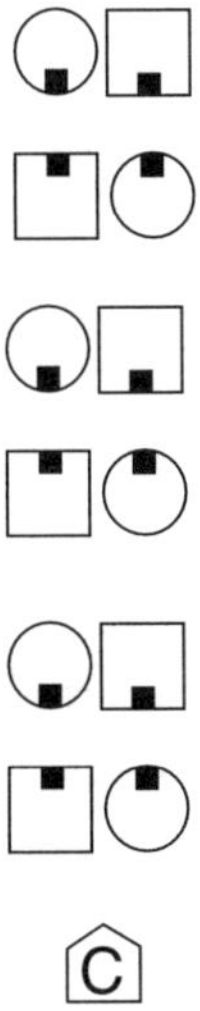

The dances listed in this section are all prompted 64-beat routines. They are arranged in a rough teaching sequence. Keep in mind that dances from this section should be mixed in with other formations and music styles to provide a good balance in variety.

First Night Sicilian Circle

Calvin Campbell

Formation: Couples facing couples around the hall like spokes of a wheel. #1 couple (shaded) facing counterclockwise, #2 couple (unshaded) facing clockwise .

Record: Grenn 12241 "Yankee Doodle Dandy"

Prompts

Intro	*- - - -, Turn the opposite Right Hand Around*
1-8	**- - - -, Turn the opposite Left Hand Around**
9-16	**- - - -, Join hands & Circle Left**
17-24	**- - - -, Circle Right**
25-32	**- - - -, Two men** (left ends) **Turn by the Right**
33-40	**- - - -, Two ladies** (right ends) **Turn by the Left**
41-48	**- - - -, Everybody Forward & Back**
49-56	**- - - -, 1's arch & 2's duck thru to the next**
57-64	**- - - -, Turn the opposite Right Hand Around**

Description

1-8	Facing dancers Arm Turn Right.
9-16	Facing dancers Arm Turn Left.
17-24	Facing couples Circle Left.
25-32	Facing couples Circle Right back to their original facing position around the circle.
33-40	Two men or whoever is on the left, turn the other diagonal left person by a Right Arm Turn.
41-48	Two ladies or whoever is on the right, turn the other diagonal right person with a Left Arm Turn.
49-56	Everybody Forward & Back.
57-64	#1 couple (shaded) arch with the adjacent hands and #2 couple (unshaded) duck through the arch, move on to the next couple and bow.

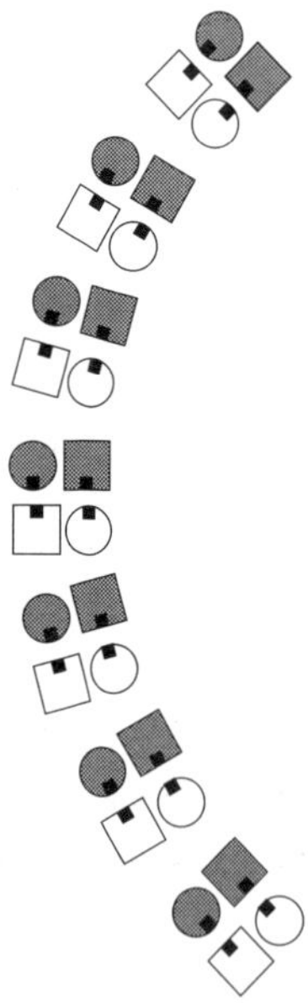

Note: As the name implies, this dance is designed to be used on the first night of dancing. If the dance is done in a stacked formation, the #1 couples face the caller at the head of the hall and will make an arch for the #2 couple to duck under.

Scottish Man 'O' War

Vickie Goodloe

Formation: Couples facing couples around the hall like spokes of a wheel. #1 couple (shaded) facing counterclockwise, #2 couple (unshaded) facing clockwise.
Record: LS 193/194 "Dashing White Sergeant"

Prompts

Intro	*- - - -, - - Circle Left*
1-8	**- - - -, - - Circle Right**
9-16	**- - - -, Two men Turn Right Hand around**
17-24	**- - - -, Two men Turn Left Hand around**
25-32	**- - - -, Two ladies Turn Right Hand around**
33-40	**- - - -, Two ladies Turn Left Hand around**
41-48	**- - - -, #1's arch & #2's duck under**
49-56	**#2's arch & #1's duck under, Repeat twice more.**
57-64	**- - - -, - - Circle Left**

Description

1-8	Circle 4 to the left with the opposite couple.
9-16	Circle Right back to original facing positions.
17-24	Two men Arm Turn Right.
25-32	Two men Arm Turn Left.
33-40	Two ladies Arm Turn Right.
41-48	Two ladies Arm Turn Left.
49-56	#1 couple arch with inside hands and #2 couple ducks through the arch and proceed to the next couple around the large circle. Then the #2 couple makes an arch and the #1 couple duck through this arch and proceed to the next couple around the large circle.
57-64	Repeat 49-56.

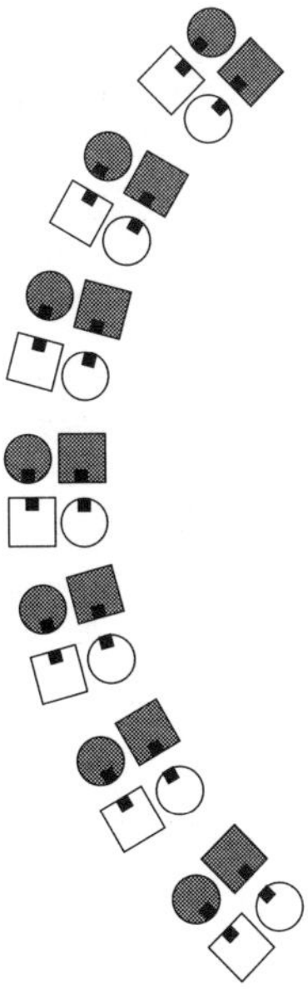

Note: The dance action in 49-64 travels through 4 couples and stops with the fifth couple. In traditional square dancing this is call a Dip & Dive.

Cecily Circle

Ken Kernen

Formation: Couples facing couples around the hall like spokes of a wheel.
Record: LS "St Anne's Reel"

Prompts

Intro	*- - - -, Facing couples Star Right*
1-8	**- - - -, - - Star Left**
9-16	**- - - -, Two ladies DoSaDo**
17-24	**- - - -, Two men DoSaDo**
25-32	**- - - -, - - Circle Left**
33-40	**- - - -, - - Circle Right**
41-48	**- - - -, - - Swing partner**
49-56	**- - - -, Pass Thru & bow to new two**
57-64	**- - - -, - - Star Right**

Description

1-8	Facing couples Right Hand Star.
9-16	Same couples Star Left.
17-24	Two facing ladies DoSaDo.
25-32	Two facing men DoSaDo.
33-40	Facing couples join hands and Circle Left.
41-48	Circle Right back to original facing positions around the big circle.
49-56	Swing your partner and face the opposite couple.
57-64	Pass Thru to a new couple and bow.

Scones & Tea

Ken Kernen

Formation: Couples facing couples around the hall like spokes of a wheel.
Record: LS-38 "Lighted Sconce"

Prompts

Intro	*- - - -, Facing couples Star Right*
1-8	**- - - -, - - Star Left**
9-16	**- - - -, Two ladies DoSaDo**
17-24	**- - - -, Two men DoSaDo**
25-32	**- - - -, As couples DoSaDo**
33-40	**- - - -, Circle Left once around**
41-48	**- - - -, - - Swing your partner**
49-56	**- - - -, Pass Thru on to the next**
57-64	**- - - -, Facing couples Star Right**

Description

1-8	Facing couples Right Hand Star.
9-16	Same four Star Left back to original facing positions.
17-24	Two ladies DoSaDo.
25-32	Two men DoSaDo.
33-40	As a couple DoSaDo around the other couple. Couples can link arms or put arms around each others' waist.
41-48	Circle Left with the opposite couple once around.
49-56	Everyone Swing their partner and finish facing the opposite couple.
57-64	Pass Thru the opposite couple and move onto the next couple around the big circle.

Happy Circle

Bob Howell

Formation: Couples facing couples around the hall like spokes of a wheel.
Record: TNT 192 "Make Someone Happy"

Prompts

Intro	*- - - -, - - Circle Left*
1-8	**- - - -, - - Circle Right**
9-16	**- - - -, - - DoSaDo opposite**
17-24	**- - - -, - - Swing partner**
25-32	**- - - -, - - Star Right**
33-40	**- - - -, - - Star Left**
41-48	**- - - -, - - Forward & Back**
49-56	**- - - -, Pass Thru on to the next**
57-64	**- - - -, - - Circle Left**

Description

1-8	Circle 4 to the left with the facing couple.
9-16	Circle Right back to original facing positions.
17-24	DoSaDo the opposite person.
25-32	Swing your partner.
33-40	Make a four hand Right Hand Star.
41-48	Star Left and finish back in original facing positions around the big circle
49-56	Everybody Forward & Back
57-64	Pass Thru the facing couple and proceed to the next couple.

Weathervane Promenade

Glen Nickerson

Formation: Couples facing couples around the hall like spokes of a wheel.
Record: Red Boot 2155 "Patriotic Medley" or TNT 250 "76 Trombones"

Prompts

Intro	*- - - -, - - Circle Left*
1-8	**- - - -, - - Circle Right**
9-16	**- - - -, Outside two Promenade in**
17-24	**- - - -, Same two Promenade back out**
25-32	**- - - -, Inside two Promenade out**
33-40	**- - - -, Same two Promenade in**
41-48	**- - - -, Couples weathervane once around**
49-56	**- - - -, - - - -**
57-64	**- - - -, On to the next & Circle Left**

Description

1-8	Circle Four to the left with the facing couple.
9-16	Circle Four to the right with the facing couple.
17-24	The two dancers on the outside edge of the big circle Promenade toward the center of the hall passing between the inside pair.
25-32	The same people U-turn Back and Promenade back out to their original facing position around the big circle
33-40	The two dancers on the inside edge of the big circle Promenade out toward the wall passing between the outside pair.
41-48	The same people U-turn Back and Promenade back in to their original facing position.
49-56	Each couple should link inside arms and then the men will hook left elbows. The two-faced lines will then rotate around the hooked left elbows.
57-64	The two faced line will continue to turn until the men can release left elbows and each couple can move onto the next couple and face.

Sicilian Circle #37

Jerry Helt

Formation: Couples facing couples around the hall like spokes of a wheel.
Record: E-Z 722 "Tunnel of Love" or LS E-40 "Tunnel Contra"

Prompts

Intro	*- - - -, - - Circle Left*
1-8	**- - - -, - - Circle Right**
9-16	**- - - -, - - 2 Ladies Chain**
17-24	**- - - -, - - Ladies Chain back**
25-32	**- - - -, - - Star Right**
33-40	**- - - -, - - Star Left**
41-48	**- - - -, - - Promenade once & a little bit more**
49-56	**- - - -, - - - -**
57-64	**- - - -, Onto to the next & Circle 4**

Description

1-8	Circle 4 to the Left with the facing couple.
9-16	Circle Right.
17-24	2 Ladies Chain.
25-32	2 Ladies Chain back.
33-40	Same four Star Right.
41-48	Star Left.
49-56	Couple Promenade with the men shoulder to shoulder once around.
57-64	Continue the Couple Promenade until each couple can proceed to the next couple and stop.

Grand Star Circle

Rod Linnell

Formation: Couples facing couples around the hall like spokes of a wheel.
Record: TNT 111 "Lemon Tree"

Prompts

Intro	*- - - -, - - Circle Left*
1-8	**- - - -, - - Circle Right**
9-16	**- - - -, - - 2 Ladies Chain**
17-24	**- - - -, - - Ladies Chain back**
25-32	**- - - -, - - DoSaDo opposite**
33-40	**- - - -, - - DoSaDo partner**
41-48	**- - - -, - - Star Right half**
49-56	**To the next Star Left half - , To the next Star Right half -**
57-64	**Next Left half - , Next Right half & Circle Left**

Description

1-8	Circle Left with the opposite couple once around.
9-16	Circle Right with the opposite couple once around.
17-24	2 Ladies Chain.
25-32	2 Ladies Chain.
33-40	DoSaDo the opposite person.
41-48	DoSaDo your partner and finish facing the opposite couple.
49-56	Star Right halfway with the facing couple and move on to the next couple. Star Left halfway with the 2nd couple and move on to the 3rd couple.
57-64	Star Right with the 3rd couple and move on to the next and Star Left with the 4th couple. Finish by moving on to the 5th couple and face them ready to Circle Left.

Note: In the four Stars in 49-64 the man will be leading his partner.

AL-Burke-Q

Ken Kernen

Formation: Couples facing couples around the hall like spokes of a wheel.
Record: Mountain Records MR 88 "Tijuana Lady"

Prompts

Intro	*- - - -, - - Circle Left*
1-8	**- - - -, - - Star Left**
9-16	**- - - - , - - Partner pattycake**
17-24	**- - - - , - - Opposite pattycake**
25-32	**- - - - , - - Men DoSaDo**
33-40	**Right Hand step by , - - Ladies DoSaDo**
41-48	**Right Hand step by , - - Men DoSaDo**
49-56	**Right Hand step by , - - Ladies DoSaDo**
57-64	**Right Hand step by , - - Circle Left**

Description

1-8	Circle 4 with the opposite couple
9-16	Same four Star Left.
17-24	Face your partner and clap right hands, with the opposite dancer, 3 times in first 2 beats of music. Clap left hands, with this same dancer, 3 times in the next 2 beats of music. Clap both hands with this same dancer 3 times in 2 beats of music, then stamp your feet 3 times in 2 beats of music.
25-32	Face the opposite dancer and clap right hands 3 times, clap left hands 3 times, clap both hands with the opposite person 3 times, then stamp feet 3 times.
33-40	Face the opposite couple and the two men DoSaDo. On the last 2 counts, the same men take right hands and step by each other and move on to the next pair.
41-48	The facing ladies DoSaDo. On the last 2 counts, the same facing ladies take right hands and step by each other.
49-56	Two men DoSaDo. On the last 2 counts the same two men take right hands and step by and move on to the next couple
57-64	The facing ladies DoSaDo. The ladies finish by taking right hands and stepping by to face the new couple with their original partner.

Siege of Carrick

Traditional

Formation: Couples facing couples around the hall like spokes of a wheel. (#1 couple facing counterclockwise, #2 couple facing clockwise as shown on page 224)

Record: LS 303 or Grenn 12204 "Sherbrooke"

Counts

Intro	*- - - -, - - Circle Left*
1-8	**- - - -, - - Circle Right**
9-16	**- - - -, - - Right Hand Star**
17-24	**- - - -, - - Left Hand Star**
25-32	**- - - -, - -#1's Split #2's**
33-40	**- - Around one, face partner clap twice Right Arm Turn**
41-48	**- - - -, - - #2's Split 1's**
49-56	**- - Around one, face partner clap 4 times Pass Thru**
57-64	**- - - Bow, - - Circle Left**

Description

1-8	With the opposite couple Circle Left
9-16	Same four Circle Right
17-24	Same four Star Right
25-32	Same four Star Left to finish back in original positions and facing the opposite couple.
33-40	The couples facing counterclockwise (#1) Split the couple facing clockwise and Separate around that couple to face partner in 6 steps. Each person claps their own hands together twice.
41-48	Right Arm Turn your partner once around to finish facing the opposite pair.
49-56	The couple facing clockwise (#2) Split the first couple and Separate around one in 4 steps to face their partner and clap their own hands together 4 times.
57-64	Pass Thru the facing couple and proceed to the next couple and bow.

Note: The original dance had the numbered couples reversed. The modification was made to minimize any possible confusion with two other dances used in this section.

Pittsfield Circle

Ken Kernen

Formation: Couples facing couples around the hall like spokes of a wheel.
Record: Ute UR-1 "Pittsfield Drum & Bugle Corp"

Prompts

Intro	*- - - -, - - Star Right*
1-8	**- - - -, - - Star Left**
9-16	**- - - -, Two ladies DoSaDo**
17-24	**- - - -, Two ladies Star Right**
25-32	**- - - -, Star Promenade the men back home**
33-40	**- - - -, Two men Star Left**
41-48	**- - - -, Star Promenade the ladies back home**
49-56	**- - - -, Pass Thru to a new two**
57-64	**- - - -, - - Star Right**

Description

1-8	Facing couples Right Hand Star.
9-16	Same couples Star Left back to facing couple positions.
17-24	Two facing ladies DoSaDo.
25-32	Same two ladies Star Right once around and a little bit more.
33-40	Pickup the opposite man with an arm around and Star Promenade to the ladies original position.
41-48	Two men Star Left once around and a little bit more.
49-56	Pickup the original partner with an arm around and Star Promenade back to the man's original position.
57-64	Pass Thru to a new couple and bow.

Mescolanzas

Mescolanzas are done in lines of four facing lines of four as shown below. In a large hall with a large crowd, several sets may be formed. Mescolanzas should probably not be attempted with less than twelve couples.

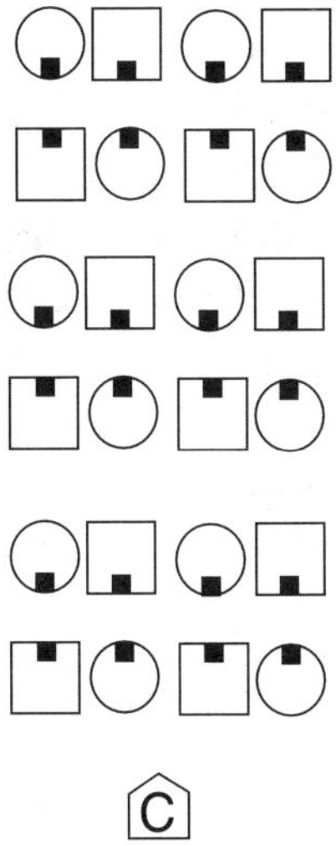

Many of these dances can be done with any combination of men and ladies in each line of four. **ONS Party Mescolanza** (Pg. 236), **Dumbarton Drums** (Pg. 237), and **Siege of Ennis** (Pg. 238) all fit into this category. This makes them very appropriate for parties where the mixture of people is heavily one gender or the other.

Every other time through some dance routines (**Dumbarton Drums**), a line of four at the head of the hall nearest the prompter and a line of four at the foot of the hall will have no facing line. The people in these lines should *Wheel Around* as a couple to face the opposite direction. They then wait until the current dance routine finishes and a new line of four moves forward to join them.

In other dances, the lines of four *Pass Thru* two lines (**ONS Party Mescolanza**). The couples at the head and foot of the hall must *Wheel Around* and be ready to meet the approaching line and start the next dance routine.

In very large halls with a large crowd, it is possible to setup the facing lines of fours like spokes of a wheel similar to Trios or a Sicilian Circle. In this configuration, each line of four proceeds only one direction.

The dances are arranged in the same instruction order as used in the square dance section. Mescolanzas can be used from the first teaching session on.

ONS Party Mescolanza

Les Henkel

Formation: Lines of four facing lines of four in columns. The lines nearest the caller have their backs to the caller.
Record: TNT 148 "Merry Oldsmobile"

Prompts

Intro	*- - - -, All 8 Circle Left*
1-8	**- - - -, - - - -**
9-16	**- - - -, - - Circle Right**
17-24	**- - - -, - - - -**
25-32	**- - - -, With your partner DoSaDo**
33-40	**- - - -, With the opposite couple Star Right**
41-48	**- - - -, Same four Star Left to home**
49-56	**- - - -, Pass Thru 2 lines**
57-64	**- - - -, All 8 Circle Left**

Description

1-16	Facing lines of four join hands and all 8 Circle Left once around.
17-32	Circle Right once around.
33-40	Face your partner and DoSaDo.
41-48	Face the opposite line and Star Right with the opposite couple.
49-56	Same four Star Left back to original facing lines of four.
57-64	Lines of four Pass Thru 2 facing lines of four and stop facing the 3rd line of four.

Note: The dance can be done with any combination of men and ladies in each line of four. When the lines reach the head or the foot of the hall, couples (pairs) Wheel Around and face the opposite direction and the approaching line of four.

Dumbarton Drums

Dorothy Shaw

Formation: Lines of four facing lines of four in columns. The lines nearest the caller have their backs to the caller.
Record: LS 172 "Dumbarton Drums"

Prompts

Intro	*- - - -, With the music Forward & Back*
1-8	**- - - -, Right couple in front sashay over**
9-16	**- - - -, With the music Forward & Back**
17-24	**- - - -, Right couple in front sashay back**
25-32	**- - - -, With the opposites Right Hand Star**
33-40	**- - - -, Same four Left Hand Star**
41-48	**- - - -, Back to lines then Forward & Back**
49-56	**- - - -, Arch to the head & duck to the foot**
57-64	**- - - -, With the music Forward & Back**

Description

1-8	Lines of four walk Forward & Back.
9-16	The right hand pair take a short step forward and sashay (slide) to the left 6 steps and then stamp 3 times. At the same time the left hand pair slide (sashay) to the right behind the other pair. Finish back in lines of four.
17-24	The lines of four go Forward & Back
25-32	The new right hand pair take a short step forward and sashay (slide) to the left 6 steps and stamp 3 times. At the same time the new left hand pair slide (sashay) to the right behind the other pair. Finish back in lines of four.
33-40	Facing pairs on each end of the lines of four should Star Right. All should finish facing across the set in their original facing lines of four.
41-48	Same four should Star Left. All should finish facing across the set in their original lines of four.
49-56	Lines of four Forward & Back
57-64	The lines facing the prompter should raise their hands to make two arches. The people in the lines with their backs to the prompter should duck through these arches and everyone proceeds forward to face a new line of four.

Note: When a line gets to the head or foot of the hall, the people face back the other way. If the couples are a male/female pair the man should put the woman back on his right side.

Siege of Ennis

Formation: Lines of four facing lines of four in columns. The lines nearest the caller have their backs to the caller.
Record: Folkcraft 1148 "Davy Davy Nick-Nock"

Prompts

Intro	*- - - -, All go Forward & Back*
1-8	**- - - -, Right couple in front sashay over**
9-16	**- - - -, All go Forward & Back**
17-24	**- - - -, Right couple in front sashay back**
25-32	**- - - -, Center 4 Star Right & ends Swing**
33-40	**- - - -, Centers Star Left & ends still Swing**
41-48	**- - - -, All go Forward & Back**
49-56	**- - - -, Arch to the head & duck to the foot**
57-64	**- - - -, All go Forward & Back**

Description

1-8	Lines of four walk Forward & Back.
9-16	The right hand pair take a short step forward and sashay (slide) to the left 6 or 8 short steps. At the same time the left hand pair slide (sashay) to the right behind the other pair. Finish back in lines of four.
17-24	The lines of four go Forward & Back
25-32	The new right hand pair take a short step forward and sashay (slide) to the left 6 or 8 short steps. At the same time the new left hand pair slide (sashay) to the right behind the other pair. Finish back in lines of four.
33-40	The center two people in each line form a Right Hand Star, while the end four people Swing the opposite person.
41-48	The center four people reverse to a Left Hand Star while the end people continue to Swing. All should finish facing across the set in their original lines of four.
49-56	Lines of four Forward & Back
57-64	The lines facing the prompter should raise their hands to form 2 arches. The people in the lines with their backs to the prompter should duck through these arches and everyone proceed forward to face a new line of four.

Note: Lines of four who do not have a facing line at the head or the foot of the hall should Wheel Around as a couple and wait for one sequence of the dance routine and then rejoin the action on the next sequence.

Ma-Bell Mescolanza

Doris & Jim Howatt & Art Seele

Formation: Lines of four facing lines of four in columns. The lines nearest the caller have their backs to the caller.
Record: Gold Star GS 712 "God Bless America"

Prompts

Intro	*- - - -, Right couple in front sashay over*
1-8	**- - - -, Right couple in front sashay back**
9-16	**- - - -, With the couple across DoSaDo**
17-24	**- - - -, Once and a half walk ahead**
25-32	**- - - -, Next couple Right & Left Thru**
33-40	**- - - -, - - Right & Left Back**
41-48	**- - - -, Same 2 Ladies Chain**
49-56	**- - - -, - - Chain Back**
57-64	**- - - -, Right couple in front sashay over**

Description

1-8	The right hand pair take a short step forward and sashay (slide) to the left 6 or 8 short steps. At the same time the left hand pair slide (sashay) to the right behind the other pair. Finish back in lines of four.
9-16	The new right hand pair take a short step forward and sashay (slide) to the left 6 or 8 short steps. At the same time the new left hand pair slide or Sashay to the right behind the other pair. Finish back in lines of four.
17-24	DoSaDo the opposite person once around.
25-32	Continue the DoSaDo one half more until the original facing people are now back to back and then each person walk forward to the next line of four.
33-40	Right & Left Thru with the facing couple.
41-48	Right & Left Thru with the same facing couple.
49-56	2 Ladies Chain across.
57-64	2 Ladies Chain back.

Note: The sashay over can be completed easily in 6 beats of music. This leaves 2 beats of music for a stamp-stamp-stamp-and.

Keene Anniversary

Chip Hendrickson

Formation: Lines of four facing lines of four in columns. The lines nearest the caller have their backs to the caller.
Record: Southerners Plus 2 RP 500 "McQuillen's Squeezebox"

Prompts

Intro	*- - - -, All go Forward & Back*
1-8	**- - - -, Straight across Right & Left Thru**
9-16	**- - - -, 2 Ladies Chain across**
17-24	**- - - -, 2 Ladies Chain along the line**
25-32	**- - - -, 4 Ladies Chain across**
33-40	**- - - -, All go Forward & Back**
41-48	**- - - -, Right & Left Thru across**
49-56	**- - - -, Pass Thru & onto the next**
57-64	**- - - -, All go Forward & Back**

Description

1-8	Lines of four go Forward & Back.
9-16	Right & Left Thru with the couple across.
17-24	2 Ladies Chain across to the opposite line.
25-32	2 Ladies Chain along the same line.
33-40	4 Ladies Chain back to their original partner.
41-48	Lines of four go Forward & Back.
49-56	Right & Left Thru with the couple across.
57-64	Lines of four Pass Thru and proceed to the next line of four.

Star Weaver

Calvin Campbell

Formation: Lines of four facing lines of four in columns. The lines nearest the caller have their backs to the caller.
Record: E-Z 714 "Stars & Stripes Forever"

Prompts

Intro	*- - - -, Center four Star Right*
1-8	**- - - -, Star Left with the outside two**
9-16	**- - - -, Star Right in the middle**
17-24	**Star Left with the other two, - - - -**
25-32	**Star Right - -, - - Partner Swing**
33-40	**- - - -, All go Forward & Back**
41-48	**- - - -, Pass Thru 2 lines**
49-56	**- - - -, DoSaDo with the opposite**
57-64	**- - - -,**

Description

1-8	Center four Star Right once around.
9-16	Each center person join their partner to Star Left with the outside four.
17-24	The same center four Star Right once and a half to the opposite end of the line and Star Left with the opposite ends.
25-32	The end Left Hand Stars complete their turn and the centers Star Right again until each couple is in their home line.
33-40	Swing your partner and finish facing the opposite line of four.
41-48	Lines go Forward & Back.
49-56	Pass Thru two lines and proceed to the third line of four.
57-64	DoSaDo the opposite person.

Note: In this routine, the couples move from one Star to the next and back in one flowing motion. The exact number of steps alotted to each Star will not be an exact 8 steps.

Portland Fancy

Unknown

Formation: Lines of four facing lines of four in columns. The lines nearest the caller have their backs to the caller.
Record: Blue Star 1585 "Midnight" **or** New England Chestnuts Side A Band 2 or Folkcraft 1243B "Portland Fancy"

Prompts

Intro	*- - - -, Join hands & Circle 8*
1-8	**- - - -, - - Full around**
9-16	**- - - -, Straight across Right & Left Thru**
17-24	**- - - -, Same four Right & Left Back**
25-32	**- - - -, Straight across 2 Ladies Chain**
33-40	**- - - -, - - Chain back**
41-48	**- - - -, All go Forward & Back**
49-56	**- - - -, Pass Thru on to the next**
57-64	**- - - -, - - Circle 8**

Description

1-16	Lines of four join hands with the opposite line of four and Circle 8 once around. Finish back in the original lines of four.
17-24	Facing couples Right & Left Thru.
25-32	Facing couples Right & Left Thru.
33-40	Facing couples 2 Ladies Chain.
41-48	Facing couples 2 Ladies Chain.
49-56	Lines of four go Forward & Back.
57-64	Pass Thru the facing line and proceed to the next lines of four.

Note: Lines of four who do not have a facing line at the head or the foot of the hall should Wheel Around as a couple and wait for one sequence of the dance routine and then rejoin the action on the next sequence.

Double Devil

Glenn & Flo Nickerson

Formation: Lines of four facing lines of four in columns. The lines nearest the caller have their backs to the caller.
Record: LS-186 "Happy Wanderer"

Prompts

Intro	*- - - -, With the opposite DoSaDo*
1-8	**- - - -, All 8 Circle Left**
9-16	**- - - -, All 8 Star Left**
17-24	**- - - -, Single File Promenade across**
25-32	**- - - -, U-turn Back & Promenade back**
33-40	**- - - -, Face across & 2 Ladies Chain**
41-48	**- - - -, - - Chain back**
49-56	**- - - -, Pass Thru 2 lines**
57-64	**- - - -, With the opposite DoSaDo**

Description

1-8	DoSaDo the dancer in the opposite line of four.
9-16	Both lines of four join hands and Circle 8 to the left.
17-24	All 8 Star Left back to the original lines of four.
25-32	Promenade Single File to the opposite side.
33-40	U-turn Back and Promenade Single File back to the original facing positions of the lines.
41-48	2 Ladies Chain across to the opposite line.
49-56	2 Ladies Chain back to their original lines.
57-64	Pass Thru two lines of four to face the third line of four.

Don's Mescolanza

Don Armstrong

Formation: Lines of four facing lines of four in columns. The lines nearest the caller have their backs to the caller.
Record: LS 308/200 "Ocean View Reel" or Grenn 12236 "Macnamara's Band"

Prompts

Intro	*- - - -, Right hand couples Right & Left Thru*
1-8	**- - - -, Same couples Right & Left back**
9-16	**- - - -, Left hand couples 2 Ladies Chain**
17-24	**- - - -, Same 2 Ladies Chain back**
25-32	**- - - -, Star Right with the couple you face**
33-40	**- - - -, Same four Star Left**
41-48	**- - - -, Everybody Forward & Back**
49-56	**- - - -, Pass Thru 2 lines**
57-64	**- - - -, Right hand couples Right & Left Thru**

Description

1-8	The right hand couples in each line of four face eachother diagonally and Right & Left Thru.
9-16	Same couples Right & Left Thru back to their original positions.
17-24	The left hand couples in each line of four face eachother diagonally and 2 Ladies Chain.
25-32	The same 2 Ladies Chain back to their original positions.
33-40	Each couple Star Right with the facing couple straight across in the opposite line.
41-48	Same four Star Left back to original lines.
49-56	Lines of four go Forward & Back.
57-64	Lines of four Pass Thru two lines and stop facing the third line of four.

Note: To add variety, switch the roles of which couples do the Right & Left Thru and the 2 Ladies Chain.

Swap Ends

Calvin Campbell

Formation: Lines of four facing lines of four in columns. The lines nearest the caller have their backs to the caller.
Record: Grenn 32053 "Ride Ride Ride"

Prompts

Intro	*- - - -, Diagonal end 2 Ladies Chain*
1-8	**- - - -, Other 2 Ladies Chain**
9-16	**- - - -, Diagonal right ends Right & Left Thru**
17-24	**- - - -, Diagonal left ends Right & Left Thru**
25-32	**- - - -, 4 Ladies Chain**
33-40	**- - - -, Lines go Forward & Back**
41-48	**- - - -, Straight across Right & Left Thru**
49-56	**- - - -, Pass Thru 2 lines**
57-64	**- - - -, Diagonal end 2 Ladies Chain**

Description

1-8	The 2 Ladies on the right ends of each line of four Chain to the opposite line.
9-16	The 2 Ladies in the center of each line of four Chain to the opposite line.
17-24	The right hand couples in each line of four Right & Left Thru with the couple diagonally to their right in the opposite line.
25-32	The left hand couple in each line of four Right & Left Thru with the couple diagonally to their left in the opposite line.
33-40	All 4 Ladies Chain back to their original partner.
41-48	Lines of four go Forward & Back.
49-56	Couples Right & Left Thru across. Everyone is now in their original line of four with their partner, but on the opposite end of the line of four.
57-64	Couples Pass Thru 2 lines of four and proceed to the third.

Route 271

Carol Kopp

Formation: Lines of four facing lines of four in columns. The lines nearest the caller have their backs to the caller.
Record: LS 322 "Cobb's Hill Reel"

Prompts

Intro	*- - - -, Two right hand couples Circle Left*
1-8	**- - - -, Two left hand couples Circle Left**
9-16	**- - - -, Two right hand couples Right & Left Thru**
17-24	**- - - -, Straight across Right & Left Thru**
25-32	**New right hand couples Right & Left Thru**
33-40	**Straight across Right & Left Thru**
41-48	**All join hands & Circle Left halfway**
49-56	**Right & Left Thru with a full turn**
57-64	**Two right hand couples Circle Left**

Description

1-8	The right hand couple in each line of four Circle Left once around with the right hand couple in the opposite line of four.
9-16	The left hand couple in each line of four Circle left once around with the left hand couple in the opposite line of four.
17-24	The right hand couple in each line of four Right & Left Thru with the right hand couple in the opposite line of four. Finish facing the opposite line of four.
25-32	Right & Left Thru with the couple in the opposite line.
33-40	The new right hand couple in each line of four Right & Left Thru with the right hand couple in the opposite line of four. Finish facing the opposite line of four.
41-48	Right & Left Thru with the couple in the opposite line.
49-56	All join hands and Circle 8 halfway.
57-64	Right & Left Thru with a full turn (see Pg. 69) and then proceed to the next line of four.

Round Dance Mixers

Mixers are dances where partners are exchanged several times during the dance. Couples dance in a large circle facing counterclockwise around the hall. The mixers chosen for this book feature routines that do not require any knowledge of how to waltz or two-step. Most of the dances only require that you be able to walk and turn around with reasonable grace. This will encourage many more people to get onto the dance floor and to enjoy good music including some mixers danced to waltz or two-step rhythm.

The real enjoyment of 'mixers' is dancing with different people to good music. For this reason, leaders may choose to use the same dance routine with different music for different groups. Teenagers are probably going to enjoy different music than people in a retirement community. Always carefully fit the music and the routine to each other. When you are trying out a new piece of music, always dance the routine through the entire recording before using it with a live audience. Some arrangements of music have extra pauses, codas, etc. thrown in at various places that can make them awkward for dancing a set routine.

Every mixer should be walked at least once before it is danced. After this walk-thru the dancers are expected to generally remember how the routine goes. The purpose of the cues is only to remind them of the sequence. As such, far fewer words are needed and the words used are only key phrases to remind the dancers what comes next. Several choices of words are illustrated in different mixers. Choose the wording that best fits your delivery.

When the dancers appear to be confident in their knowledge of the dance routine, the leader should shorten the cues. Eventually, the leader should be able to let the dancers do the routine from memory with only an occasional reminder to those who need a little extra help. The end goal is to let the dancers enjoy the music and the dance without the infringement of spoken directions any more than is absolutely necessary.

Blue Stars & Stripes Mixer

Jerry Helt

Formation: A circle of couples facing counterclockwise around the hall. Lady on the man's right hand side with near hands joined.
Record: Grenn 15011 "In the Good Old Summertime" or E-Z-174 "Stars & Stripes Forever"

Cues

Intro - - - -, - - Walk forward

1-8 - - - -, Face partner & back away
9-16 - - To the right, - - Walk forward

Description

1-8 All couples walk 7 steps forward counterclockwise around the hall. Face your partner on the 8th step.

9-16 Back away from your partner 4 steps. The men will back toward the center of the hall and the ladies will back toward the wall. Each person will walk forward diagonally to their right to meet a new partner in 4 steps to finish facing counterclockwise around the hall with the lady on the man's right hand side.

The next four mixers use only square dance terminology so the description section is not needed. They can be used to many singing call records. All of them can be used at beginner parties and during the first few learning sessions for new dancers.

Cielito Lindo Mixer

Jerry Helt

Formation: A single circle of couples facing the center of the hall, hands joined with adjacent dancers.
Record: E-Z 724 "Cielito Lindo"

Cues

Intro - - - -, Everybody Forward & Back

1-8 - - - -, With your partner DoSaDo
9-16 - - - -, All join hands & Circle Left
17-24 - - - -, - - Corner Swing
25-32 - - - -, Face center & Forward & Back

I Don't Know Why

Ken Kernen

Formation: A single circle of couples all facing the center of the hall, with hands joined with adjacent dancers.
Record: Lloyd Shaw LS E-37 or MacGregor MGR 2403 "I Don't Know Why"

Cues

Intro	*- - - -, - - Circle Left*
1-8	**- - - -, - - Circle Right**
9-16	**- - - -, Everybody Forward & Back**
17-24	**- - - -, Just the ladies Forward & Back**
25-32	**- - - -, Face the corner & DoSaDo**
33-40	**- - - -, - - - Swing**
41-48	**- - - -, - - Promenade & sing**
49-56	**- - - -, - - - -**
57-64	**- - - -, - - Circle Left**

Molly Mixer

Ken Kernen

Formation: Couples in a single circle, adjacent hands joined and facing the center of the hall.
Record: MacGregor 2028

Prompts

Intro	*- - - -, Join hands Circle Left*
1-8	**- - - -, - - Circle Right**
9-16	**- - - -, Everybody Forward & Back**
17-24	**- - - -, Face your partner & DoSaDo**
25-32	**- - - -, With your corner DoSaDo**
33-40	**- - - -, Same corner Swing**
41-48	**- - - -, - - All Promenade**
49-56	**- - - -, - - - -**
57-64	**- - Back out, join hands & Circle Left**

Bubbles Mixer

Bob Howell

Formation: A single circle of couples all facing the center of the hall and with hands joined with adjacent dancers.
Record: Grenn 15005 "I'm Forever Blowing Bubbles"

Cues

Intro	*- - - -, - - Circle Left*
1-8	**- - - -, - - Circle Right**
9-16	**- - - -, Face your partner Star Right**
17-24	**- - - -, - - Star Left**
25-32	**- - - -, - - Corner DoSaDo**
33-40	**- - - -, - - - Swing**
41-48	**- - - -, - - - Promenade**
49-56	**- - - -, - - - -**
57-64	**- - - -, - - Circle Left**

E-Z Mixer

Jack and Helen Todd

Formation: A single circle of couples all facing counterclockwise around the hall.
Record: Grenn 15008 "Sherbrooke"

Cues

Intro	*- - - -, - - Walk forward 4*
1-8	**- - Form a circle, - - Ladies to the center**
9-16	**- - Back out, - - Men to the center**
17-24	**- - Face out, new partner Swing**
25-32	**- - - -, Face forward & walk 4**

Description

1-8	Walk counterclockwise around the hall 4 steps. On the next 4 steps, couples rotate to face the center of the hall. Both people back away from the center of the hall on the last 2 steps.
9-16	The ladies walk 4 steps toward the center of the hall and then back up 4 steps to the same position in the circle.
17-24	The men walk 4 steps toward the center of the hall and turn to their left almost half around. On the next 4 steps the men walk to the corner lady diagonally to their right.
25-32	Swing the corner and finish facing counterclockwise around the hall with the lady on the man's right hand side.

Flip Flop Mixer

Jack & Helen Todd

Formation: Double circle of dancers facing partners. Men in the inside circle facing the wall. Ladies in the outside circle facing the center of the hall.
Record: Grenn 15016 "Moonlight Saving Time"

<u>Cues</u> (Two-step rhythm)

Intro - - - -, - - - Back away 3

1-4 - New partner, - Ladies clap
5-8 - Men clap , - Right elbow twice
9-12 - Left elbow twice, - Right hip twice
13-16 - Turn & Stamp, - Back away 3

<u>Description</u>

1-4 Men and ladies back away 3 quick steps in 2 beats of music. Then run forward to your new partner 3 quick steps.

5-8 The man holds out both hands with palms turned up. The lady will clap the man's right palm with her right hand on the 1st beat and will clap the man's left palm with her left hand on the 2nd beat. The lady then holds out both hands with palms turned up. The man will clap the lady's right palm with his right hand on the 3rd beat and will clap the lady's left palm with his left hand on the 4th beat.

9-12 Facing dancers touch right elbows together twice on 2 beats of music. Then dancers touch left elbows together on 2 beats of music.

13-16 Dancers touch right hips together on 2 slow beats of music. Turn 1/4 to face this partner in 2 slow steps and then stamp 3 times in 2 slow beats of music.

Note: This dance needs to be reserved for groups where rough dancing can be controlled. If you don't, someone may get over zealous with either the hand claps or bumps.

Lancash Barn Dance

Formation: Double circle of dancers. All facing partners and standing about 6 feet apart. The ladies will be in the outside circle facing the center of the hall and the men will be in the inside circle facing the wall.
Record: Lloyd Shaw LS E-35 (special 48-count music)

Cues

Intro	*On the starting musical chord bow to partner, then all Forward & Back*
1-8	**- - - -, - - Forward & Back**
9-16	**- - - -, - - Right Hand Turn**
17-24	**- - - -, - - Left Hand Turn**
25-32	**- - - -, - - Two Hand Turn**
33-40	**- - - -, - - DoSaDo**
41-48	**- - Move to the left, - - Forward & Back**

Description

1-8	Walk toward your partner 3 steps and stamp, then back away 3 steps and clap your hands twice (fast) on the 4th count.
9-16	Repeat 1-8.
17-24	Turn your partner with a Right Arm Turn. You can also use a pigeon-wing grip (fingers up, elbows down).
25-32	Partner Left Arm Turn.
33-40	Partner two hand turn. Walk around right hip to right hip.
41-48	All DoSaDo partners and back away. While backing away, move to your own left to face a new partner.

The dance goes through 4 times. To end, repeat counts 1-16 and bow to that partner.

The next two mixers are variations on a theme using the same recording and the same gimmick.

Hyll's Phrase Craze Mixer

Lou Hyll

Formation: Circle of couples facing counterclockwise around the hall. Inside hands joined, lady on man's right. Begin the dance on outside feet.
Record: Lloyd Shaw LS E-17 or LS 3323 "Phrase Craze"

Cues

Intro	*- - - Walk forward*
1-8	**- - - -, - - Face back away**
9-16	**- - Clap & stamp, One on the right DoSaDo**
17-24	**- - - -, - - - Swing**
25-32	**- - - -, - - - Walk forward**

Description

1-8	Walk forward 7 steps and face your partner on the 8th step
9-16	Back away from your partner 4 steps. On beats 5 and 6 clap hands 3 times quickly. On beats 7 and 8 stamp feet 3 times quickly. The claps and the stamps occur during the four beat long pause in the music.
17-24	Walk forward diagonally to the right to a new person and DoSaDo.
25-32	Swing this same person (new partner). Finish facing counterclockwise with the lady on the man's right and inside hands joined.

Note: The recording has a pause in the music from beats 12-16 each time through the melody. The hand claps and the stamps occur during this 4 beat pause. It is the gimmick that makes the dance different. The routine can be danced to different music, but without as great an effect.

New Craze

Ken Kernen

Formation: Couples, threesomes, or any combination of men and ladies in lines facing counterclockwise around the hall with near hands joined.
Record: Lloyd Shaw 3323 "Phrase Craze"

Cues

Intro	*- - - Promenade*
1-8	**- - - -, - - Face & back away**
9-16	**- - Clap 3 stamp 3, - - Star Right**
17-24	**- - - -, - - Star Left**
25-32	**- - Open to lines, - - - Promenade**

Description (New Craze)

1-8	Lines of people facing counterclockwise around the hall walk forward 7 steps. Each individual then faces the center of their line
9-16	In the direction you are now facing backup 4 steps. Clap your hands 3 times in 2 beats of music. Stamp your feet 3 times in 2 beats of music. These will occur during a pause in sound.
17-24	Star Right with the other dancers in your line.
25-32	Star Left and on the last 2 beats of music open out into lines facing counterclockwise around the hall. It doesn't make any difference who opens out so the arrangement of people in the line can vary each time through the dance.

Note: There is a third variation on this theme named Circle Craze in the No-Partner Dance section (Pg. 272). The three versions show how the same idea and music can be applied to different dance situations.

All Spice Mixer

Bob Howell

Formation: A single circle of couples all facing the center of the hall and with near hands joined with adjacent dancers.
Record: Grenn 15015 "Gingersnap"

Cues (Steps are slow)

Intro - - - -, - - Circle Right

1-8 - - Side close twice, - - Circle Right
9-16 - - Side close twice, - - Ladies in
17-24 - - Curtsy & back out left, - - Men in
25-32 - - Back out right, - - Circle right

Description

1-8 All join hands in a big circle and Circle Right 4 steps. Face to the center of the hall and continue to move to the right by stepping to right on right foot, close left to right, step right to side again and close with the left foot. (Side, Close, Side, Close)

9-16 Repeat 1-8

17-24 Just the ladies walk toward the center of the hall 4 steps. The ladies back away from the center of the hall 4 steps as they move to their left to stand between their former partner on the right and a new man on the left.

25-32 The men walk toward the center of the hall 4 steps. The men back away from the center of 4 steps as they move to their right to stand between two new ladies. Everyone has moved two positions around the circle.

Hi Neighbor

Jack Murtha

Formation: Couples facing counterclockwise around the hall with near hands joined. Opposite footwork for the man and the lady.
Record: Square Dancetime SD-500 or Jewel 700 "Hi Neighbor"

Cues

Intro	*- - - -, - - - Walk forward*
1-8	**- Face & slide twice, - - - Walk forward**
9-16	**- Face & slide twice, - - Back away & clap**
17-24	**- - Move right & clap, - - Back away & clap**
25-32	**- - Move right & clap, - - Walk forward**

Description

1-8	Starting on man's left foot and lady's right foot, walk forward 4 steps. Face your partner and slide to the man's left (lady's right) twice in 4 counts. (Side, Close, Side, Close)
9-16	Repeat 1-8
17-24	Back away from your partner 4 steps. Clap your hands on the 4th step. Face diagonally to your right to face a new person and walk forward 4 steps. Clap the opposite person's hands on the 4th step.
25-32	Repeat 17-24 and finish with the lady on the man's right hand side facing counterclockwise around the hall. Each dancer has now moved two positions around the hall.

Notes: A clever addition to this routine is to have people wave to each other on beat 24 and say, "Hi!". The Jewel recording has "Bay Boogie" (Pg. 267) on the flip side.

Patty Cake Polka

Formation: Double circle, facing partners, butterfly dance position, men facing the wall and ladies facing the center of the hall. Footwork is opposite for the ladies and the men throughout the dance. Instructions are given for the man. The ladies footwork is opposite

Record: Lloyd Shaw LS-228 or Windsor 4624 "Patty Cake Polka "

Cues

Intro	*- - - -, With your partner heel & toe*
1-8	**- - - Slide, - - Heel & toe**
9-16	**- - - Slide, - - - Clap hands**
17-24	**- - - -, - - - Turn Right**
25-32	**- - - -, Slide to the right & heel & toe**

Description

1-8 In butterfly position (partners facing, both hands joined, out to sides, shoulder high) touch left heel out to left, then touch left toe along side right foot. Repeat. Slide quickly counterclockwise by stepping to left on left foot, close right to left, step to left on left foot, close right to left, step left to side again and touch right alongside of left, keeping weight on left. (Heel, Toe, Heel, Toe, Slide, Slide, Slide, Touch)

9-16 Touch right heel out to right, then touch right toe along side left foot. Repeat. Slide clockwise by stepping to right on right foot, close left to right, step to right on right foot, close left to right, step right to side again and touch right alongside of left, keeping weight on left. (Heel, Toe, Heel, Toe, Slide, Slide, Slide, Close)

17-24 Clap partner's right hand 3 times, left hand 3 times, both hands 3 times, your own knees 3 times.

25-32 Hook right elbows (or Right Arm Turn) and turn your partner one full turn in 4 steps. Release and each dancer moves to the left to face the next person in 2 steps. Stamp 3 times in place (Right, Left, Right). Take butterfly position with this new partner.

Note: This dance has been modified from the original instructions to simplify the movements so the dance can be used in a larger variety of party situations. When used with adults and small children dancing together, place the children on the inside of the set and the adults on the outside. If the three hand claps are too difficult for the younger people have then clap just once for each hand. You may also want to eliminate the changing of partners.

Jiffy Mixer

Jerry & Kathy Helt

Formation: Double circle, partners facing in butterfly position. The man's back is to the center of the hall. Directions are given for the man.
Record: Lloyd Shaw LS E-35 or Windsor 4684 "Jiffy Mixer"

Cues

Intro	*- - - -, Heel & toe then side close side*
1-8	**- - - -, - - The other way back**
9-16	**- - - -, - - Chug & clap**
17-24	**- - - -, Slant right get a new partner**
25-32	**- - - -, - - Heel & toe**

Description

1-8	In butterfly position (partners facing, both hands joined, out to sides, shoulder high) touch left heel out to left, then touch left toe along side right foot. Repeat. (Heel, Toe, Heel, Toe) Move counter-clockwise by stepping to left on left foot, close right to left, step left to side again and touch right alongside of left, keeping weight on left. (Side, Close, Side, Touch) (Ladies footwork is opposite the man's)
9-16	Repeat the above action using the other foot and moving in the opposite direction.
17-24	Drop hands, partners "chug" (with weight on both feet take a short jump backwards) away from each other 4 times, man backing in towards the center of the hall, lady backing away toward the wall. Both "chug" on the down-beat of the music and clap hands on the up-beat of the music. (Chug, Clap, Chug, Clap, etc.)
25-32	Start with the left foot and move, diagonally right, to a new partner with 4 slow swaggering steps. Finish in a butterfly position to begin the dance again.

Note: People that have knee problems can just back away in 4 slow steps instead of Chug. Jiffy Mixer is an excellent dance to use where children are dancing with adults. Place the children in the middle of the circle facing the adults on the outside of the circle. You can also eliminate changing partners.

White Silver Sands

Manning & Nita Smith

Formation: Couples facing counterclockwise around the hall with near hands joined. Opposite footwork for the man and the lady.
Record: Jewel 703 or Grenn 15006 or Virgo VO-1016 "White Silver Sands"

Cues

Intro - - - -, - - Walk forward

1-8	**- - Turn backup, - - - Walk forward**
9-16	**- - Turn backup, - - - Step apart**
17-24	**- Together - Apart, - Together & ladies roll back**
25-32	**- - Step left & right, - - - Walk forward**

Description

1-8	Starting with outside feet, couples walk counterclockwise around the hall 3 steps. Turn on the 4th step to face clockwise. Backup 4 steps counterclockwise around the hall.
9-16	Couples reverse their direction of travel and walk clockwise around the hall 3 steps. Turn on the 4th step to face counterclockwise. Backup 4 steps clockwise around the hall.
17-24	Still facing counterclockwise couples step apart on the outside feet and touch the inside foot next to the outside foot in 2 beats of music. Step together on the inside feet and touch the outside foot beside the inside foot in 2 beats. Repeat the apart and together action one more time.
25-32	The lady rolls back over her right shoulder to the following man as he turns 1/4 to face her in 4 beats of music. Then they step to the man's left and touch and then to the man's right and touch. Couples should then quickly face counterclockwise arond the hall to start the dance once again.

Note: This dance routine can be used to many other records. The music should have a medium beat.

10 O'Clock Mixer

Al Brozek

Formation: Single circle of couples all facing the center of the hall. Lady on the man's right hand side.

Record: Grenn 12180 "Lay Some Happiness On Me"

Cues

Intro	*- - - -, Everybody Forward & Back*
1-8	**- - - -, Forward & Back again -**
9-16	**- - - -, Face & Heel & toe in**
17-24	**- - Heel & toe out , - - Heel & toe in**
25-32	**- - Heel & toe out, Step to the Left & all walk**
33-40	**- - - -, U-turn Back & find your partner**
41-48	**- - - -, Turn partner Left all the way around**
49-56	**- - - -, Swing new corner round & round**
57-64	**- - Face center, everybody Forward & Back**

Description

1-8	With all hands joined, starting with man's right foot and ladies left foot, everyone walk 4 steps toward the center of the hall. Then back away from the center of the hall 4 steps
9-16	Repeat 1-8 to end with the man and the lady turning 1/4 to face each other. All the ladies will be facing clockwise around the hall and the men will be facing counterclockwise.
17-24	Beginning with man's left foot and ladies right foot, do a heel and toe and then slide 2 steps toward the center of the hall. Change lead to the other foot and heel and toe and slide 2 steps toward the wall.
25-32	Repeat 17-24
33-40	Each person steps to their left to Single File Promenade around the circle. Men moving counterclockwise in the inside circle and ladies moving clockwise in the outside circle.
41-48	U-turn Back and walk the opposite direction (Men clockwise and ladies counterclockwise) until they reach their partner.
49-56	Turn partner with a Left Arm Turn once around and proceed to the new corner.
57-64	Swing the corner, put her on the man's right hand side to end facing the center of the hall as new partners.

Notes: See "Patty Cake Polka" (Pg 259) for more detail on heel & toe step. The flip side to this record also contains an easy level singing call.

Sunshine Mixer

Marie Armstrong

Formation: Couples in a circle, lady on man's right, facing counterclockwise around the circle, with near hands joined. The footwork is opposite throughout the dance with each person starting on the outside foot. Directions are given for the man.

Record: Lloyd Shaw LS E-35 "You Are My Sunshine"

Cues

Intro	*- - - -, - - Forward 4*
1-8	**- - Side close twice, - - Forward 4**
9-16	**- - Side close twice, - - Clap right & left**
17-24	**- - Both & knees, - - DoSaDo**
25-32	**- - Move right, - - Forward 4**

Description

1-8	Starting on outside foot for both the man and the lady, walk forward 3 steps. Face your partner on the 4th step and join both hands with your partner. The facing couples move counterclockwise around the circle with a step to the man's left on left foot, close right foot to left foot, step again to left on left foot, close right foot to left foot. (Side, Close, Side, Close) Finish by quickly facing counterclockwise around the circle.
9-16	Repeat 1-8 but finish facing partner.
17-24	Clap your partner's right hands 3 times, left hands 3 times, both hands 3 times, clap your own knees 3 times.
25-32	DoSaDo this partner and slide to the left to meet a new partner. Face counterclockwisearound the hall with this new partner.

Note: If people have difficulty with the hand clap sequence, replace this sequence with a slower version. Alternate hand clap sequence: Clap own hands once, clap right hands with (new) partner once; Clap own hands once, clap left hands with partner once; Clap own hands, clap both hands with partner; Clap own hands three times in the rhythm: clap...clap, clap. The cues will fit both versions.

C. J. Mixer

Calvin & Judy Campbell

Formation: Couples in a circle, lady on man's right, facing counterclockwise around the hall. Varsouvianna dance position (see note). Footwork is the same for the man and the lady. Directions are given for the man.
Record: LS 3316 "C.J. Mixer"

Cues

Intro	*- - - -, - - - -, - - - -, - - - Walk Forward*
1-8	**- - Turn backup, - - - Go forward**
9-16	**- - Turn backup, - - - Star Left**
17-24	**- - - -, - - - Star Right**
25-32	**- - - -, With new partner walk forward**

Description

1-8	In varsouvianna position, walk forward 3 steps counterclockwise around the hall. While maintaining the hand holds, turn 1/2 right face individually on 4th step to face clockwise with lady on outside and the man on inside. The lady is now on the left side of the man. Back up 4 steps counterclockwise around the circle. (A total of 8 steps traveling counterclockwise.)
9-16	Walk forward around the circle clockwise 3 steps and turn 1/2 left face on the 4th step to face counterclockwise. This places the lady back on the right side of the man. Back-up clockwise with 4 steps. (A total of 8 steps traveling clockwise.)
17-24	Drop right hands, but keep left hands joined and guide the lady to the inside of the circle making a Left Hand Star (2 hand Star). Turn the Two Hand Star for 6 steps; then turn around in 2 steps and Star Right.
25-32	Turn the Right Hand Star for 6 steps. On steps 7 and 8, the man moves back (clockwise) and lady forward (counterclockwise) to a new partner and resume varsouvianna position ready to repeat the dance.
Ending	Walk forward 3 steps and turn. Backup 4 steps. Walk forward 3 steps and turn. Backup 3 steps. Face your partner & bow.

Note: Varsouvianna position–The lady is on the man's right hand side. The man's right hand and arm is extended behind the lady's back slightly above the shoulder of the lady and holding the lady's right hand. The man should be careful to not rest his right arm on the lady's right shoulder. The lady's left hand and arm is in front of the man at waist level holding the man's left hand.

Bye Bye Blues

Ken Kernen

Formation: Circle of couples facing counterclockwise around the hall. Lady on the man's right and near hands joined. Directions are written for the man's position.
Record: Grenn 15009 "Bye Bye Blues"

Cues

Intro	*- - - - , - - - Forward 4*
1-8	**- - Face & Slide, - - Walk the other way**
9-16	**- - Face & Slide, - - Rock & Touch**
17-24	**- Twice - -, - - DoSaDo**
25-32	**- - Slide to the Right, - - Forward 4**

Description

1-8 Starting on the outside feet, couples walk 3 steps counterclockwise around the hall. On the 4th step face your partner and move counterclockwise around the big circle with a step to the left on left foot, close right foot to left foot, step again to left on left foot, touch right foot to left foot. (Side, Close, Side, Touch) Finish by quickly facing clockwise around the circle.

9-16 Starting on the outside foot, couples walk 3 steps clockwise around the hall. On the 4th step face your partner and move clockwise around the circle with a step to the right on right foot, close left foot to right foot, step again to right on right foot, close left foot to right foot. (Side, Close, Side, Touch)

17-24 The facing couples step left (counterclockwise) on the left foot (right for lady) and touch right foot beside left. Step right and touch left foot beside right. Step left and touch right foot beside left. Step right and touch left foot beside right. (Rock Left, Rock Right, Rock Left, Rock Right)

25-32 DoSaDo your partner. On the last 2 beats of the phrase, slide to the right and face counterclockwise around the hall with a new partner. Lady on the man's right hand side.

Dixie Melody Mixer

Bob Van Antwerp

Formation: Circle of couples facing counterclockwise around the hall. Lady on the man's right hand side and near hands joined.
Record: Grenn 16013 or CEM 37036 "Dixie Melody"

Cues

Intro	*- - - -, - - Walk 3*
1-8	**Backup 3 turn one quarter, - - Chase the men**
9-16	**- - Chase the ladies, - - Rock Left & Right**
17-24	**- - Rock again, - - Back away 4**
25-32	**- - To the right 4, - - Walk 3**

Description

1-8 Starting on outside feet, couples walk forward 3 steps and touch on the 4th. Backup 3 steps and both dancers turn 1/4 left face to face the center of the hall with the lady Single File behind the man.

9-16 The lady chases the man 3 steps toward the center of the hall and both pivot around on the 4th step. The man chases the lady 3 steps toward the wall. The lady turns to face the man on the 4th step.

17-24 In butterfly hand position, the couples step to the man's left (lady's right) and touch and then to the man's right and touch in 4 beats of music (Rock Left, Rock Right). Repeat the same left and right rocking motions in the next 4 beats of music.

25-32 Dancers back away 3 steps and touch. The ladies will be backing toward the wall and the men will be backing toward the center of the hall. All dancers face diagonally to the right and walk 4 steps to meet a new partner. Finish by facing counterclockwise around the hall with the lady on the man's right hand side near hands joined.

Bay Boogie

Calvin & Judy Campbell

Formation: A single circle of couples all facing the center of the hall, with hands joined with adjacent dancers.
Record: Jewel 700 "San Francisco Bay Blues"

__Cues__

Intro	*- - - -, - - Circle Left*
1-8	**Roll Away 1/2 Sashay, - - Circle Left**
9-16	**Roll Away 1/2 Sashay, - - Just the men forward**
17-24	**- - Just the ladies forward, - - All backup**
25-32	**- - Face & clap, - - - DoSaDo**
33-40	**- - - -, - - Swing**
41-48	**- - - -, - - - Walk forward & kick**
49-56	**- - Back & touch, - - - Promenade**
57-64	**- - - -, Back out Circle Left**

__Description__

1-8	Couples Circle Left 4 steps. Roll Away 1/2 Sashay with the lady on the right in 4 steps.
9-16	Repeat 1-8
17-24	Just the men walk toward the center of the hall 4 steps and stop. Just the ladies walk forward toward the center of the hall 4 steps to join the man.
25-32	Both the men and the ladies backup together 3 steps and turn to face each other on the 4th step. Clap right hands with your partner on 5. Clap left hands with your partner on 6. Clap both hands with your partner on 7. Lean back and snap your fingers on 8 and say "Hey". (Right, Left, Both, Hey)
33-40	DoSaDo your partner
41-48	Swing your partner. Finish facing counterclockwise around the hall with the lady on the man's right hand side and near hands joined.
49-56	Walk 3 steps forward & kick (swing) on the 4th beat. Backup 3 steps and touch on the 4th beat.
57-64	Promenade 6 steps. On steps 7 and 8 back out to form the big circle.

Note: Hi Neighbor (Pg. 258) is on the flip side of this record.

The Light in the Window

Dorothy Stott Shaw

Formation: Couples in a circle, lady on man's right, facing counterclockwise around the hall. Varsouvianna dance position. Footwork opposite throughout, each starting with outside foot.
Record: Lloyd Shaw LS- 220 "The Light in the Window"

<u>Cues</u> (waltz)

Intro *- - -, - - -, - - -, - - Run forward*

1-12 **- - Turn, - - Backup, - - Pause, - - Run forward**
13-24 **- - Turn, - - Backup, - - Hands over, - - Balance apart**
25-36 **- - Change places, - - Apart, - - Change places, - Apart - Star Right**
37-48 **- - -, - - New partner, - - Get set, - - Run forward**

<u>Description</u>

1-12 Run forward 3 steps counterclockwise around the hall. While maintaining varsouvianna position each person should turn right face with 3 steps to end facing clockwise around the hall. (The lady is now on the man's left hand side.) Backup 5 steps counterclockwise around the hall and pause on the 6th step.

13-24 Without turning around, run forward 3 steps clockwise around the hall. Each person should turn left face to end facing counterclockwise around the hall (The lady is now on the man's right hand side again.) Back-up clockwise around the hall 3 steps. On the next 3 steps lift the joined right hands over the lady's head dropping the left hands and turn to face each other keeping the right hands joined. The man's back is to the center of the hall and the lady is facing him. You should be standing almost nose to nose with your partner.

25-36 Step away from your partner on man's left foot (lady's right foot), touch toe to floor and hold 2 counts. Change places with the lady turning left face under the joined right hands while the man turns right face. Both people take 3 steps. (The man is on outside of circle and the lady is on inside.) Repeat these two measures back to place keeping right hands joined.

37-48 Step away from your partner on man's left foot (lady's right foot), touch toe to floor and hold 2 counts. Change places with the lady turning left face under the joined right hands while the man turns right face. Both people take 3 steps. (The man is on outside of circle and the lady is on inside.) Step apart & Star Right about 3/4 around in 3 steps. Offer your free left hand to on-coming new partner. The man moves clockwise around the hall to the new lady. The lady moves counterclockwise around the hall to the new man. With a sweeping left face turn the man takes the lady's right hand in his right and using 3 steps (lady steps in place) moves back to varsouvianna position facing counterclockwise around the hall.

Note: The first half of "C. J. Mixer" (Pg. 264) and "Light in the Window use the same dance position and body movement. "C. J. Mixer" should be taught first to enable the dancers to master the body motion before waltz rhythm is added.

Manning's Mixer

Manning & Nita Smith

(Modified slightly by Calvin Campbell)

Formation: Circle of couples facing counterclockwise around the hall. Lady on the man's right hand side and near hands joined.
Record: Grenn 15011 or LS 3319/3320 "In the Good Old Summertime"

Cues

Intro	*- - - -, - - Walk forward*
1-8	**- - Side close twice, - - Walk forward**
9-16	**- - Side close twice, - - Walk forward**
17-24	**- - Back away, lady on your right DoSaDo**
25-32	**- - Two faced circle, Step forward & step back**
33-40	**- - Half by the Left, Step forward & step back**
41-48	**- - Half by the Left, Wrong Way Right & Left Grand**
49-56	**- - Five hands, - - Swing number 5**
57-64	**- - - -, - - Walk forward**

Description

1-8	Starting on outside feet, couples walk forward 4 steps. Turn to face your partner and side close to the man's left 2 times. (In the original dance this was a vine step)
9-16	Repeat 1-8
17-24	Walk forward 3 steps and turn on the 4th step to face partner. Back way from your partner 4 steps. Men backing toward the center of the hall and ladies toward the wall.
25-32	Face diagonally to the right and DoSaDo a new person in 8 steps. Finish in a big circle with men facing out and the ladies facing in with adjacent hands joined (elbows should be slightly bent and palms of the hands should be touching with fingers pointing up). The new person is on the right hand of the man and the former partner is on the left.
33-40	Step forward on left, close right foot to left, step back on left, close right to left in 4 beats of music. Turn the original partner Half Left in 4 steps and join right hands with a new person to complete the circle. Men are now facing the center of the hall and the ladies are facing the wall.
41-48	Repeat 33-40. Finish with the men facing the wall and the ladies facing the center of the hall.
49-56	Beginning with the right hand do a wrong way Right & Left Grand (clockwise for men and counterclockwise for ladies) for 4 hands (8 steps).
57-64	Swing the 5th Lady you meet. Finish the Swing by placing the lady on the man's right hand side and face counterclockwise around the hall
Ending:	In open position walk forward 3 steps and turn to face your partner on 4th step. Back away 3 steps and bow.

Vine step—face partner and step to the side on the man's (lady's right) foot, cross right behind left, step to left on left counterclockwise, cross right in front of left to end facing counterclockwise.

No-Partner Dances

Dances that do not require a partner are essential for any community style dance program. Some people attend the dance without partners. Some people with partners have times when they wish to rest and their partner does not wish to rest. No-partner dances enable people to participate as much as they choose.

Many no-partner dances are referred to as "line dances" because people tend to form long lines facing in the same direction when they begin the dance. They are also called "solo dances", which is another way of saying no partner is needed.

This section also includes no-partner dances done from circles. Many international folk dances also do not require partners, but usually folk dancers tend to specialize in folk-dancing and so these dances will be left to their pleasure.

The collection of no-partner dances included in this text book is limited to dances that do not require complicated footwork. Whenever possible, technical dance terminology was eliminated. Any one of these dances should be able to be learned by the average dancer in 3-5 minutes.

You will notice that the dances do not include cues or prompts. All of them can be taught by demonstrating the dance routine and walking the dancers through the steps. Following this, the dancers usually need only an occasional reminder word or two to help them remember the routine.

The music recommended for each dance has proven to be popular over a long period of time. Keep in mind that the same dance routine may dance very well to more modern music. One of the advantages to using no-partner dances is the ability to dance the same routine to a number of different tunes.

Amos Moses #1

Formation: No partners. All start facing the same direction in loose lines.
Record: RCA 447-0896 "Amos Moses"

Description

1-4 Touch the right heel to the floor and bring the foot back and stand on it. Touch the left heel to the floor and bring the foot back and stand on it.

5-8 Starting with the right foot, walk 2 steps forward and pivot on the 3rd step to make a 1/4 right face turn. End with your weight on the left foot for the 4th count.

Circle Craze

Ken Kernen

Formation: Circle of dancers in Single File Promenade position.
Record: Lloyd Shaw 3323 "Phrase Craze"

Description

1-8 All Promenade Single File 7 steps counterclockwise around the hall and face the center of the hall.

9-16 Back away from the center of the hall 4 steps. Clap your hands 3 times in 2 beats of music. Stamp your feet 3 times in 2 beats of music. This will occur during a pause in sound.

17-24 Ladies walk into the center 4 long steps and clap their hands on the 4th step. Back out 4 short steps.

25-32 Men walk into the center 4 long steps and stamp their foot on the 4th step. Back out 4 short steps to join the ladies. All face quickly to the right to start the dance over again.

The Texas Freeze

Formation: No partners. All start facing the same direction in loose lines.
Record: MCA 53546 "Elvira "

Description

1-4 Step to the right. Close the left foot to the right and change weight to the left foot, step to the right again and touch the left toe beside the right foot. (Side, Close, Side, Touch)

5-8 Step to the left. Close the right foot to the left and change weight the right foot. Step to the left again and touch the right toe beside the right foot. (Side, Close, Side, Touch)

9-16 Starting with the right foot back up 3 steps and wait for 1 beat. Step forward on the left foot and freeze in place for 3 beats and then quickly turn 1/4 left face on the planted left foot.

Raunchy

(Texas Hustle)

Formation: No partners. All start facing the same direction in loose lines.
Record: Circle D 702B "Raunchy"

Description

1-4 Starting with the right foot. Step to the right. Close the left foot to the right and change weight to the left foot. Step to the right again and touch the left toe beside the right foot (Side, Close, Side, Touch).

5-8 Starting with the left foot. Step to the left. Close the right foot to the left and change weight to the right foot. Step to the left again and touch the right toe beside the right foot (Side, Close, Side, Touch).

9-12 Starting with the right foot back up 3 steps (Right, Left, Right) and touch left beside right foot.

13-16 Rock forward on left foot, rock back on right foot. Rock forward on left foot and pivot 1/4 left face.

San Antonio Stroll

Formation: Dancers in a circle, facing around the hall counterclockwise.
Record: MCA-60188 or Red Boot 195 "San Antonio Stroll"

Description

1-8 Step to the left, cross right foot behind the right foot. Step to the left again. Swing right foot across in front of left (Vine Left). Step to the right, cross left foot behind the right foot. Step to the right again. Swing left foot across in front of the left (Vine Right).

9-16 In place, step left and touch right toe to left instep. Step right and touch left toe to right instep. Repeat again (Rock Left, Rock Right).

17-24 Walk 3 steps toward the center of the hall the hall (starting with left foot) and kick right foot forward (Left, Right, Left, Kick). Backup 3 steps and touch left toe to floor. (Right, Left, Right, Touch)

25-32 Face counterclockwise and stroll 4 slow steps forward and finish facing the center of the hall again.

Hully Gully

Ben Highberger

Formation: Scattered around the floor all facing the same wall to start.
Record: RB-3017 "Pink Cadillac " or Col 4-42529 "Little Black Book"

Description

1-8 Starting with the right foot, step to right. Step behind with the left foot. Step to the side with the right foot (Vine Right). The 4th step is a short kick with the left foot. The same action is repeated moving to the left and starting with the left foot, crossing behind with the right foot, stepping to the side with the left foot and kicking forward with the right foot. (Vine Left)

9-20 Starting with the right foot take 2 slow steps forward, then 3 quick steps with a right face turn on the 3rd quickstep & kick forward with the left foot on the 4th count. Back up 3 steps and pause 1 beat with the weight on the left foot.

Notes: Some people have problems with the vine step in counts 1-8. This step can easily be replaced with a side, close, side, touch as used in the "Texas Freeze" on page 272.

Amos Moses #2

Description

1-4 Touch the right heel to the floor and bring the foot back and stand on it. Touch the left heel to the floor and bring the foot back and stand on it.

5-8 The general direction of the first 3 steps is forward from the starting point. The following body movements keep your feet from getting tangled. Starting with the right foot step forward and turn your body left so the next step can be taken with the left foot passing behind the right foot. The 3rd step with the right foot moves straight to the side. On the 4th step turn halfway around. The entire movement finishes with everyone facing the original right hand wall.

Note: There are probably a dozen other variations to this dance. The two main rules are: 1) Don't interfere with anyone else and 2) Everyone should end facing the same direction.

Rocky Mountain Scramble

Calvin & Judy Campbell

Formation: No partners. All start facing the same direction in loose lines.
Record: YR 102 "Popps Hoedown"or Columbia "Wild Man" 38-74748

Description

1-4 Step to right with right foot, step behind right foot with left foot, step to right with right foot and touch the toe of the left foot beside the right foot (Vine Right).

5-8 Step to left with left foot, step behind left foot with right foot, step to left with left foot and touch the toe of the right foot to the floor beside the left foot (Vine Left).

9-12 Starting with the right foot, take 3 steps forward (Right, Left, Right) and swing the left foot forward.

13-16 Starting with the left foot, take 3 steps backward (Left, Right, Left) and touch the right toe to the floor beside the left foot.

17-20 Lightly touch the right toe to the floor 3 times, moving in a diamond pattern (forward, to the side and on to the back). Finish by bringing the right foot up beside the left foot and changing weight to the right foot (Point, Point, Point, Close).

21-24 Lightly touch the left toe to the floor 3 times, moving in a diamond pattern (forward, to the side and on to the back). Finish by bringing the left foot up beside the right foot and touch the left toe to the floor (Point, Point, Point, Touch).

25-28 Starting with the left foot, take 2 slow steps forward (Left, Right) in 4 beats of music.

29-32 Take 3 quick steps (Left, Right, Left) forward and on the 3rd step with the left foot, turn 1/4 left face to end with the weight on the left foot and the right knee lifted slightly, ready for the routine to begin again.

Note: This dance has more of the country or western (CW) feel and dancing very nicely to many CW recordings.

Alley Cat

Formation: No partners. All start facing the same direction in loose lines.
Record: Atco 62-6059 "Ally Cat" or Collectables 3170B "Popcorn"

Description

1-4 Point right toe to right and then touch right toe to the instep of the left foot. Repeat a second time (Right foot twice).

5-8 Repeat the above using the left foot. (Left foot twice)

9-12 Point right toe back and then touch right toe to the instep of the left foot. Repeat a second time. (Touch back right twice)

13-16 Repeat 9-12 using the left foot (Touch back left twice).

17-20 Raise the right foot and cross the right knee in front of the left knee twice. Finish with your weight on the right foot (Right knee twice).

21-24 Raise the left foot and cross the left knee in front of the right knee twice. Finish with your weight on the left foot (Left knee twice).

25-28 Raise right foot and cross the right knee in front of the left knee. Finish with weight on the right foot. Raise left foot and cross left knee in front of right knee. Finish with weight on both feet (Right knee then Left knee).

29-32 Clap both hands on the first count and wait one count. Bend knees slightly and jump 1/4 turn facing to the right. On the last beat of the phrase, shift the weight to the left foot ready to begin the dance over (Turn & Clap).

Electric Slide

Formation: No partners. All start facing the same direction in loose lines.
Record: Col 2607 "Electric Boogie" or Capitol S7-57797 "Old Time Rock & Roll"

Description

1-4 Starting with the right foot, slide 3 short steps to the right and pause on the 4th.

5-8 Starting with the left foot, slide 3 short steps to the left and pause on the 4th.

9-16 Starting with the right foot back up 3 steps and wait for one beat. Step forward on the left foot and tap the right foot in place on the floor. It helps to also lean forward. Step back on the right foot and tap the left foot on the floor.

17-18 Step forward on the right foot and then quickly turn 1/4 left face on the planted left foot.

Notice that the last action is only 2 beats of music. The dance starts at a different place in the musical phrase each time. The title "Electric Slide" has been applied to several dance routines and the steps modified to meet the mood of the music. In some areas, the slide steps to the right and the left are changed to a vine right and a vine left. The actions and music described above are the original dance and still the best choice when used with younger people.

Chap Slap

Jerry & Kathy Helt

Formation: No partners. All start facing the same direction in loose lines.
Record: RCA GB-11986 "East Bound and Down"

Description

Intro	8 beats
1-8	With the right foot heel & toe twice. Slide to the right 4 times.
9-16	Repeat 1-8 with the left foot.
17-24	Slap right thigh (chap) with right hand 3 times in 2 beats of music. Slap left thigh (chap) with left hand 3 times in 2 beats of music. Slap both thighs (chaps) 3 times in 2 beats of music. Clap hands together 3 times in 2 beats of music.
25-32	Circle to the right with 3 quick steps followed by a pause on the 4th count (two-step). Repeat 4 times to finish 3/4 of the way around and facing the original left hand wall.

New York, New York

Formation: No partners. All start facing the same direction in loose lines.
Record: MCA 60194

Description

1-4	Step to right with right foot, step behind with left foot, step to right with right foot and touch the toe of the left foot beside the right foot (Vine Right) .
5-8	Step to left with left foot, step behind with right foot, step to left with left foot and touch the toe of the right foot to the floor beside the left foot (Vine Left) .
9-12	Step forward on right foot. Rock back on left foot. Step forward on right foot and kick left foot forward.
13-16	Step on left foot and pivot 1/4 right face with 2 more steps (Right, Left). Touch right toe to the floor on the 4th count.

Ghostbusters

Formation: No partners. All start facing the same direction in loose lines.
Record: ASF-9344 "Ghostbusters"

Description

1-4	Touch the right heel to the floor and bring the foot back and stand on it. Touch the left heel to the floor and bring the foot back and stand on it.
5-8	Repeat with right & left foot.
9-12	Strut 3 steps forward. Turn 1/4 right face on the 4th step.
13-16	Step backward 4 steps (Right, Left, Right, Left).

Sunny Mood

Grant Longley

Formation: No partners. All start facing the same direction in loose lines.
Record: Grenn 15015 "Gingersnap"

Description

1-4	Starting with the right foot. Step to the right. Close the left foot to the right and change weight to the left foot. Step to the right again and touch the left toe beside the right foot (Side, Close, Side, Touch).
5-8	Starting with the left foot. Step to the left. Close the right foot to the left and change weight to the right foot. Step to the left again and touch the right toe beside the right foot (Side, Close, Side, Touch).
9-16	Strut 4 slow steps forward.
17-20	Step to the right, cross right foot behind the left foot. Step to the right again. Swing left foot across in front of the left (Vine Right).
21-24	Step to the left, cross left foot behind the right foot. Step to the left again. Swing right foot across in front of left (Vine Left).
25-32	Walk in a semicircle to the right in 4 slow strutting steps and finish facing the opposite direction.

Bye Bye Blues

Grant Longley

Formation: No partners. All start facing the same direction in loose lines.
Record: Grenn 15009 "Bye Bye Blues"

Description

1-4 Touch the left heel to the floor and bring the foot back to place and stand on it. Touch the right heel to the floor and bring the foot back to place and stand on it.

5-8 With feet together, lean forward until you weight is off your heels and separate the heels and then bring them back together 2 times.

9-16 Repeat 1-8.

17-24 Step forward on the left foot, touch right toe forward, step backward on the right foot and touch the left toe backward (Charleston step). Repeat one more time.

25-32 Strut in a small circle moving to the left 8 steps, waving both hands in the air and return to face forward again.

The Lion Sleeps Tonight

Formation: No partners. All start facing the same direction in loose lines.
Record: OS 13119 "The Lion Sleeps Tonight"

Description

1-4 Starting with the right foot. Step to the right. Close the left foot to the right and change weight to the left foot. Step to the right again and touch the left toe beside the right foot. (Side, Close, Side, Touch)

5-8 Starting with the left foot. Step to the left. Close the right foot to the left and change weight to the right foot. Step to the left again and touch the right toe beside the right foot. (Side, Close, Side, Touch)

9-12 Run forward 2 steps (Right, Left). On the 3rd step with the right foot, pivot 1/4 right face. On the 4th count hop backward on the same right foot. (Chug)

13-16 Backup 3 steps (Left, Right, Left) and touch the right foot to the floor.

California Strut

Ken Kernen

Formation: No partners. All start facing the same direction in loose lines.
Record: Eric 2024 "California Strut" or 2023 "A Fifth of Beethoven"

Description

1-4	Starting with the left foot, take 3 steps forward (Left, Right, Left) and touch the right toe to the floor beside the left foot.
5-8	Starting with the right foot, take 3 steps backward (Right, Left, Right) and touch the left toe to the floor beside the left foot.
9-16	Repeat 1-8.
17-20	Rock diagonally left forward as you step on the left foot. Rock back on the right. Repeat one more time (Rock, Rock, Rock, Rock).
21-24	Roll left face one complete turn in 3 steps (Left, Right, Left) and touch right foot next to left foot or 4th count. Also clap hands together on 4th count.
25-28	Rock 4 times starting with the right foot. See 17-20.
29-32	Roll right one complete turn in 3 steps (Right, Left, Right) and touch left foot next to right foot on 4th count as you again clap hands together.

Cotton-Eyed Joe

Formation: Lines or couples, hands joined, arms around waist, or hands on shoulders of adjacent dancers, all facing same direction. Identical footwork.
Record: LS E-35 or PAD 137 (2 vocal versions) "Cotton-Eyed Joe"

Description

1-4	With weight on left foot swing right foot across in front of left, keeping right knee bent and right foot almost touching left, then kick forward with right foot, straightening right leg.
5-8	Backup 3 short steps (Right, Left, Right, Pause).
9-12	Repeat the action in counts 1-2 using opposite footwork.
13-16	Backup 3 short steps (Left, Right, Left, Pause).
17-32	Repeat all the above.
33-64	Run forward 3 quick steps and pause on the 4th count (Two-step). Repeat 8 times.

Note: This is the Texas version of this popular dance and it is danced with much enthusiasm and vigor! It can also be danced as a couple dance and in several other combinations of people.

The Bunny Hop

Formation: No partners. All join in a line behind the leader. Each person places their hands on the hips of the person in front of them (conga line).
Record: LS E-47 or Capitol 6026 or MacGregor 6995 "The Bunny Hop"

Description

1-4 All touch right heel to the right. Bring foot back along-side left foot. Repeat and then finish with the weight on the right foot.
5-8 All touch left heel to the left. Bring foot back along-side right foot. Repeat and finish with weight on both feet.
9-12 On both feet jump forward, pause, jump back, pause.
13-16 Then jump (quickly) forward 3 times and pause.

Hokey Pokey

Formation: Single circle, everyone facing the center. It can also be done in scattered groups.
Record: LS E-38 or Capitol 6026 or MacGregor 6995 "Hokey Pokey"

Song:

You put your right foot in. You put your right foot out. You put your right foot in and you shake it all about. You do the Hokey Pokey and you turn yourself about. That's what it's all about.

Description

1-8 Each person turns to place their right foot toward the center of the circle and then turns halfway around to place the right foot away from the center of the circle.
9-16 Turn halfway again and place the right foot in and then lift the foot and shake it.
17-24 Hold your hands over your head and turn once around while shaking your hands in the air.
25-32 Clap your hands 4 or more times.

Note: You may wish to reverse direction to keep from getting dizzy. In place of the Right Foot you can substitute Left Foot, Right Hand, Left Hand, Right Elbow, Left Elbow, Head, Whole Self and Backside. The Capitol Records version has a vocal.

Ding Dong Daddy

Formation: Seated, or standing, in a circle facing center,or in lines facing the leader. The leader demonstrates the dance and the audience follows.
Record: LS 3324 or E-14 "Ding Dong Daddy"

Description

Intro Wait 8 counts

Part A

1-4 Clap knees twice. Clap hands twice.
5-8 Slide right hand over left twice (palms down). Slide left hand over right twice.
9-12 Pound right fist over left fist twice. Pound left fist over right fist twice.
13-16 Touch right palm to left elbow twice. Touch left palm to right elbow twice.
17-32 Repeat all of the above from 1-16.

Part B

1-4 Make swimming motion (crawl stoke) with right arm (2 beats) then with left arm (2 beats).
5-8 Make swimming motion (breast stroke) with both arms twice.
9-12 Make motion of twirling a lasso with right arm, 4 times.
13-16 Twirl lasso with left arm, 4 times.
17-20 Make hitchhike motion with right arm, thumb extended (4 beats).
21-24 Hitchhike motion with left arm (4 beats).
25-28 Make motion of catching a fly (2 beats), place the fly on the opposite hand (2 beats).
29-32 Swat the fly (2 beats) and blow it away (2 beats).

Note: The final time through the tune there is a extra line. You catch the fly a second time, swat it and lick it off your hand.

Dance of the Little Birds

Formation: With or without partner, usually done in a circle.
Record: LS E-39 or Satril SA-1006 "Dance of the Little Birds"

Description

Part A

1-2	Tap fingers together like a beak of a chick, "Cheep, cheep, cheep, cheep."
3-4	Flap your elbows up and down, "Flap, flap, flap, flap."
5-6	Wiggle your hips, "Wiggle, wiggle, wiggle, wiggle."
7-8	Clap your hands, "Clap, clap, clap, clap ."
9-32	Repeat 3 more times.

Part B

1-16	Find a partner and join right elbows and turn clockwise.
17-32	Turn by the left elbow and turn counterclockwise.

Note: The elbow turn can be replaced by stars with any number of people or circle left and right in a group of four or more, etc. The leader can also have people change partners. With small children, try having them extend their arms like wings and swoop about.

Hallelujah

Formation: No partners. All start facing the same direction in loose lines.
Record: Curb WBS8877 "Hallelujah"

Description

1-4	Sway left, right, left, right with hands raised up.
5-8	Face 1/4 right face and walk 4 slow steps.
9-12	Face the center of the Repeat 1-4.
13-16	Face 1/4 left face and walk 4 slow steps.
17-20	Face the front of the hall and walk 4 slow steps forward. On the last step stretch right heel forward and lean back with your hands out.
21-24	Backup 3 steps and on the 4th beat touch your right toe to the floor in back.
25-28	Walk forward left, right and then cut left foot over right and step back on the right foot.
29-32	Repeat 25-28

Slush

Formation: No partners. All start facing the same direction in loose lines.
Record: Oldies F-2005 "Ya Ya"

Description

1-4 Step to left with left foot, step behind with right foot, step to left with left foot and touch the toe of the right foot beside the left foot (Vine Left) .

5-8 Step to right with right foot, step behind with left foot, step to right with right foot and touch the toe of the left foot to the floor beside the right foot (Vine Right) .

9-12 Repeat 1-4

13-16 Step to right with right foot, step behind with left foot, step to right with right foot. (Vine Right) On the last beat (16) you lift the left arm up and arch it over your head, while you lift the left heel up behind the right knee and slap it with your right hand. (The Old Soft Shoe style)

17 Step on the left foot while you bring the right knee up waist high in front of you. At the same time touch the raised knee with your right elbow and touch your forehead with your right fist. (Thinker's pose)

18 Step on the right foot while turning 1/4 to the right and kick the left leg straight out in front while you clap your hands under the raised leg.

Note: The last 3 steps occur quickly and will require some coordination. Once the moves are mastered they balance each other very well.

Other Dance Formations

Some dance formations do not either fit easily into a category or there aren't enough good examples to warrant a separate section. These dances have ended up in this section.

Clopton Bridge

English

Formation: Four couple contra lines. Four men on the prompter's right facing four ladies on the prompter's left.
Record: LS E-27 "Clopton Bridge"

Prompts

Intro	*- - First lady, fourth man turn Right Hand Around*
1-8	**- - - -, Same two Left Hand Around**
9-16	**- - 1st man, 4th lady Right Hand Around**
17-24	**- - - -, Same two Left Hand Around**
25-32	**- - - -, Center four Star Right**
33-40	**- - - -, Same four Star Left**
41-48	**- - - -, Head couple slide to the foot**
49-56	**- - - -, All two hand turn your partner**
57-64	**- - 1st lady, 4th man turn Right Hand Around**

Description

1-8	The lady in each line of four closest to the prompter (top lady) and the man in the opposite line of four on the far end away from the prompter (foot man) Arm Turn Right.
9-16	Same four Arm Turn Left and finish back in a line of four.
17-24	The man in each line of four closest to the prompter (top man) and the lady in the opposite line of four on the far end away from the prompter (foot lady) Arm Turn Right.
25-32	Same four Arm Turn Left and finish back in a line of four.
33-40	The center two people in each facing line of four Star Right.
41-48	The same four Star Left and finish back in own line of four.
49-56	The top or head couple will join both hands with the opposite and slide (sashay) to the foot of the set and step back into their line of four.
57-64	Everyone will turn the opposite person with a two hand turn once around and finish back in their line of four.

Marching to Pretoria

Bob Howell

Formation: Couples facing couple in a double circle. One couple in each foursome with their backs toward the wall. One couple in each foursome with their back toward the center of the hall.

Record: LS-183 "Marching to Pretoria"

Prompts

Intro	*- - - -, - - 2 Ladies Chain*
1-8	**- - - -, - - Chain back**
9-16	**- - - -, Same four Star Left**
17-24	**- - - -, - - Star Right**
25-32	**- - - -, In your big circle march Single File**
33-40	**- - - -, Come back to the same couple**
41-48	**- - - -, - - Right & Left Thru**
49-56	**- - - -, - - Pass Thru**
57-64	**- - Wheel left, - - 2 Ladies Chain**

Description

1-8	2 Ladies Chain with the facing couple.
9-16	2 Ladies Chain back.
17-24	Same 4 Star Left
25-32	Same 4 Star Right
33-40	The inside couples Promenade Single File counterclockwise with the ladies following their partner. The outside couples Promenade Single File clockwise with the ladies following their partner.
41-48	Reverse the direction of both circles and Promenade Single File until you reach the same couple.
49-56	Right & Left Thru with this couple.
57-64	Pass Thru the same couple and then each couple wheel to the left to meet a new couple.

Note: Do not attempt to dance this dance with less then 24 couples.

Levi Jackson Rag

Pat Shaw

Formation: Five couples in a U shape formation. One head couple stands with their back to the caller. The other four couples form facing lines of four on the sides. (See below)

Record: LS E-28 "Levi Jackson Rag"

Prompts

Intro	*When the music starts, lines Right & Left Thru*
1-8	**- Ones down halfway, lines Right & Left Thru back**
9-16	**- Ones down & Separate, lines Circle Four across**
17-24	**- Ones go home alone, - Partners DoSaDo**
25-32	**- - - -, 5 Ladies Chain 2 places**
33-40	**- - - -, 5 Ladies Chain 2 places**
41-48	**- - - -, Keep her & Promenade one place**
49-56	**- - - -, - - - Swing**
57-64	**- - - -, New lines Right & Left Thru**

Description

1-8	The facing couples in the lines Right & Left Thru across the set. As these couples Courtesy Turn, the head couple walk half way down the set and pause.
9-16	The facing couples in the lines Right & Left Thru back across the set. As they Courtesy Turn, the head couple moves to the foot of the set and Separate, man going left and the lady going right.
17-24	The facing couples then Circle Four once around while the head man and the head lady walk up the outside of the set back to head position.
25-32	All couples DoSaDo their partners.
33-40	All 5 ladies chain 2 places clockwise. (Leave the partner, pass the next man and Courtesy Turn with the 2nd man)
41-48	Repeat 33-40
49-56	Each couple Promenades one place to the right to occupy a new position.
57-64	All couples Swing to finish facing the center of the formation.

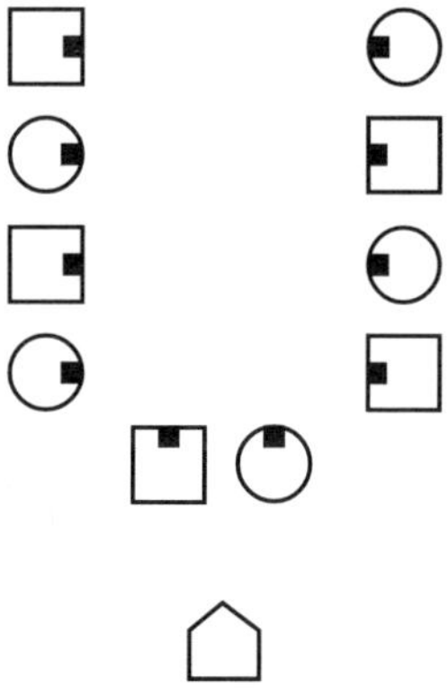

Notes: The timing on "Levi Jackson Rag" is so close that dancers often fail to keep up with the music until they become familiar with the dance. There are two points in the routine where you can temporarily eliminate a call to give the dancers time to stabilize. The first point is during counts 25-32 where a DoSaDo can be eliminated and just allow the people to stand for the same amount of time. The second point is just after the second Ladies Chain and all the couples Promenade one position. By temporarily eliminating the Swing, the people have time to recognize that they have changed positions and think a bit about what their next move will be.

Kingston Flyer

Iain Boyd

Formation: Four men facing four ladies.
Record: Blue Star 2410 "Freight Train"

Prompts

Intro	*- - - -, Head lady lead your line around*
1-8	*- - - -, - - - -*
9-16	**- - - -, Head man lead your line around**
17-24	**- - - -, - - - -**
25-32	**- - - -, Head couple down the center**
33-40	**- - - Turn, Come back to place**
41-48	**- - - -, Separate & down the outside**
49-56	**- - - -, DoSaDo at the foot**
57-64	**- - - -, Head man lead your line around**

Description

1-16	The head lady in each line leads the line of four ladies around the line of four men. They pass behind the line of men.
17-32	The head man in each line leads the line of four men around the line of four ladies. They pass behind the line of ladies.
33-40	Head couple walk down the center of the set 8 steps.
41-48	The same couple U-Turn Back and return to the head of the set.
49-56	The head couple Separate and walk down the outside of the set to the foot of the set.
57-64	At the foot of the set the same couple will DoSaDo and then remain at the foot of the set.

Kiwi Ring

A Scottish Country Dance Mixer from New Zealand

Formation: Couples, lady on man's right in a single circle.
Record: LS E-40 (special 80-count jig) "Kiwi Ring"

Prompts

Intro	*- - - -, - - Circle Left*
1-8	**- - - -, - - Circle Right**
9-16	**- - - -, Ladies figure 8 with the men**
17-24	**- - - -, - - - -**
25-32	**- - - -, Men figure 8 with the ladies**
33-40	**- - - -, - - - -**
41-48	**- - - -, Face partner clap & stamp**
49-56	**- - Right hand step by, - - clap & stamp**
57-64	**- - Left hand step by, - - clap & stamp**
65-72	**- - Right hand step by, - - clap & stamp**
73-80	**- - Left hand step by, - - Circle Left**

Description

1- 8	All hands joined, shoulder high, arms bent slightly at elbow, Circle Left 8 steps.
9-16	All Circle Right 8 steps.
17-32	The ladies walk a "figure of eight" around the standing men (first their partner and then their corner) beginning by moving to the left in front of their partner, around him, then in front of their corner, around him, and return to place. (32 steps)
33-48	The men walk a "figure of eight" around the standing ladies (first their partner and then their corner) beginning by moving to the right in front of their partner, around her, then in front of their corner, around her, and return to place. End facing partners, men facing counterclockwise. (32 steps)
49-56	Start an "interrupted Grand Right and Left." Partners clap own hands twice, then stamp right foot twice, then join right hands and pass each other by in 4 steps to face the next.
57-64	Repeat the hand claps and stamps, join left hands and pass each other by in 4 steps.
65-72	Repeat actions in 49-56.
73-80	Repeat actions in 57-64 and end by Circling Left in a big ring.

T.A.G

Roger Whynot

Formation: Four couple contra lines. Men on the caller's right and ladies on the caller's left.
Record: LS E-27 "T.A.G"

Prompts

Intro	*- - - -, First Couple go down the center*
1-8	**- - - -, - - And back**
9-16	**- - Cast out & men Star Left ladies Star Right**
17-24	**- - - -, Change the Stars -**
25-32	**- - - -, - - And change them back**
33-40	**- - - -, - - Promenade up**
41-48	**- - - -, Separate & march to the foot**
49-56	**- - Make an arch, other duck thru & move to the top**
57-64	**- - - -, Next top couple down the center**

Description

1-8 The first couple (closest to the prompter) step into the center of the set, face down toward the foot of the set as a couple and walk down the center of the set 6 steps and U-turn Back in 2 steps.

9-16 The same people walk back toward the head of the set six steps and finish with the man turning left and the lady turning right to start a Left Hand Star for the men and a Right Hand Star for the ladies.

17-48 The other three people in each line should face the head of the set and follow the leader into Stars. The men will form a Left Hand Star and the ladies will form a Right Hand Star. As soon as the first man and the first lady meet, the lady should proceed in front of her partner to the Left Hand Star and the man should proceed to pass behind the lady to the Right Hand Star. All the following people should follow until all the men are in a Right Hand Star and all the ladies are in a Left Hand Star. As soon as the first couple meet again, the lady should proceed in front of her partner back to the Right Hand Star and the man should proceed to pass behind the lady back to the Left Hand Star. All the following people should follow until all the men are back in the Left Hand Star and all the ladies are in a Right Hand Star. When the first couple reaches the foot of the set, they leave their Star and Promenade up the set toward the head of the hall.

49-56 All the other couples follow them and Promenade toward the head of the hall. The lead couple should Separate and proceed down the outside of the set Single File to the foot of the set and form a two hand arch. All the other people should Promenade Single File, men behind men and ladies behind ladies.

57-64 The trailing three couples duck through the arch formed by the leading couple and Promenade to the head of the set and finish facing across the set ready to start the dance with a new couple at the head of the set.

Note: On the "cast out" the first man turns away from the center (LF) and down the outside to form a Left Hand Star with the other men as the first lady turns away (right face) and down the outside to form a Right Hand Star with the other ladies.

Additional References for Dances

Publications

CD Journal, 343 Turf Lane, Castle Rock, Colorado, 80108 Calvin Campbell, editor. This quarterly publication of CALLERLAB contains articles, dances and news about the Community Dancing. You must be a member of CALLERLAB to subscribe, but members may distribute the publication to anyone else.

"**CALLERLAB Community Dance Program Handbook**", 467 Forrest Ave #118, Cocoa. Fl 32922. This handbook explains the concepts behind the creation of the Community Dance Program. Numerous dance examples are included and a sample teaching plan is provided.

"**Easy Level Solo Dances, The Bob Howell Collection**" Published by Siddle & Ray Publications for Dance, 1017 Williamsburg Dr., Charleston, IL 61920. This is a collection of over 130 solo dances originally published in the "**Easy Level**" column of American Square Dance Magazine over 23 years. Each dance has music recommendations, concise directions for all levels of ability, including educational level, plus an interesting history of each dance.

"**Sharing A Treasure of Dances**" Les Henkel, 301 Oak St. Box 18, Tobias, NE 68453-0018. This book is filled with many dances suitable for the Community Dancing. The book includes sections on: One Night Parties, Solo/Line, Couple Dances, Couple Mixers, Three Person Dances, Mescolanza (4 Person) Dances, Five Couple Dances, Easy Contras, Community Dance Program

Bob Dalsemer, PO Box 181, Brasstown, NC 28902-0181 has several publications."**When the Work's All Done**", "**A Square dance party for Beginners and Old Hands**" and "**Smoke on the Water**" are aimed at the traditional style of square dancing and contain music and chords for use by a live band. Most of the material fits within the 24 square dance basic recommended for the CDP. Music is available on cassettes. A third booklet titled "**New England Quadrilles**" contains instructions for how to call traditional square dances and prompt quadrilles as well as many good solid routines.

"**Contra Dancing**", Don Armstrong, Lloyd Shaw Foundation Sales Division, PO Box 11, Macks Creek, MO, 65786. This book has over 100 contra dances along with pictures, diagrams and descriptions.

"**First Steps to Contra**" Walt Cole, American Square Dance Magazine, 661 Middlefield Rd, Salinas, CA 939062. The small booklet contains general information about contra dancing and several example contras.

New England Caller, PO Box 8069, Lowell, MA 01853 has several handbooks that contain material suitable for the Community Dance Program. This includes line dances, rounds and squares and the original American Square Dance Society manuals.

American Square Dance Magazine, 661 Middlefield Rd., Salinas, CA, 93906-1004. While this magazine is largely devoted to square dancing, it is an excellent source for finding records, books etc. It also has a monthly column "**Easy Level**" by Bob Howell.

Record Companies

Grenn Inc., Box 216, Bath, OH 44210 produces four record labels. Several catalogue combinations are available that list dances suitable for the CDP. The dances are even graded as to the difficulty so leaders have the opportunity to pick and choose records that will fit within the skills of your dancers. They have several series tailored to fit the the basics listed in this text book.

The Lloyd Shaw Foundation Sales Division, PO Box 11, Macks Creek, MO, 65786 produces a wide variety of records for contras, squares, quadrilles, rounds and folk dancing.

Wagon Wheel/Windsor Records, Po Box 5576, Whittier, CA 90607-55765. Records can be ordered directly.

Other Record/Equipment Sources

Supreme Audio, Po Box 50, Marlborough, NH, 03455-0050. Has one of the largest stocks of records, books, PA equipment,. etc. A catalogue is available. www.Dosado.com

Palomino Records Inc. 2905 Scenic Dr., Marion, OH, 43302-8386.

The Country Dance & Song Society, 17 New South St, Northampton, MA, 01060 has an extensive catalogue of records, books, etc. Much of the material fits in the area of traditional dancing.

Videos

"**An Introduction to CONTRA DANCING**", R&R Video International, 3649 Whittier Blvd., Los Angles, CA 9002. The package includes a video, two cassettes tapes and a 49 page booklet containing 17 contras, 1 mescolanza and 1 quadrille. Mike Seastrom prompts the dances with added commentary by Bob Osgood. The video is a product of the California Contra Callers Association.

The package is an excellent introduction to contras for anyone who is unfamiliar with this dance form. Both dancers and leaders can use the video to learn the mechanics. Then the cassette tapes can be used to actually dance the routines. Finally, the new leaders have a quick written reference for each of the dances that will enable them to prompt the dances in person.

"**Jerry Helt's Dance Party**", Kentucky Dance Foundation,C/O Stew Shaklette. 460 Long Needle Rd., Brandenburg, KY 40108. This video is worth getting just to study Jerry's presentation techniques.

Appendix A

General Styling, Steps & Handholds

Arches—In a couple arch, the dancers, standing side by side, join their inside hands and raise them to form an arch. In a two hand arch, dancers face and join both hands and raise them high enough to form an arch of sufficient height for people to duck under.

Arms in Natural Dance Position— Arms should be held slightly bent at the elbow in comfortable position in anticipation of the next movement.

Bow to Partner or to Corner—Men turn slightly to face their partner and make eye contact. The left hand should be placed behind the back or at the left hip, palm out. Place the right foot in front of left foot. The right foot should be pointed toward the lady with the toe touching the floor. The lady's left hand is held by the man's right hand. Both legs are straight, with weight on the back foot.

Ladies turn slightly to face their partner and make eye contact. The right hand should be used to pick up the right side of the skirt or the hand held out gracefully to the side. The left foot should be pointed forward with toe touching floor, right foot in back. The man's right is held by the lady's left hand. Both legs are straight with weight on back foot. [In an acceptable traditional variation of styling, the men bow slightly from the waist as the ladies acknowledge with a curtsy.]

Couple Handhold—Inside hands joined. Men with palm up, ladies palm down. In the event of a same sex couple, the left-hand dancer places their palm up, the right-hand dancer places their palm down. Arms should be bent at the elbow with hands held slightly higher than the elbow of the shorter person.

Dance Step—Should be smooth and gliding. The ball of the foot should touch and then slide along the surface of the floor before the heel touches the floor. The length of stride should be comfortable for an average height lady. Dance steps should be in time with the musical beat. The objective is smooth gliding steps where the dancers appear to float around the floor with little or no bobbing up and down.

Forearm Grip—Dancers are facing and holding the opposite person's arm midway between the wrist and the elbow. Each dancer places their hand on the inside of the arm of the opposite person. Firm support should be provided, but dancers should not grip the arm tightly. The center of the turn will be where the arms are joined. While turning, each dancer is moving equally around the other.

Handshake Hold—Use a comfortable handshake grip, i.e. firm, but not tight. The thumb should overlap the back of the opposite dancer's hand. It is important in a Right & Left Grand to release hand holds prior to passing shoulders.

Posture—Dancers should stand erect and tall, shoulders back. The body weight should be forward on the balls of the feet with the heels just touching the floor.

Promenade Ending Twirl—Square dancing - Man raises his right hand holding the lady's right hand loosely as she turns clockwise underneath, ending in a squared up couple position.

Sashay Step—A quick sliding step to the right or to the left. Basic action is a side, close, side, close, etc. The movement is used primarily in prompted dances and mixers.

Skirt Work—With the free hand, pickup the skirt between the thumb and index finger and roll the hand under the fabric. The thumb should be on top of the fabric. Hold skirt in free hand about waist high using very slight rhythmical flourishes to move skirt in front and back, right hand moving with left foot, left hand moving with right foot.

Star (Box or Packsaddle)—4 to 6 dancers place the hand over the wrist of the person ahead of them to form a box. The palm is down. (Palm Star)—Place inside hands together with the other dancers with fingers pointing up and thumbs closed gently over the back of the adjacent dancer's hand. Arms should be bent slightly at the elbow so the height of the handgrip is at average eye level.

Step By—The movement brings two facing people past each other. If hands are held, the handhold should be dropped before their bodies cross a common plane.

Basic Square and Prompted Dance Movements

The basic dance movement definitions listed below are arranged in alphabetical order. A suggested order for instruction is listed in the front of the manual. The same general order is used in the dances presented in other formations. The goal is to provide a means to easily enable leaders to combine squares, contras, quadrilles, trios, etc. into one program and to still have a wide selection of dances available at each stage of the development of the dancers.

The following descriptions are detailed. It is usually not necessary for all this detail to be orally communicated to the dancers. Demonstrations and the correct choice of words should enable any basic (even Grand Square) to be explained quickly. Be prepared to explain each basic using several different choices of words.

Allemande Left—Starting formation - facing dancers. Dancers face their corner and turn by the left forearm (Arm Turn). The corner for the man is always the lady in the first position clockwise around the set. The corner for the lady is the man in the first position counterclockwise around the set. Release arm holds and each person step by and face his or her partner.

<u>Styling</u>: See Arm Turns

<u>Timing</u>: **Square or Contra line with corner** = 8 steps.

<u>Teaching Tips</u>: Point out that an Allemande Left is really just a version of an Arm Turn.

Arm Turn Right/Left—Starting formation - dancers facing. Dancers join specified forearms (left or right) and walk forward around each other the distance specified; e.g. half (180°), three quarters (270°), full (360°), etc.

<u>Styling</u>: The arms are held midway between the wrist and the elbow. Each dancer places his hand on the inside of the arm of the opposite person. The fingers and thumb are kept close together. The center of the turn will be at the joined arms. While turning, each dancer moves equally around the other.

<u>Timing:</u> **Square or Prompted Dances**—Full around = 8 steps; three quarters = 6; one half = 4; one quarter = 2.

Teaching Tips: Teach from a big circle and change partners several times. Encourage eye contact. This will assist in keeping the facing people turning around a center point between the two dancers.

Bend the Line—Starting formation - any line with an even number of dancers. Dancers in each half of the line must be facing in the same direction. The center dancers in the line drop hands with each other. With each half of the line working as a unit, the ends move forward while the centers back up until both halves of the line are facing each other.

Styling: As ends move forward, centers back up equally. Use normal couple handhold and in the event a new line is formed, immediately join hands in the new line.

Timing: Lines of four, six or eight = 4 steps.

Teaching Tips: In square dancing, *Bend the Line* results in the formation of new lines. In contra dancing, *Bend the Line* usually results in the formation of long lines. Have the dancers back away from the center of the set on the last 2 steps to spread the long lines apart.

Circle Left/Right—Starting formation - two or more dancers. Dancers join hands to form a circle. Face slightly left or right, as directed, and move forward around the circle. When left or right is not specified, then Circle Left.

Styling: All dancers walk (dance) with joined hands, men's palms up and lady's palms down, elbows bent comfortably so that hands can be held above the level of the elbow of the shortest person. When adjoining dancers are the same sex, the right hand person in the pair should place their hand palm down and the left hand person in the pair should place their hand palm up.

Timing: *Standing or static square of 8 people*—Circle full around = 16 steps; Circle three quarters = 12 steps; Circle one half = 8 steps; Circle one quarter = 4 steps.

Square or Prompted Dance—sets of 4 Circle full around = 8 steps; Circle one half = 4 steps; Circle 3/4 = 6 steps

Teaching Tips: Usually taught from a large circle. Try to avoid the grapevine step action because it tends to throw off the balance of other people in the circle.

Circle to a Line—Starting formation - facing couples. The lead couple is on the inside of the set facing the outside couple. Couples Circle Left one half (180°). The lead dancer in the couple who started on the inside (man's position) release the left handhold, but retain the handhold of the dancer on the right. This lead dancer becomes the left end dancer of the line of four. The released dancer (usually, but not always a lady) will move forward under the raised arm arch formed by that dancer and the adjacent dancer to become the right end dancer in the line of four.

Styling: The Circle portion of the movement is the same styling as in *Circle Left*. As the man breaks with his left hand to form a line, he should lead the line several steps before turning. After the end lady has released her right hand, and while retaining the right hand of the man beside her, together they will raise their joined hands and make an arch. Then as the line begins to straighten out, the lady will move forward under this arch, turning left face gradually under her own left arm so that instead of backing up she is moving forward to the end of the line.

Timing: 8 steps. (Circle Half takes 4 steps, make the line of four takes 4 steps)

Teaching Tips: The end result will be two lines of four facing across the set. In a square dance, the active man will be on the end of the line closest to his home position .

Courtesy Turn—Starting formation - couple, facing dancers. The man (left hand dancer) takes the lady's (right hand dancer) left hand (palm down) in his left (palm up) and places his right hand in the small of the lady's back. Moving as a unit, the couple turns around (180°) with the left hand dancer backing up and right hand dancer walking forward. Unless otherwise specified, the couple faces the center of the set or the center of the formation.

Styling: The man's extended left hand serves as a direction indicator and the man uses his left hand to lead, not pull, the lady around. The man should place his the right hand in the small of the lady's back and push gently. Ladies use the right hand to work her skirt or she can place her right hand in the middle of her back where she wants the man's hand to be placed. The call *Courtesy Turn* is limited to turning a woman on the man's right.

Timing: 4 steps.

Teaching Tips: The word 'courtesy' implies being gentle. Emphasize this to the dancers. Tell them, "Ladies do not like to be pushed around. Be gentle about it."

DoSaDo— Starting formation - facing dancers. Dancers advance and pass right shoulders. Without turning around, each dancer moves to their right passing in back of the other dancer (slide back to back). Then step backwards, dancers pass left shoulders and return to starting positions.

Styling: Men - arms are held in natural dance position, right shoulders turned forward as right shoulders pass, left shoulders turned forward as left shoulders pass. Ladies - both hands on skirt, moving her skirt forward and back, right hand moving forward as right shoulders pass, left hand moving forward as left shoulders pass.

Timing: *Square and Prompted Dances*—DoSaDo with corner = 6 steps; DoSaDo with partner = 6 steps; DoSaDo from a box formation (couple facing couple close enough to easily touch hands with the facing person) = 6 steps; DoSaDo across the set = 8 steps.

Teaching Tips: A DoSaDo once around starts and ends with the participants facing each other. Adding following calls that emphasize these positions will help in keeping the dancers from developing sloppy positioning habits.

Forward & Back— Starting formation - single dancer. Each dancer walks forward 3 steps. On the 4th beat of music, bring the free foot forward and touch the toe to the floor beside the weight bearing foot without transferring the weight. Each dancer moves backward 3 steps beginning with the free foot. On the 4th beat of music, touch the free foot beside the weight-bearing foot. From facing lines of four or similar situations where 8 steps are not appropriate, each dancer steps forward 1 step and pauses while bringing the other foot forward and touching it to the floor without transferring weight. Each dancer then steps back on the free foot and pauses while touching the other foot beside it. This is sometime referred to as Balance Forward & Back.

Styling: Couples have inside hands joined. As couples meet in the center, outside hands of the facing people may be touched palm to palm. Eye contact with the opposite person is encouraged. As the foot is brought to touch on the 8th count, it should remain on the floor and weight returned to both feet.

Timing : **SS (static square) or Contra lines**— All Forward & Back = 8 steps, heads or sides or lines Forward & Back = 8 steps, rock Forward & Back = 4 steps; balance Forward & Back = 4 steps.

Teaching Tips: Vocal cues are often helpful in perfecting the timing. Have the dancers walk forward three steps and say "Whoa" and then back up three steps and "Hey".

Grand Square—Starting formation - square. In the dance movement the heads dance one part (1a & 1b) while at the same time the sides dance another (2a & 2b).

Part 1a—Number of steps =16.

Heads move forward to the center of the square (4 steps), turning one quarter (90°) on the 4th step to face partners and back away to the sides of the square (4 steps). Turn one quarter (90°) to face the original opposites. Back away to the corners of the square (4 steps) and turn one quarter (90°) to face original partners and walk forward to home (4 steps). Do not turn around.

Part 1b—Number of steps =16.

From this point the action is reversed. Heads back away from their partners (4 steps), turn one quarter (90°) on the 4th step and walk forward to the opposites (4 steps). Turn one quarter and walk forward into the center toward partners (4 steps). Turn one quarter (90°) to face opposites and back up to home. Total steps 1a + 1b =32.

Part 2a—While the head couples are doing the first 16 steps, the sides start by facing their partners to back away and do the second 16 steps *(Part 1b)*.

Part 2b—Then the sides do the first 16 steps *(Part 1a)*, while the heads are doing the last 16. The two parts interlock. The principle of walking 3 steps and then turning (or reversing) on the 4th step is followed throughout. Total steps = 32.

Styling: Mens' arms in natural dance position; ladies work skirt with natural swinging action. When moving forward and backward as a couple, normal couple handhold is desired.

Timing: 32 steps.

Teaching Tips: Notice that dancers are either moving toward or away from their partner or the opposite person. After each 90° turn there is only one choice. If dancers are standing face to face, they must back away 4 steps. If facing dancers are across the set, they walk forward 4 steps. This simple piece of logic usually enables a Grand Square to be taught in a very short period of time. Grand Square may be broken into fractional parts by the caller directing the number of steps required. The call may also start with the heads, or other designated dancers, directed to face.

Ladies Chain—2 Ladies Chain: Starting formation - facing couples (man on the left, lady on the right). The ladies step forward, extend right hands to each other and step by. Each man should step slightly forward and to the right. The lady coming toward the man extends a left hand to the man for a *Courtesy Turn.* Couples finish facing each other. 4 Ladies Chain: Starting formation - square or circle of 8 dancers. Similar to 2 Ladies Chain except that all four ladies step to the center and form a *Right Hand Star*. They turn the *Star* halfway around to their opposite men. All four couples *Courtesy Turn* to face the center of the set. Two (or Four) Ladies Chain 3/4: Starting formation - facing couples, a square or circle of 8 dancers. The directed ladies step to the center, form a *Right Hand Star* and turn the star three quarters and *Courtesy Turn* to face the center of the set.

Styling: Men release partner then turn right shoulder slightly toward the center of the square to begin the *Courtesy Turn* portion of the call, step back with the left foot. Ladies use handshake and step by for 2 Ladies Chain. No skirt work except as part of the *Courtesy Turn*. In 3/4 and 4 Ladies Chain, the ladies use the hands up palm star, touching right hands in the star pattern. It is important that the man clear a path for receiving the lady after the chain by moving slightly to the right and starting the *Courtesy Turn* motion before the lady arrives.

Timing: *Squares or Prompted dances*, 2 Ladies Chain across set = 8 steps; *Squares*, Ladies Chain 3/4 = 10 steps; 4 Ladies Chain across the set = 8 steps; three quarters = 10 steps.

Teaching Tips: This movement is defined with terminology used in other movements. Be sure the dancers are comfortable with *Courtesy Turn* and with *Right/Left Hand Stars* before attempting to teach a Ladies Chain.

Lead Right/Left—Starting formation - couple. The directed couple(s) take a step forward and, as a unit, turn to the right 90° and move forward.

Styling: Normal couple handhold between the man and lady, outside hands in normal dance position.

Timing: 4 steps.

Teaching Tips: Most of the dances which feature Lead Right are in the square dance section. This means the active couples will end facing the couple to their right.

Pass Thru—Starting formation - facing dancers. Dancers move forward, passing right shoulders with each other. Each person ends in the opposite persons starting position (back to back) but neither dancer changes facing direction.

Styling: The right shoulder should be turned slightly forward as right shoulders pass. Arms are held in natural dance position or ladies can work skirts with both hands, right hand leading as right shoulders pass.

Timing: **Square or facing lines,** Pass Thru across the set = 4 steps; Pass Thru from a box formation = 2 steps.

Teaching Tips: When dancers Pass Thru and face out, many dancers will want to turn around and not remain facing away from the center of the set. Use choreography that leave them facing out for 4-8 beats of music.

Promenade (Couple)—Starting formation - two people side by side. Couples walk forward as a unit in the direction indicated. Unless otherwise specified, Couples Promenade until they reach the man's (left hand person's) home position. *Square dance special rules:* The normal direction of movement is around the circle counterclockwise. At the end of the Promenade, the couple turns, as a unit, to face the center of the set. If Promenading to the man's home position, the couple always goes at least one quarter around the square. If need be, they continue past the man's home position for another full time around. *Contra dance special rules*: Dancers may be asked to Couple Promenade up or down the hall and Half Promenade across the set. See individual dances for further description.

Styling: Both the man's hands are palm up, right forearm above the lady's left arm. Lady's hands are palm down in man's hand. Joined hands should be positioned equally between partners and at a comfortable height for the lady. Discourage any pumping actions.

Timing: *Square Dances*—Couples Promenade full around = 16 steps; three quarters = 12 steps; one half = 8 steps; one quarter = 4 steps; Promenading inside = 8 steps. *Prompted dances*—Promenade Half from facing lines or couples = 8 steps.

Teaching Tips: Teach from a big circle. Use a *Single File Promenade* preceding teaching the Couple Promenade. From a *Single File Promenade* position have the men move to the inside of the circle and up beside their partner. Shake right hands with their partner without facing them. Join left hands under the joined right hands and walk forward. This can often be done while people continue to walk forward. Point out that a Couple Promenade is one of the few times during a dance where there is time to have a little conversation with the other person. Smile and talk a while.

Promenade (Single File)—Starting formation - 2 or more dancers in any line or circle. Dancers walk forward in single file (one behind the other) in the direction indicated.

Styling: Man's arms are held in natural dance position; lady's hands on skirt, working with the natural swinging motion.

Timing: *Square Dances*—Promenade full around = 16 steps; three quarters = 12; one half = 8; one quarter = 4; Four people Promenade inside as square = 8 steps. *Prompted dances*— usually Promenade for 8 steps.

Teaching Tips: Teach from a big circle. If *Circle Right* is called previous to teaching a Single File Promenade, people will all ready be traveling in the correct direction. Ladies in the lead 'Indian style' is also a term many people still recognize.

Star Thru—Starting formation - facing dancers (man and lady). Man's right hand is placed against the lady's left, palm to palm with fingers up, to make an arch. As the dancers move forward the lady moves under the arch and does a one quarter (90°) left face turn, while the man does a one quarter (90°) turn to the right moving behind the lady. They end side by side with the lady on the man's right.

Styling: Hands are touched in the arch, palm to palm, fingers pointed up. The hand grip should be readjusted to couple handhold after the movement is completed. Join hands in raised position approximately eye level. It is important that hands not be joined before that point. Man's hand should be used to stabilize as the lady provides her own momentum. It is equally important that the man's arm remain well above the lady's head.

Timing: 4 steps from point of contact.

Teaching Tips: Some people have physical problems raising their arms above shoulder height. If this is true, the same movement can be done without the hand/arm action.

Right & Left Grand—Starting formation - square, circle, line or any position where dancers can conveniently turn 90° or less (if needed) to face opposite sex and men are facing counterclockwise and ladies are facing clockwise around the circle. Join right hands (if not already joined) and step by the facing dancer. Give a left hand to the next and step by, a right to the next and step by, a left to the next, until each dancer meets the person with whom they started. *Wrong Way Grand*: Like Right & Left Grand, but men move clockwise and ladies move counterclockwise.

Styling: Alternating hands are used with alternating step-by movements. Hand holds should be supportive, but not tight. Arms should be held in natural dance position and the handhold should be released just as dancers pass each other. Both men and women should stand tall and resist the temptation to lean over and stretch out their hand to the next person. Use just a comfortable extension of the arm and hand. Brief eye contact should be made as they meet each dancer.

Timing: Until you meet your partner = 10 steps. This will be on the far side of the square.

Teaching Tips: Counting the partner, each dancer in the square must pass 4 people and touch 4 hands. The partner is then the 5th person. Have the dancers count hands out loud as they proceed. Change partners frequently.

Right & Left Thru—Starting formation - facing couples. Dancers step forward, join right hands with the dancer directly ahead and step by. Each couple then does a *Courtesy Turn* (180°) to face the other couple in the foursome.

Styling: Each dancer takes regular handshake hold (right hands) with opposite person as they move by each other. They release hands as they step by. For *Courtesy Turn* styling, refer to that basic.

Timing: **Squares or Prompted dances** heads or sides across the set = 8 steps; box formation (couples standing closer together) = 6 steps.

Teaching Tips: This movement has another movement as part of the definition. Be sure the dancers are comfortable with *Courtesy Turn* before teaching Right & Left Thru. Use *Pass Thru* and *Courtesy Turn* routines to pre-teach correct styling. Once the dancers are comfortable dancing a *Pass Thru* and *Courtesy Turn,* all that needs to be added, for a *Right & Left Thru,* is a light touch with the right hands in the middle.

Roll Away Half Sashay—Starting formation - couple. The directed dancer (dancer on the right) rolls across a full turn (360°) in front of the dancer on the left, as they sidestep to the right. The two dancers exchange places. When dancers are momentarily face to face they should join both hands. The ladies roll left face across in front of the men unless otherwise directed.

Styling: Hands are held in normal couple handhold. The man and lady should each use a slight pulling motion toward each other as they initiate the roll. The man should pull the lady slightly as both man and lady reach to join hands and then continue the pulling motion with the left hand. Man steps back with left foot, to the side and across.

Timing: 4 steps

Teaching Tips: The men should provide good support to the ladies as they roll. Teach from a standing square before trying it from a Circle Left.

Star Promenade—Starting formation - varies. Directed dancers form a Star (left/right) and place the other arm around the waist of another directed dancer. Turn the Star Promenade the distance directed by the caller.

Styling: Men's inside hands joined the same as in a standard *Star*. The outside arm is around the lady's waist. Lady's inside arm is around man's waist under his arm. The outside hand of the lady can be used to work the skirt.

Timing: Squares, Four couples full around = 12 steps; three quarters = 9 steps; one half = 6 steps; one quarter = 3 steps. Four couples full around with a back out at home = 16 steps.

Teaching Tips: A Star Promenade is usually preceded by a *Left Hand Star*. The ladies should anticipate the arrival of the men and face the direction the *Star* will be traveling.

Separate—Starting formation - couple. Each dancer turns individually away from other person in the couple until they are back to back with each other. Then each person moves forward to the position designated by the caller. The distance traveled is determined by the next instruction.

Styling: Men's arms in natural dance position. Any skirt work by the ladies is optional.

Timing: 2 steps to stand back to back.

Teaching Tips: The caller or prompter must always provide immediate directions on where the dancers are to proceed after they Separate.

Split the Couple/Ring—Starting formation - facing couples. The active or directed couple move forward and pass between the outside couple. The outside couple must step apart enough to let them through then step back together again.

Styling: Men's arms held in natural dance position; ladies may work their skirts. The inactive couple that is Split by the active couple simply moves out of the way with a couple of sidesteps so that the active couple can walk between them. Once the active couple has moved through and is out of the way, the inactive couple will move together once again.

Timing: Squares, individual couples Split Two around one to a line = 8 steps; around two to a line = 10 steps; to home = 12 steps. From a box formation, the inside people Split outsides to a line = 4 steps; to home position = 6 steps.

Teaching Tips: Dance as *Split the Ring* first. The outside couple must counter dance and anticipate the need to slide apart, let the inside pair through and then slide back together.

Star Left/Right—Starting formation - facing dancers or facing couples. The directed dancers step forward and extend designated hands to form a left or right hand palm star. Dancers should be facing clockwise for a Right Hand Star and counterclockwise for a Left Hand Star. The dancers walk forward, turning around the center point of the star where the inside hands touch. Turning distance of the star may be specified in fractions of one quarter, one half, three quarters, or a complete revolution.

Styling: In a forward moving Star, inside hands should be joined in a 'palm star' position (hands of those making the star are held about average eye level - palms touching), arms bent at the elbow. Men's outside arm in natural dance position, the lady's outside hand can be used to work her skirt.

Timing: Four person Stars full around = 8 steps; three quarters = 6 steps; one half = 4 steps; one quarter = 2 steps. Eight person Stars full around = 16 steps; three quarters = 12 steps; one half = 8 steps; one quarter = 4 steps.

Teaching Tips: Tell people to put their right hand in the Star and walk the easiest direction. Only a very few will attempt to walk the wrong way. Repeat using a left hand.

Swing—Starting formation - facing dancers (man and lady). Dancers move forward and to the left until they are right hip to right hip with the adjacent dancer. Move around each other turning in a clockwise direction for 4 to 8 beats of music. To break out of the Swing, the man relaxes the tension on the waist hand, while still providing some support, and the lady continues turning to her right until she is facing the same direction as the man. The lady should be on the man's right hand side and the couple facing the direction indicated by the caller.

Styling: Men - left arm bent at the elbow, palm slightly up. Right hand on lady's back slightly above the waist. Posture should be erect. Ladies - right hand palm down on man's left hand. Left hand on man's right shoulder, arm resting on man's right arm. Footwork: *Walk Around Swing* - use short walking or shuffling steps around a central point. *Buzz Step* - right foot moves in small steps around the pivot point between the two dancers while the left foot pushes, as in a scooter motion (similar to pushing a skate board). Ending position: Lady rolls off man's right arm blending smoothly to position for the next call or twirls (to a *Promenade* position only - lady's option). To twirl, the man raises his left hand over the lady's head, holding lady's right hand loosely. Her hand should revolve around his for stability as she turns clockwise moving down line of dance three steps, into a *Promenade* position, joining inside hands on the 4th step. While the lady turns, the man will move forward down the line of dance to be in position for the *Promenade*.

Timing: *Square Dancing*—usually 4 to 8 beats of music. *Prompted dances*— Swing for 8 beats of music or longer if directed.

Teaching Tips: Make sure couples are standing right side to right side. If the lady leans back lightly into the man's right arm around her waist and the man counter balances the weight, the Swing action is much easier and smoother. It also helps if people maintain eye contact as they Swing. This helps control dizziness and improves the appearance of coordinated action.

U-turn Back—Starting formation - single dancer. Each directed dancer does an in-place about-face turn (180°), turning toward their partner unless the body flow dictates otherwise. If alone (i.e. no partner), the dancer turns toward the center of the set. If the dancer is facing directly toward or away from the center of the set, they may turn in either direction.

Styling: Arms in natural dance position.

Timing: 2 steps.

Teaching Tips: Use a memory jogger to help people remember which way to turn such as, "It's not polite to turn your back on a lady."

Weave The Ring—A *R*ight *& Left G*rand without touching hands. You can also Weave the Ring the wrong way around with men traveling clockwise and ladies traveling counterclockwise.

Styling: As you meet each person, turn slightly to face them and make eye contact. A nod and a smile are also nice touches. Ladies can work both sides of their skirt. Men can *W*eave the Ring with both hands behind their back or hanging naturally at their sides.

Timing: Same as *Grand Right & Left.*

Teaching Tips: Always teach *Right & Left Grand* first. *W*eave the Ring can be substituted for Right & Left Grand in many figures.

Wheel Around—Starting formation - couple. The couple, moving as a unit, turns halfway around (180°). The left hand dancer backs up while the right hand dancer moves forward. The pivot point is the handhold between the two dancers.

Styling: Same as in *Couple Promenade.*

Timing: 4 steps.

Teaching Tips: Wheel Around is used mainly in prompted dances or from a *Promenade* in square dancing. The man (left hand person of the pair) will frequently need to be reminded that they back up.

Appendix B

Open Dance Lesson Plan

The following lesson plan is designed to teach a total of 24 basics over 8 lessons. Each 2 hour session covers a selection of 12 basics and the dances are arranged to allow new dancers, with no experience in dancing, to enter the program at the start of any one of the 8 sessions.

Some people will also be teaching sessions of 45-50 minutes in length at schools and recreation departments. Each session can be split approximately in half to fit these time restrictions. In some cases, you may only want to cover 1/3 of the dances in a 45 minute session. Just remember to keep it simple and keep it fun.

Each of the 8 sessions can become a stand alone dance experience and could be used as a beginner party plan or as a single lesson plan. Some modification may be necessary based on the assumption that most beginner parties last only 90 minutes or less.

Dancers who attend more than one session will dance both material and basics that are familiar from previous session and new dance routines which they have not danced before. During each session they will learn several new basics out of the set of 24 basics. Once the dancers have completed a rotation of 8 sessions/dances, they will have enough knowledge and experience to attend any Community Dance Program which uses these 24 basics.

The goal of the lesson plan is to present a flexible learning program which can be adapted to a variety of audiences without the necessity of imposing rigid lesson attendance requirements. By allowing new dancers to enter the program at the beginning of any session, the dancers choose when to start and how often to attend.

Session 1	Page #	Circle L/R	Fwd & Back	Swing	Prom Sing File	Arm Turn L/R	Sashay/Slide	Cpl Promenade	DoSaDo	R&L Grand	Star R/L	Pass Thru	Ladies Chain
Big Circle		x	x	x	x	x		x					
Virginia NoReel Contra	146		x		x	x	x						
NoName Contra	147		x	x		x	x						
Break													
Patter Square		x	x	x	x	x		x	x	x	x		
Singing Call	47	x		x	x			x	x				
Raunchy Solo	273												
Break													
Wild Turkey Trio	210					x							
Do-Ci-Dizzy Trio	212	x	x						x				
Break													
Patter Sicilian Cir		x	x			x			x		x	x	x
1st Night Sicilian Cir	226	x	x		x								
Cielito Lindo Mxr	250	x	x	x					x				
Break													
Patter Square		x	x	x		x		x		x	x		x
Singing Call	66	x		x		x		x	x	x			x
Break													
Dumbarton Drums Mes	239		x				x				x	x	
Texas Freeze Solo	272												
Break													
Clopton Bridge 4Fc4	285					x					x		
Blue Strs & Strps Mxr	250												
Extra New Dances													
Thru Whte & Drftd Snow	188			x					x		x		x
Ladies Star Turn Quad	121					x		x	x		x		
Tip Top Quad	123				x			x	x		x		x
Dances Repeated Earlier or Later													
Coronado Quad (5)	122	x						x					x
Mason's Apron Trio (5)	216	x	x					x			x	x	
Bubbles Mixer (5)	252	x		x				x	x				
Lcash Brn Dnc Mxr (5)	254		x			x		x					
Rky Mtn Scrmbl Solo	274												
Chap Slap Solo	277												

Session 2	Page #	Circle L/R	Fwd & Back	Swing	Prom Sing File	Cpl Promenade	DoSaDo	Allemande Left	Star R/L	Pass Thru	U-turn Back	Courtesy Turn	Separate
Big Circle #2		X	X		X	X	X	X					
Patter Square		X	X	X		X	X	X	X				
Singing Call	43	X	X	X		X	X	X	X				
Break													
Kingston Flyer 4Fc4	288				X		X				X		X
ONS Contra	158		X	X	X		X		X				
Break													
Amos Moses #1 (Solo)	272												
Tres Trio	213		X	X			X			X			
TBC Trio	217		X		X		X			X	X		
Break													
Cecily Cir Sis Cir	228	X		X			X		X	X			
Scones & Tea Sis Cir	229	X		X			X		X	X			
Hi Neighbor Mrx	258												
Break													
Patter Square	60	X	X	X						X	X	X	X
Singing Call	61	X	X	X		X	X			X	X		
Raunchy (repeat)	273												
Break													
Molly Mixer	251	X	X	X		X	X						
San Antonio Stroll Solo	273												
Extra New Dances													
Jefferson's Reel Contra	187	X							X		X		
Hand Maze Trio	220	X	X				X			X			
Star Weaver Mesco	243		X	X					X	X			
Dances Repeated Earlier or Later													
One Horse Reel (4)	160	X		X			X	X	X				
Dos Plus One Trio (6)	221	X	X						X	X			
Happy Cir Sicilian (6)	230	X	X	X			X		X	X			
ONS Party Mesco (6)	238	X					X		X	X			
E-X Mixer (6)	252												

Session 3	Page #	Circle L/R	Fwd & Back	Swing	Arm Turn L/R	Cpl Promenade	DoSaDo	Allemande Left	Grand R & L	Right & Left Thru	Separate	Split	Roll Away 1/2 Sh
Big Circle		x	x		x	x	x						x
Patter Square	81	x	x	x		x		x	x				x
Singing Call		x		x		x		x					x
Break													
Patter Sicilian Cir		x		x	x		x			x	x	x	x
Scottish Man O'War	227	x			x								
Electric Slide Solo	276												
Break													
I Don't Know Why Mxr	251	x	x	x		x	x						
Theil's Trio	211				x								
Do-Ci-Dizzy	212	x				x							
Break													
Beginner's Luck Contra	159	x		x	x		x						
High Five Contra	161		x	x		x	x						
Break													
Patter Square		x	x	x		x	x	x	x	x			x
Pretty Baby Quadrille	124	x	x			x				x			
Texas Freeze repeat	272												
Break													
Kiwi Ring	290	x							x				
Jiffy Mixer	260												
Extra New Dances													
Sunshine Mxr	263				x	x							
Bay Boogie Mxr	267	x	x	x		x							x
Route 271 Mesco	248	x								x			
Dances Repeated Earlier or Later													
Happy Snds Quad (7)	131					x		x		x			
Wthrvne Prm SCr (6)	231	x				x							
White Slvr Snd Mxr (7)	261												
Hully Gully Solo(7)	274												
Ghost Busters (7)	278												

Session 4	Page #	Circle L/R	Fwd & Back	Swing	Arm Turn L/R	Cpl Promenade	DoSaDo	Pass Thru	Ladies Chain	Right & Left Thru	Separate	Split	Lead Right
Big Circle		x	x	x	x	x	x						
Alternate Trios	214	x	x		x		x	x					
Three Legged Stool	215	x	x		x		x	x					
Break													
Patter Square	68	x	x	x		x		x	x	x			
Singing Call	71	x		x	x	x			x	x			
Ally Cat Solo	276												
Break													
Who's in the Middle	192	x		x	x	x				x	x		
Caller's Wife	181	x	x	x	x	x			x	x	x		
Break													
Patter Call	87	x	x	x	x	x		x				x	x
Gordo's Quadrille	128	x			x	x				x	x	x	x
Electric Slide Solo	276												
Break													
Portland Fancy Mesco	244	x	x					x	x	x			
Keene Anniversary Mesc	242		x					x	x	x			
Patty Cake Polka Mxr	259				x								
Break													
Levi Jackson Rag	287	x				x			x	x	x		
Extra New Dances													
Market Lass Contra	208		x		x					x			
Swap Ends Mesco	247		x					x	x	x			
Dances Repeated Earlier or Later													
Prtlnd Fncy Mesco (8)	244	x	x					x	x	x			
Keene Aniv Mesco (8)	242	x						x	x	x			
All Spice Mxr (8)	257	x	x										
Quarter Chain Quad(8)	127					x			x	x			
Cotton Eyed Joe	280												
Ding Dong Daddy	282												

Session 5

Session 5	Page #	Circle L/R	Fwd & Back	Swing	Cpl Promenade	DoSaDo	Allemande Left	Star R/L	Pass Thru	Ladies Chain	Right & Left Thru	Lead Right	Circle to a Line
Big Circle	x	x	x	x	x		x						
Patter Sicilian Circle	x	x	x			x		x	x	x	x		
Sicilian Circle #37	232	x			x			x		x			
Break													
Patter Square	91	x	x	x	x					x	x	x	x
Coronado Quadrille	122	x			x					x			
Rocky Mtn Scramble	275												
Break													
Skontra Contra	195	x	x					x		x	x		
Contra-Action	162			x		x		x		x	x		
Bubbles Mxr	252	x		x	x	x		x					
Break													
Three's Greet Trio	218	x	x			x			x				
Mason's Apron Trio	216	x	x			x		x	x				
Chap Slap (Solo)	277												
Break													
Patter Call	91	x	x	x	x	x	x		x	x	x	x	x
Singing Call	93		x	x	x					x	x	x	x
Queen's Quardille	125			x	x					x	x		
Extra New Dances													
Caller's Grlfrnd Cntra	180	x	x	x		x	x	x	x	x			
Homosassa HrnP Cntra	163			x	x	x		x		x	x		
Taos Trio (tough)	222		x			x		x	x	x		x	x
Gnd Str Cir Siscilian	233	x				x		x		x			
Don's Mesco	246		x					x	x	x	x		
Dances Repeated Earlier or Later													
First Night Siscillian (1)	227	x	x										
Blue Strs & Strp Mxr (1)	250			x									
Cielito Lindo Mxr (1)	250	x	x	x		x							

Session 6	Page #	Circle L/R	Fwd & Back	Swing	Prom Sing File	Sashay/Slide	Cpl Promenade	DoSaDo	Allemande Left	R & L Grand	Star R/L	Pass Thru	U-turn Back
Big Circle		x	x	x			x	x	x	x			
Patter Call	60			x				x	x		x	x	x
Singing Call	61	x		x			x	x	x			x	x
Break													
OXO Reel	150	x	x		x	x					x		
Tunnel Contra	148		x			x						x	x
Phrase Craze Mxr	255			x			x	x					
Break													
ONS Party Mesco	238	x						x			x	x	
Siege of Ennis Mesco	240		x	x		x					x		
Amos Moses #2 (Solo)	274												
Break													
Patter Square	60								x	x		x	x
Singing Call	61	x	x						x			x	x
E-Z Mixer	252	x	x	x									
Break													
Dos Plus 1 Trio	221	x	x			x		x			x	x	
TBC Trio	217		x		x			x			x	x	
Lion Sleeps (Solo)	279												
Break													
Happy Circle Siscilian	230	x	x	x				x			x	x	
Weathervane Prom	231	x					x						
Extra New Dances													
First Night Quad	120	x	x					x	x	x	x		
Jefferson's Reel	187	x			x				x				x
Toot's Trio	224	x	x			x		x					
C.J. Mxr	264												
Dances Repeated Earlier or Later													
Scones & Tea Siscil (2)	228	x		x				x			x	x	
Cecily Cir Siscilian (2)	228	x		x				x			x	x	
Hi Neighbor Mxr	258												
San Antonio Strool	273												

Session 7	Page #	Circle L/R	Fwd & Back	Swing	Arm Turn L/R	Cpl Poomenade	DoSaDo	Star R/L	Pass Thru	Ladies Chain	Right & Left Thru	Star Promenade	Grand Square
Big Circle		x	x	x	x	x	x						
Patter Siscilian Cir		x	x	x	x	x	x	x	x	x			
Pittsfield Circle	236							x		x		x	
Break													
Patter Square	97	x	x	x		x			x		x	x	
Singing Call	99	x		x		x	x					x	
White Silver Sands Mxr	261												
Break													
ONS Contra	158	x	x	x			x	x					
Who's in the Mid Cntra	192	x		x	x	x				x	x		
Ghost Busters Solo	278												
Break													
Tres Trio	213	x	x				x		x				
Hully Gully Solo	274												
Break													
Patter Square													x
Happy Sounds Quad	131				x	x		x					x
Singing Call										x			x
Break													
Siscilian Circle #37	232	x				x				x			
Extra New Dances													
Stars & Strips Quad	126		x		x	x	x	x		x	x		
Farmer's Quad	132					x	x			x	x		x
Wheel's Quad	137						x			x	x		x
Granny's Pearls Cntra	164				x	x			x	x	x		
Callison Hall Jig Cntra	190	x				x	x	x	x		x		
Dances Repeated Earlier or Later													
I don't know wy Mxr (3)	251	x	x	x		x		x					
10 O'Clock Mx (3)r	262	x	x			x							
Jiffy Mxr	260												

Session 8	Page #	Circle L/R	Fwd & Back	Swing	Arm Turn L/R	Cpl Promenade	DoSaDo	Pass Thru	U-turn Back	Ladies Chain	Right & Left Thru	Separate	Bend the Line
Big Circle		x	x	x	x	x	x						
Patter Siscilian Clr		x	x	x	x	x	x	x		x	x		
Scottish Man O'War	227	x			x								
Break													
Patter Square	94							x	x	x	x	x	x
Singing Call		x						x		x			x
I Don' Know Why Mxr	251	x	x	x		x							
Break													
Beginner's Luck Cntra	159	x		x	x		x						
Murphy's Helper Cntra	166			x	x	x	x		x			x	
Amos Moses #1 Solo	272												
Break													
Portland Fancy Mesco	244	x	x						x		x	x	
Keene Anniv Mesco	242		x					x		x	x		
All Spice Mixer	257												
Break													
Patter Call		x	x	x		x		x		x	x	x	x
Quarter Chain Quadrille	127					x					x	x	
Cotton Eyed Joe													
Break													
Ding Dong Daddy													
Extra New Dances													
Lighted Sconce Cntra	193	x		x	x				x	x			x
Chain Reaction	199	x	x	x		x				x			
La Semilla HrnP Cntra	203	x	x						x		x	x	
Dances Repeated Earlier or Later													
Patty Cake Polka (4)	259												
Ally Cat Solo (4)	276												
Wild Turkey Trio (4)	210				x	x							
Alternate Trios (4)	214	x	x		x		x	x					
3 Legged Stool Trio (4)	215	x	x		x		x	x					
Levi Jackson Rag (4)	287	x			x		x				x	x	